Women in Southern Culture

Margaret Ripley Wolfe, SERIES EDITOR

Creeker

A WOMAN'S JOURNEY

Linda Scott DeRosier

THE UNIVERSITY PRESS OF KENTUCKY

Publication of this volume was made possible in part by
a grant from the National Endowment for the Humanities.

Editorial and Sales Offices: The University Press of Kentucky
663 South Limestone Street, Lexington, Kentucky 40508–4008

03 02 01 00 99 5 4 3 2

Frontispiece: Linda Sue Preston, ca. 1946

Library of Congress Cataloging-in-Publication Data
DeRosier, Linda Scott, 1941–
     Creeker : a woman's journey / Linda Scott DeRosier.
        p. cm.
     ISBN 0-8131-2123-X (alk. paper)
     1. DeRosier, Linda Scott, 1941– . 2. Mountain whites
(Southern States)—Kentucky—Social life and customs.
3. Kentucky—Biography. 4. Appalachian Region, Southern—
Biography. 5. Appalachian Region, Southern—Social life and
customs. I. Title.
CT275.D3664A3   1999
976.9'14   98-32029
[B]—DC21

This book is printed on acid-free recycled paper
meeting the requirements of the American National Standard
for Permanence of Paper for Printed Library Materials.
♾ ✺

Manufactured in the United States of America

For Momma and Daddy,

who filled my tousled head with a sense of

adventure and possibility and filled our homeplace

with tall tales and summer songs.

And

For Arthur,

best friend and life's companion,

whose love and laughter help me live with the past

and whose generosity of spirit continues to brighten

every day of my life.

Two bits, four bits

Six bits, a dollar;

Send those creekers

Back up the holler!

Paintsville High cheer, 1950s

CONTENTS

Illustrations follow pages 46, 110, and 198.

EDITOR'S PREFACE

Women in Southern Culture is dedicated to the experiences of women across the vast range of southern history. The publication of *Creeker: A Woman's Journey* marks the appearance of the inaugural volume of the series. It seems particularly fitting that the first book comes from the edges of the American South and the margins of southern womanhood. *Creeker* is a highly personal and refreshingly honest account of a human life—that of a scrawny kid from Two-Mile Creek, Kentucky, who is now a middle-aged professor of psychology, a wife two times over, a mother, and a college president's spouse. Linda Scott DeRosier's autobiography, both humorous and poignant, tells the story of an educated and cultured American woman who came of age in Appalachia; hers is a fresh new voice from the ranks of contemporary twentieth-century women.

*Creeke*r resonates with the folkways of a rural South that is rapidly receding into the past. It is reminiscent of Anne Moody's *Coming of Age in Mississippi* and Shirley Abbott's *Womenfolks: Growing up Down South*. Linda Scott DeRosier is just as appealing in her metier as Sharyn McCrumb and Lee Smith are in theirs. All of them hail from the southern highlands, and McCrumb and Smith routinely draw on their Appalachian heritage for the characters and settings of their fiction.

The Southern Appalachians have changed dramatically during the course of the twentieth century, but remnants of the folk persist, vestiges of an American subculture that has moved into a high-tech society without completely divesting itself of the old ways and values. These beliefs survive in the shadows of interstate highway bridges and industrial smokestacks. One catches passing glimpses—the fierce individualism and independence of someone boasting of paying cash and not owing a cent; the political aversion to experts and intellectuals, nowhere more apparent than in some school board races; the reluctance to make a will, an admission of human mortality in black and white; and the adherence to a prescribed and expected ritual of grief at funerals, a ritual often derided by the more sophisticated. The strength of the rural patriarchy persists at family gatherings where men eat first and women get the leftovers.

With a new century dawning, considerable confusion still surrounds Appalachian women. Homespun grannies, "yarb" doctors, "fotched-on" women, Dogpatch cuties, and coal-miners' daughters capture the popular imagination. But Linda Scott DeRosier reveals the complexities of family life, femininity, and feminism in the mountains. *Creeker* is a remarkable alternative to much of what has been published about the Appalachian region and its women. DeRosier is an academic, but *Creeker* is not a conventional scholarly work; nor is it intended to be. Bereft of footnotes and bibliography, it provides a unique perspective filled with universal truths.

Margaret Ripley Wolfe

ACKNOWLEDGMENTS

This blend of remembrance and reality is a tale of a family—mine—and of a time and place that delineated it. I have long been fond of telling my students, "You are the greatest authority on you." Until I began this effort, I honestly believed that. Without the bounty of other folks' memories, however, this book would have been much less accurate—and far less pleasurable to create. I have been fortunate in the excavation of this story to have had my own reminiscences restored—and on occasion remedied—by Pat and Michael Greer, Brett Dorse Scott, and Gwen Holbrook. Indeed, I have drawn so heavily on the goodwill, professional skills, and memories of friends and family that I find myself beholden to a host of folks whose faith in me helped turn this effort into reality. A few of those whose support I appreciate are Heather Haas and Jeanette Morris, trusted associates who read every line time after time and whose thoughtful reviews significantly improved this work; Barbara Vail, friend and colleague for nearly twenty years, whose perpetual constancy, joyous friendship, and professional support I simply take for granted; Margaret Ripley Wolfe, series editor, who always cleared a place for my manuscript in her packed schedule and gave time, skill, and constant encouragement, however often it was needed; Thomas Appleton, *uber*-reader, whose kind attention to my every comma splice brought clarity to this effort; Gwen Holbrook, oldest friend and witness to the early years, whose voice over the long-distance lines always brings Two-Mile back to me, and me back to Two-Mile; the DeRosier girls—Deborah, Marsha, and Melissa—who granted me the splendid opportunity of having daughters and whose presence has immeasurably enriched my life; Pat Greer, Baby Sister, whose support never wavered and whose recollections I counted upon to add her voice to mine in resurrecting memories of the parents and past we share; Brett Dorse Scott, who helped me reconstitute the essence and structure of a match that, while it may have been made in heaven, did not remain forever within those pearly gates; Brett Preston Scott, Sunner, whose entrance into this world created a place in my heart that didn't exist before him and whose idealism everlastingly restores my hope; and Casey Joans, she of the shining lantern, who has always stood ready to help a creeker learn to bake a new pie.

FAMILY GENEALOGY

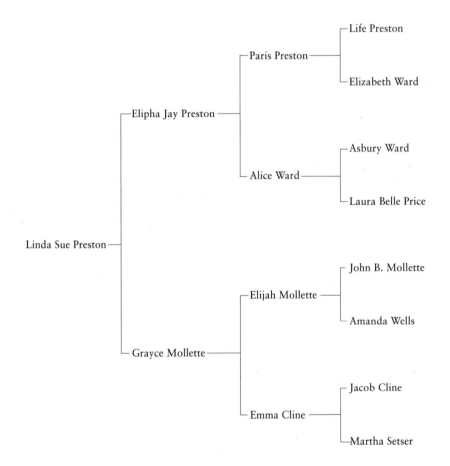

Asbury Ward
m.
Laura Belle Price

- Bum Ward

- Alice Ward
m.
Paris Preston
  - Mitchell Preston
m.
Viola Fannin
    - Christine Preston
    - Herbert Preston
    - Ray Preston
    - Chester Preston
    - Woodrow Preston
  - Glen Preston
m.
Ruth Williams
    - Glenna Lee Preston
  - Irene Preston
m. Ernie Potts
    - Robert Jay Potts
    - Roby Lee Potts
  - Elipha Jay Preston
m.
Grayce Mollette
    - Linda Sue Preston
    - Patricia Jaye Preston
  - Jo Imogene Preston

- Ella Ward
m. —— Johnson
  - Delphie Johnson
  - Annalee Johnson

- Sally Ward
m.
Milroy Daniels
  - Ena Mae Daniel

- Lizzie Ward
m. Guy B. Meade
  - Guy Bandi Meade
  - Jink Meade

- Mack Ward

- Hettie Ward
m. —— Daniels
  - Mack Daniels

- Exer Ward
m.
Keenis Holbrook
  - Dorothy Holbrook
  - Doris Holbrook
  - Cathleen Holbrook
  - Pauleen Holbrook
  - Juanita Holbrook
  - Betty Holbrook
  - Keenis Holbrook, Jr.
  - Gwen Holbrook

Elijah Mollette
m.
Emma Cline

- Lizzie Mollette
  m.
  Ray Colvin
  - Gene Ray Colvin
  - Frances Colvin
  - Fred Thomas Colvin
  - Roy Mitchell Colvin
  - Lois Ann Colvin

- Fred Mollette
  m.
  1. Alma —— — Leon Mollette
  2. Laurie —— — Burns Mollette
             Donald Mollette

- Stella Mollette
  m.
  Tom Fletcher —— Veva Fletcher

- John B. Mollette
  m.
  1. Maggie Williams —— Betty Ann Mollette
  2. Loretta ——

- Amanda Mollette
  m.
  J. Kash Holbrook

- Burns O. Mollette
  m.
  1. Elizabeth Baldridge
  2. Lillian Hicks —— Burns A. Mollette
  3. Liz ——

- Gladys Mollette

- Grayce Mollette
  m. Elipha Jay Preston
  - Linda Sue Preston
  - Patricia Jaye Preston

MY PLACE

*M*ine was not the Kentucky of bluegrass, juleps, and cotillions; the Kentucky of my youth was one of coal banks, crawdads, and country music. I grew up in the Appalachian Mountains of eastern Kentucky between the small towns of Paintsville and Inez in a place called Two-Mile Creek. This is my postcard from Appalachia written from the beginning of the "Big War" through the "Age of Aquarius" and running head-long, as quickly as all my baggage will allow, into the twenty-first century.

I was born February 20, 1941, on a feather bed in the upper room of my Grandma Emmy's log house on the left-hand fork of Greasy Creek in what is now Boons Camp, Kentucky. The small birthing room was heated by a coal fire, illuminated by coal oil lamps, and permeated by the aroma of cured hams hanging above the bed. Dr. Frank Picklesimer drove the fifteen or so miles from Paintsville over winding dirt roads to deliver what he judged to be about four pounds of Linda Sue Preston. At that time it was considered unusual for a doctor to be in attendance to deliver a child in families of our circumstance; but my mother was sickly, and it was thought that one of us might well not make it through the experience.

My daddy's name was Life; my momma's name was Grace. Who could ask for a more auspicious beginning? Daddy worked in the coal mines. We bred Hampshire hogs—those are the big black ones with a white stripe around their midsection—and raised most of our food on a couple of acres that Grandma Emmy Mollette owned. We got electric lights when I was in the second grade; indoor plumbing came considerably later. I come from a rural community in deep eastern Kentucky, and I am one of those who went away and stayed—but I never got away, not really.

I am not only *from* Appalachia; I am *of* Appalachia. My attitudes and behaviors were shaped by having grown up in that family, in that place, and in that time. Although I left home at age seventeen, my definition of what community means as well as my expectations of myself and others were formed very early in my history within my extended family. To this day, all I know of relationship is grounded in eastern Kentucky and in my sense of belonging there. On Two-Mile Creek and around on Greasy, everybody I saw or knew was in some way related to me, if not by blood then by kinship born over many generations of living together and surviving on land not famous for its generosity.

I want, at the outset, to differentiate between those Appalachians who grow up in the towns and those from rural areas—the creeks and the hollers. We tend to be lumped together by outsiders: demographers, bureaucrats who fund social programs, and academics who study the region. I would suggest to you that there is as much cultural difference between rural Appalachians and Appalachian townsfolk as between white folk and black folk who happen to live in the same city. While the difference is pervasive, it goes largely unrecognized. The prototypical hillbilly stereotype, while exaggerating the profile of rural residents, is not at all representative of those Appalachians who were brought up in the cities and small towns of that region. In terms of expectations, a woman my age born in Paintsville, Kentucky—the county seat of my home county and the nearest town to Two-Mile—would be more likely to find similarity with a cohort born in Plainville, Wisconsin, or Carthage, Alabama—or any of a thousand other little towns in the United States—

than with me. This is a story from *rural* Appalachia, recently brought to consciousness, and reported by a creeker.

In the rural areas of my home county and the three or four counties surrounding us, I knew of no Catholics, no Jews, no African-, Greek-, Italian-, Irish-, Hispanic-, Hungarian-Americans. I also was aware of no Episcopalians and not a great many Methodists or Presbyterians. Those town religions paid their preachers, and *everybody*—foot-washing Baptists, all—believed that if a man got paid to do the Lord's work, he probably didn't really get the *call* to preach anyway.

The standard of living within that area is reflected in the 1960 census, which lists two of those counties, Martin and Magoffin, as having the lowest per capita income of any all-white population in the United States. If we had known that particular statistic, it would have been interpreted by us Lord-lovin' churchfolk as a positive sign, since the Bible says, "It is easier for a camel to go through the eye of a needle than for a rich man to enter the kingdom of God." I have never worried about that particular proclamation, since I feel certain that, if any of my people do not make it through the pearly gates, it damn sure will not be because we gathered unto us too much in the way of worldly goods.

For me, looking back on my life has been a lot like reading tea leaves. I drank that tea, sip by sip, and thought myself cognizant of its most minute properties; yet, as I have sifted through my memories, I've found myself uncertain of specifics of stories I have passed on for years. Thus, I offer this work as *my own* reality, as I saw it. These tea leaves get no more legible.

I want first to take you back with me to the place of my growing up, where I learned to parse the world—to look at it and interpret it as it was processed through this body and by this mind or some earlier incarnation of same. I *am* my history; and however much I may think I have changed, in retrospect, parts of me have hardly changed at all. I believe I have always had the same desire—one that is not too unusual, although it probably shows itself in different ways—the desire to be heard. For the most part, children are not heard anywhere, and it was no different where I grew up. In my community, power was thought to come straight from the Word of God, revealed to us through biblical scriptures. Although many people probably could not read much past sixth-grade level, they believed that every word in the Bible was true and were fond of proclaiming that, often and vehemently, to cut off any questioning or curiosity.

Transgendered people speak of having felt early on that they had been born into the wrong body. Although I cannot identify with that statement in terms of sexual orientation or proclivity, it accurately describes my feelings about my early life. My world never folded around me in the way it seemed to drape itself lovingly and warmly around everybody else I grew up with. Early on, I was a bundle of curiosity, not fixed on any specific object but largely random and uncontrolled. In a world full of people who bent their shoulder to the wheel and accepted the hard life filled with the physical work and misery that God had given them, I was pretty close to worthless. As children, everyone took on the serious responsibilities of working in the fields, raising crops, and caring for the farm animals and the younger children. Although I carried out my assigned duties, I always lacked the attitude of seriousness embodied by my peers. I was like a bale of fencing wire: no matter how much I tried to roll myself into a tight little bundle, something was always springing loose, which necessitated some poor overworked grown-up's trying to put it back.

As a child, and even as an adolescent, I was far more hindrance in everybody's life than help because I had to be closely supervised to make certain that I did not waste time daydreaming or blurt out some outrageous comment that would hurt people's feelings or make them mad. The biggest problem, from my perspective, was that I could never figure out exactly what the folks who peopled my world wanted from me. I realize that it seems, upon reflection, remarkably simple, since I could, even then, repeat after folks the words they told me. But all my energies, traits, and desires kept getting in the way of my carrying out my prescribed role.

Step one of my journey back must be to revisit Two-Mile Creek in my growing-up years. Those early years taught me what to expect of myself and everybody else, and the strength of those early beliefs shaped the way I lived and gave meaning to the rest of my life. First, let us look at a map of Kentucky. If you do not remember its shape, I would refresh your memory by reminding you of the oft-repeated description that "Kentucky is shaped like a camel lying down." Now let your finger, or your mind, travel as far east as you can go without leaving the state, right nearabouts that camel's tail. If you look north of Pikeville, you will see Prestonsburg, as in Linda Sue Preston. That's me—or was. Keep traveling north to Paintsville, the county seat of Johnson County, the county where I was born and came into knowing as much as I can believe I know. Then head east toward Inez, which is hard up against the state line, if you do not count the little communities of Beauty, Lovely, and Warfield—which nobody with any sense does. Between Paintsville and Inez, you will find Meally, which is Buffalo; Williamsport, which is Two-Mile; and Boons Camp, which is Greasy. I could go on and tell you about Thelma, which is Bob's Branch; Thealka, which is Muddy Branch; and Whitehouse, which is Bee Branch, but no need. All the places have two names.

I am told that the reason the map and post office names are not the names folks who live there call them is that, way back when, government officials came through the area attaching names to places. Since the residents of those communities were mostly illiterate, the feds refused to call the places by the names common folk called them. This appears to me to be indicative of the power and credibility given my Appalachian forebears by all those well-meaning, philanthropic folk who came from Washington and the northeast to reach down and protect us from our own ignorance. That reaching-*down*-to-help-us-out attitude is, perhaps more than any other factor, what funded my pursuit of advanced degrees.

I should point out that I did not know all these things about schooling or letters such as M.A. and Ph.D. until some years after I completed my first degree and after I had come to a place where I could see the result of some of my earlier choices in life, choices made without the benefit of letters or the understanding represented by those letters. With a bunch of letters after your name, folks may still look down on you; but, since *you* know what they think about *you* while *they* don't know what you think about *them*, you win. The key to it all is to know the lower limit of your reputation, because you don't ever want anyone to be thinking you are worse than you *think* people think you are. That perspective on the world may well be what led me to psychology in the first place. Coupled with philosophy and literature, it seemed to give me some small handle on the human condition, hence a better likelihood that I could decipher what people were thinking. And that perspective had its beginnings on Two-Mile Creek in Johnson County, about as far east as you can wander and still be in Kentucky.

I want to take you back home with me to see the range of colors of the trees in autumn, when the whole country smells of wood smoke and leaves and apple butter; to see the mist that hangs in the valleys in the mornings and the glitter of the dew on spiderwebs as the sun creeps over the tops of the trees. I used to lie on my belly on the faded wooden bridge that crossed the creek by my house and stare at the water until it seemed that the bridge was moving instead of the creek. As the water streamed past me, I would imagine that I was going on a big ship to someplace exciting.

Every time I have steamed into port in some far-flung, exotic place, I have thought about my bridge and my creek and the path that led me from there to here. Seems to me that it's time for me to mark that path, so I want to take you back to Two-Mile and the well box and the bridge and the church house and the graveyard and the rock cliff and the coal bank and . . . and. . . .

MY PEOPLE

I think I must have been ten or twelve years old before I ever spoke a word to a stranger, because there literally were no strangers in my little world. When I met somebody new, I followed the pattern set by all who had gone before me and asked him, "Who are your people?" It then fell to the new person to prove he was not an outsider by tracing his history to somebody or another who lived on the creek or was close kin of somebody who was once a resident. Because of all the emphasis placed upon those who had come before me, I grew up believing that I was not only of a place but of a people; even the most distant of family connections were and are significant to me. To my son I have handed down the sense of belonging to a clan of people just as surely as I passed along my genetic code. Although I am many years gone from the creek, I remain strongly connected with my people; even those dead and buried live on in my life and in my sister's life and in the lives of our children.

My daddy had more common sense than anybody I have ever known. He was honest, kind, and generous; and he possessed an ability to laugh at himself and find fun in even the most serious situations. He was extremely hardworking, and he spent any free time he had with his family. I know this sounds idealized, and I know he had weaknesses; but I have to tell you that, for all of my life, I plain worshiped my daddy. I recall several occasions when he lost his temper and yelled a lot. But in a place where many men were routinely violent with women and children, Daddy never raised his hand to any of us. When we got out of line, he would threaten to "tan our hide," but I never felt physically afraid, since I never saw him hit anything, much less me or Sister. Although an analysis of his speech would no doubt find a good deal of profanity, he used it so naturally that it did not come across as vulgar. At his angriest, Daddy's most flagrant curse was "Goddamn my sister's red-tailed rooster." When he delivered himself of this particular profanity, Sister and I would scurry away somewhere until the fury passed; usually we were giggling as we scurried.

My daddy was the fourth of five surviving children in his family, the youngest boy. They named him Life Jay, after his paternal grandfather, Life, and his father's brother, Uncle Jay. Now, Life was an unusual name, even for the hills, so sometime in his teens he changed it to Elipha Jay. Yes, I know, Elipha is not a common name either, but Daddy never used it anyway. We could always tell by what folks called him exactly when my daddy had come to know different people in his life. Old friends and family always called him Lifie Jay, while those who met him later called him Jay or E. Jay. Pop Pop, his daddy, called him Parker, for reasons that died with the two of them.

This name thing seems significant, somehow, since much is made in certain psychological theory about the importance of name in identity. The implication is that if a person changes his name there may well be some problems with his identity formation or with acceptance of who he believes himself to be. Therefore, I should probably point out right now that all members of my immediate family have at some time tinkered with their names. In fact, I am still diddlin' around with mine. And right while I'm discussing names, you should know that throughout this work some few names will be changed to protect the privacy of the innocent—and the human.

Nobody is sure exactly when Daddy was born because he never had a birth certificate. Daddy always believed the year was 1917, while his Aunt Exer Holbrook forever insisted that he was actually born in 1918, when she was pregnant with her oldest child, Dorothy. Since he was born at home, the earliest record of his existence is the 1920 census, which listed him as three years old. It would probably surprise a lot of folks from outside the hills how often the question of Daddy's birthday came up, but we lived right across the road from Aunt Exer, and hill folk establish veracity with the stories they tell—over and over—as they remember them. Therefore, it was important to my Great-Aunt Exer that everybody accept her version of the truth.

My daddy was a coal miner, but he never actually worked digging coal. His job, for the most part, was as a carpenter at the mines, which meant he only went down inside the mine shaft itself when timbers needed shoring up or some other structure needed to be built. He did not like to go into the mine shaft and often said he was lucky that there was usually something around the mining camp that needed carpentry, plumbing, or electrical work so that he was seldom required to go underground.

The working life of a coal miner was anything but secure because layoffs, shutdowns, and strikes were a part of the job. Early in my life, my daddy often had to go off to West Virginia to get work. Sometimes we went with him and lived for a short period in boarding houses or in coal-camp houses. Most of the time, however, we stayed at our little house on Two-Mile, while Daddy left on Sunday evening and returned each Friday night. Then, when I was in the second grade, Daddy got on at Princess Elkhorn Coal Company at David, Kentucky, up in Floyd County, twenty miles from where we lived. Several other men in our community—including Ronalta Mae Pelphrey's daddy—also worked there, so Daddy hauled riders to and from the mines and picked up a little extra money that way.

When Daddy worked at David, our day began when Momma got up to cook breakfast at four o'clock each morning. At four-thirty, after she had built a fire in the coal cookstove and prepared one fried egg, two sausage patties, sawmill gravy, and a pan of homemade biscuits, she woke Daddy. He would then get out of bed, eat his breakfast, go across the branch to the toilet, and return to shave in a washpan of water Momma had heated for him on the stove.

He kept his shaving brush and soap in an old English shaving mug with a picture of a brown horse on the side, identical to my grandpa's shaving mug. My grandfather, Pop Pop, lived with us for about a year, and those horses kept company on our kitchen windowsill while he was there. I could tell the shaving mugs apart because Pop Pop's horse had two little brown lines fanning crookedly out from its left ear, where the glaze had cracked. Pop Pop shaved with a straight razor, while Daddy scraped off his beard with a safety razor. Even on weekends both men were always clean-shaven by seven in the morning. They shaved by looking at their image in a five-by-seven hand mirror that was propped on the windowsill over the sink in the kitchen. Daddy put a sink in our kitchen long before we had water in the house. We kept clean dishrags twisted to fit stuffed into the four holes on the back of the sink before we got hot and cold spigots and water to run through them.

After Daddy went off to work at five, Momma washed his dishes, made up their bed, and tidied their bedroom before preparing another breakfast of sausage, eggs, and biscuits and waking my sister and me. I do not recall ever seeing my parents' bed unmade or our house the least bit messy when I got out of bed in the morning, which could account for some of the guilt I now carry around all day if I do not spread up my own bed before I leave for work in the morning.

Since we were as well off as anybody I knew, I grew up believing that my daddy had about the best job there was. If I had been a boy, I suppose I would have aspired to work in the mines. I also knew that Daddy's and Ronalta Mae's daddy Tommy Pelphrey's jobs were better than those of Frank Ward (Easter's daddy) or Keenis Holbrook (Gwen's daddy), because Uncle Frank and Uncle Keenis were sporadically employed at smaller, nonunion mines. Another thing I learned growing up on Two-Mile was what it meant to work at the mines and how much protection the union did or did not give the miners from the vicissitudes of life. On the face of it, the union meant everything to the coal miners because they were largely unskilled and had little to offer other than strong backs and willing hearts. At the nonunion mines, they often worked for a dollar a load—digging out the coal and filling a coal car for one dollar—while the union mines paid an hourly wage however much actual work the miner did. Until Daddy went to work for Princess Elkhorn, most of his work was at nonunion mines, where coal companies often took full advantage of the power they had over the miners, so we considered his getting on at David a real blessing to our family.

Daddy joined the union the first time in the early forties, but he was always of two minds about it. He believed the union was the only thing that gave the common man a living wage, and until he died he cursed poor old Taft for the Taft-Hartley Act that gave the federal government the power to break a strike and send the miners back to work. While Daddy considered himself loyal to the union and always paid his dues, he was routinely fined for not attending union meetings. Although he never said so publicly, Daddy thought such gatherings were a waste of time; he often said these meetings were just another excuse for folks to hear themselves talk. My daddy had little patience with those who "talked big." He also believed that the unions gave a lot of lazy people an excuse to slack off on their job and that union leaders sometimes called strikes for no good reason. Whenever there was a lay-off or a shutdown at the mine, Daddy immediately found another job doing whatever kind of work he could scare up. One of the things he was proudest of was that he never took a day of "rocking chair" (unemployment compensation) in his life.

When I was about thirteen, I became a little impatient with this view when there was a big strike at David and much marching along the picket line. Whole families marched and sang together, and I was sure there was a place for me to shine in that setting. I made a sign that asked "Which side are you on?" and tucked right into a righteous rendition of "You can't change me, I'm working for the union." My daddy was not at all impressed with sign or singing and thus deprived me of the opportunity to take a stand against the oppressor, not to mention the chance to socialize with other teenagers on the picket line, which was really what I had in mind. He said he had no time for such foolishness. One of my daddy's customary sayings was "I got no time for foolishness and damn little for fun." This maxim always brought a laugh from all of us because Daddy had an abundant reservoir of both fun and foolishness. Although he was a hardworking, responsible person, my daddy also had a lot of kid in him, as evidenced by his teasing and the pleasure he took in a number of small acts, like the Orie Dutton runs.

Every so often, Daddy would load Sister and me in the car, as though we were going to the grocery store or had some other errand to run.

Then we'd head around on Greasy about a quarter-mile up the creek from Grandma Emmy's to see Orie Dutton. You have to understand that Daddy often traded out small tools or other stuff with Orie, so it was not unusual for him to go up there alone. You could almost lay money, however, that if he took Sister and me with him, the mission had a special purpose. As soon as we drove past Grandma Emmy's, thus making it apparent that the Dutton house was our destination, Sister and I would begin bouncing up and down, making the coal dust fly out of those old felt car seats, with anticipation for what surely lay ahead at Orie's. We'd roll out of the car to see Orie ambling up the path, his old hat pushed back on his head and his wife, Beunie, appearing at the front door. Most of us didn't have screens on the doors then, so in summer they just stood wide open.

Sister and I would then have to endure Beunie's efforts at hospitality as we refused something to eat or drink. Soon we'd be following Orie and Rattler, his mostly collie dog, down the path to the barn. We could never be certain what we would find there as we wandered into the darkened, hay-scented interior. Orie would lead us over to a stall, then Daddy would lift up Sister and I would stand on tiptoe so that we could peer into the stall, wherein lay a litter of puppies or sometimes kittens, their eyes just open to the world. Then came the big decision as Sister and I set about to choose one, beg for two, and make our case for three or more. With a sheepish grin, Daddy would caution, "Now your maw's gonna have a shit-fit," but Sister and I could anticipate pet-parenthood already as we kept up our pleas that we just had to have the one with the spot over his eye and how could we ever not take the tiger-striped one.

On our way back home, we'd stop by Grandma Emmy's, where Sister and I, arms full of kittens or pups, would run to greet her. Daddy followed close behind us, shaking his head as if he'd had no part in this arrangement. Grandma would laugh and shake her head too, saying, "Jay, you're in trouble now!" as she held and stroked one pup or kitten after the other.

This scenario was repeated time and again throughout my childhood, including the disapproval we faced upon our return home. My momma took pride in keeping the cleanest house on the creek, so she was not about to have a pet in the house; she always said that she'd just as soon not have one *out*side either. While her reaction was always predictably negative, I think Momma enjoyed this little charade as much as we did. She often grew more attached to the pups than all three of us; and, although she was an avowed cat-hater, she even tolerated the cats pretty well.

Daddy took a lot of pleasure from his life and the folks and creatures that inhabited it. When he was a young man, he used to relax on the porch to laugh, swap stories, play his guitar, and sing country songs. Folks would come by and say, "How you doing, Lifie Jay?" Daddy would reply, "If a man had any sense, he'd be drunk." As he got older, he was happiest when he could sit out in his yard, smoke a cigarette, and listen to some big tale somebody was telling. Just being around my daddy seemed to make most folks feel better, for laughter was his birthright and he always made light of troubles. Whatever misfortune came our way, Daddy greeted it with a rueful smile, a shake of the head, and a murmured "Aye, boys." This was Daddy's indication that the matter under discussion was one more thing that must be accepted and dealt with, though the way to proceed was not yet evident to him.

My daddy also had dreams, but he was always careful not to discuss them until he had turned the dream into a plan, the plan into action, and had succeeded in the action. He never attempted anything unless he was pretty sure he could do it, and he never, *ever* mentioned it until it was finished. He believed folks who talked big were foolish, that nothing should be claimed until it was in your pocket, and that if you proceeded quietly and did not try to overstep your bounds, you could have just about whatever you wanted before anybody who might come out ag'in you had any idea of what you were up to. He was a very thoughtful and careful man, and I do not think he made a lot of mistakes in his life. He did, however, make one colossal blunder—he married my mother.

My momma was the single most intelligent human being I have ever known. When you consider that I have spent my entire adult life in higher education, that is saying quite a lot. It is not, however, an overstatement. Although children are likely to overestimate the power of their mother, let me suggest that every person who ever had contact with my momma would attest that she was, indeed, exceptionally bright. The tragedy is that, with all that capacity, she could never think her way out of the trap that was her life.

Momma was the youngest of nine children born to a most unusual family. Every one of her brothers and sisters was extremely intelligent, but not one of them had a lick of common sense. All three of my mother's brothers were drunks. In Bible-thumping, whiskey-hating, local option territory, they did not just drink; they were dead-dog-get-down-lay-in-the-bed-for-days drunks. The females in the family did not have a drinking problem, perhaps because they were all fundamentalist Christians who never had a drink in their lives.

My momma was brilliant and spirited and passionate in a time and a place where a woman was allowed to be none of those things. She graduated from high school, passed the state teachers' exam, and was given a teaching appointment in a one-room schoolhouse on Hurricane Creek near her homeplace around on Greasy. She saved her salary, bought a car—an act absolutely unheard of in that time and place—and proceeded to get herself engaged no fewer than five times in three years before she met and married my daddy, whom she had known less than a month. Daddy was good-looking, funny, and had a car. What more could a country girl want?

Maybe if she had known him a little longer, she might have made a better choice. It's hard to figure out what *better* might have been, since Daddy made a better living, loved my momma more, and treated her better than anybody she might ever have expected to meet. That does not mean, however, that he was good for *her*. They lived together nearly sixty years, but they were just about as different as two folks could be. Daddy's world was extremely small, and, with my mother in the center of it, he could not have been happier. My momma, however, was Sarah Bernhardt performing in a small-town dinner theater; she was much too big for the stage. You see, my mother was very special and not the least bit like any other mother in our little community.

In those days, birth control often was not used successfully. Girls married early, began having babies immediately, and continued to bear a child every year or so until "the change" took them out of the baby-making business. After their first child was born, most women pulled their hair back in a bun, wore no makeup, affected big aprons from sunup to sundown, and generally adopted a very matronly appearance.

Not so with my mother. She put on bright-red lipstick first thing in the morning, chain-smoked Camels, and wore short shorts in the summertime—red short shorts. Momma was five feet, eight inches tall with chestnut hair that, much to her sorrow, had darkened as she aged. Stories and pictures suggest that she was quite a blond beauty in her youth, and I think that image, internalized in her early years, was with her until she died. She was more than a little outrageous for Two-Mile, since early on she was the only wife and mother who smoked cigarettes or drove a car. Leonie Wallen got her driver's license when I was in high school, and Pat Pelphrey (Ronalta Mae's mother) learned to drive along with Ronalta Mae in 1957, but nobody's mother smoked but mine.

The group of high-school girls just ahead of me, Bonnie and Betty Holbrook (Gwen's older sisters) and Roma Lou Ward (Easter's older sister), spent countless hours at my house, where they could confide in Momma and smoke cigarettes. There was overmuch listening to country music on the radio and laughing about exploits of one or another while Momma washed or ironed or canned or cooked. Momma carried on a veritable salon for teenagers, and at the time I resented their presence and was jealous of the attention they received from my mother. However, upon reflection, it is clear to me that Momma needed contact with people who still had some life left in them, and there was little of that to be found in her peers on the creek.

Although her given name was Grace Mollette, when she was eighteen or so Momma gave herself the middle name "Jean" after the movie star Jean Harlow. Shortly after she married Daddy, she inserted the letter Y into her first name, thus christening herself Grayce Jean Mollette Preston. Throughout her life, Momma explained that she changed the spelling of her first name to avoid being confused with another Grace Preston who lived nearby, but I doubt that was the case. I think she just wanted to have a name all her own.

Still another difference between my mother and the other mothers on the creek was that my momma never sat down in front of the fire or on the porch and just rested. There was always a magazine, book, or crossword puzzle in Momma's lap. I believe we were the only house in the community that subscribed to magazines, and, whenever we did not have physical work to do, all four of us could most often be found either reading something or napping. My family's attitude toward reading differed from that of almost everybody else because we never saw reading as a chore; it was a reward for getting our work finished. The attitude of a lot of homefolks was that folks only read things that were assigned for school, so reading was not seen as a pleasurable activity. My parents were in agreement with the community on one thing, however; they all believed that reading was a waste of time when there were chores to be done, an indication that the reader was not doing his or her share of the work necessary for survival.

Sometimes Momma went out of her way to work harder than was necessary. She was proud of using only paste wax on our linoleum floors because she believed those who used "liquid" wax were just too lazy to get down on their hands and knees and put forth the elbow grease to shine off the paste. Momma made that old house sparkle, and she was a good cook too—not as good as Aunt Exer, of course, whose biscuits and dumplings would float right away if you didn't hold them down. That the women of the community were able to excel at domestic tasks is in a way miraculous, since they were cooking on coal stoves where the heat regulation was none too precise and were keeping house without benefit of vacuum cleaners or store-bought cleaning products. When Momma got married, housekeeping became her sole occupation. She was teaching when she married Daddy, and they were married five years before I was born. Despite Daddy's many lay-offs at the mines, Momma never worked a day after they married. After Sister and I turned out the way we did (both fully employed), the subject of working women often surfaced in our conversations with our parents. Daddy's invariable opinion was "A man oughtn't to have to come home to a goddamn bowl of chili." Momma would quickly agree, and that was the end of that. Although early in their marriage there was plenty of physical work to use up my mother's energy, later in her life she had huge blocks of time that she filled with crossword puzzles, trash novels, TV soap operas, and an increased monitoring of her many illnesses, both real and imagined. Although Momma had a tendency toward hypochondria early on, it was full-blown by the time she was forty. During the course of her life, I do not recall her admitting to one day of good health.

One late summer afternoon when I was about eight years old, Momma, Sister, and I finished our chores and walked down to Leonie Wallen's store for a Pepsi-and-peanuts break. On the way home we decided to drop by and sit for a spell with our across-the-road neighbors, the Holbrooks. I can still picture the three of us climbing exuberantly up the embankment to where Aunt Exer and three of her children were drinking iced tea while relaxing on the porch. When we got about five yards from where Aunt Exer was sitting, she said, "Well, how are you, Grayce?" My mother, who up to that point had been moving along robustly, suddenly slowed her pace, slumped, and began to limp along, dragging her feet, as if it were all she could do to transport herself to the porch. Bernhardt *way* off-Broadway.

Daddy knew *exactly* what it took to make him happy, and he quietly and methodically went about getting it. Momma never had any notion what it would take to satisfy her, so she wanted everything and more—and nothing was ever enough. Her dissatisfaction was complicated by her steadfast refusal to admit to herself or anybody else that her life was not perfect, so she was never able to see what void needed filling, which in turn led to her lifelong inability to find contentment. She was fond of saying, "I have never had one moment of depression in my life." This statement was usually sandwiched between descriptions of her chronic insomnia and reports of this or that joint "going out."

My mother had lupus, which lends itself to a variety of authentic physical difficulties, so there can be no doubt that her health problems were numerous and genuine. Yet it also seems to me that the lack of intellectual stimulation or purpose in her life led to an exaggeration of her many ailments. In my opinion, just as my mother needed a name of her own, she also needed a life of her own. My poor old momma was a freight train that never could get to the station. She had a formidable intelligence and absolutely nowhere to focus it that would have been considered appropriate in that time and place.

From my mother I learned what not to do. At every juncture of my life when faced with a decision on how to proceed, I have asked myself, "What would Momma do?" Once I have answered that question, I have usually gone the opposite way. Her life has stood as an example to me of what can happen when a woman steps away from the center of her life in order to make room for a man to occupy it. However worthy my daddy was of my mother's full concentration, there was not enough substance there to sustain a woman like my momma. I got from her my curiosity and my desire to go everywhere, know everything, and sample all that is out there. From my daddy, I learned to be satisfied with what life brings me while I am trying for something more. Daddy also gave me my judgment, my sense of humor, and my ability to make myself happy wherever I happen to end up.

My baby sister was born twelve days before my sixth birthday. From the very beginning, it seemed that we could hardly have come from the same species, much less the same gene pool. At birth, I weighed in at approximately four pounds; Sister was a nine-pound baby. I was always "sickly" and fell prey to every ailment that went around, from scarlet fever to whooping cough, while Sister was robust. This resulted in my being lanky, angular, and bony throughout my childhood, while my baby sister was a little blond cherub who could have posed for baby-food ads. Sibling conflict is a fairly normal occurrence, so I suppose my feelings for Sister were normal, but they were intensified by my parents' insistence that she accompany me every moment of my life.

From my seventh summer until I left home at seventeen, I was shadowed by my baby sister; everything I did, she did with me. This usually resulted in my engaging in some sort of forbidden activity and then, despite all attempts at bribery, Sister's telling Momma and trouble abounding. It may well be that one of the reasons I liked elementary school was because I did not have to deal with my sister tagging along after me—at least all my troubles at school were self-constructed. But summer always found me with my little group of cohorts—and my sister—doing all sorts of summer things.

The group consisted of Easter Ward, so named because she was born on Easter Sunday 1939; Gwen Holbrook, born June 8, 1940; me, born February 20, 1941; and Sister, born February 8, 1947. I include these birth dates here to point out that the first three fit together as similar enough in age to form a natural group—and then there was Sister. If I felt resentment toward Baby Sister, that in no way colored my feelings for the other two members of that little group. If either Gwen Holbrook or Easter Ward had suggested I stick my head down the toilet hole, I would have run to get slime in my hair. These two individuals were the first in a long line of people who refused to love me back, thus providing me with motivation to attempt to change myself into whatever shape they deemed necessary to deserve their friendship. I do swear, I tried and tried, but nothing seemed to work.

Easter was the ninth of Frank and Edna Ward's ten children, the tenth being Hi John—whose real name was Russell Charles but nobody ever called him that—born two years after Easter. Easter, with her raven hair curling around her pale white face, was not only a beautiful child by the standards of that time and place, she was also physically tough. Gwen was the baby of the Keenis Holbrook family of eight children. With her blue eyes, freckles, and braids, she was also an endearing child. Sister was round, silky-haired, and cherubic. The only one who would not have made a Rockwell *Saturday Evening Post* cover was Linda Sue. As I look at childhood pictures of myself, I didn't really look that bad by today's standards, but everything about me—from my bone-thin body to my boundless energy—was so completely unacceptable that I always felt I was far out of the friendship loop.

"Whippoorwill" is a term used in the hills for one who is so "pore" or thin as to look unhealthy. Folks say, "Law, honey, you look just like a little whippoorwill." Well, I dwelt for all my growing-up years in whippoorwill city. And it was not a pleasant place. Gwen Holbrook recalls my mother's going to Walt Pack's store when we started third grade and buying each of us checked dresses—perhaps the only store-bought dresses we owned—in size 6X. As Gwen tells it, I wore my checked dress for several years, while she outgrew hers in about five weeks (Gwen's body type was never of the whippoorwill variety).

Anyway, I don't know whether it was because I was thin, because I was in constant motion, because I poked fun at practically everything, because Baby Sister was part of my package, because . . . because. . . . Well, it could have been any combination of the becauses that were responsible for my inability to form a bond of friendship. I had no best friend. Gwen and Easter spent a lot of time playing with me, but all of us knew they liked each other better than either of them liked me.

One of the activities our little band of four engaged in every summer until we hit puberty was to form a club. The script never changed. We would get a tablet and four pencils, climb up to the loft in Gwen's barn, and therein set out the rules for the club. I was always president, Easter was secretary, Gwen was treasurer, and Sister was vice president. Once we got to this point, each of us would take a sheet of lined tablet paper on which to write her name and her position. I would write mine—"Linda Sue Preston, President"—and help Sister write "Patsy Jaye Preston, Vice President," then all of us would display our signs to the others. Easter was one year ahead of Gwen and me in school, but she was not a crackerjack speller. Although she was not proficient, she was certainly predictable. Every single summer for at least five consecutive years, she displayed her sign: "Easter Ward, Seceratry." Unfortunately, I was just as predictable. I would immediately point to her paper, laugh, and say, as if it were the first time I had ever encountered this, "sek-er-*rat*-ry!!!" at which point Easter would proceed to whip my butt royally. This little scenario never varied year upon year. Easter never learned to spell secretary, and I never learned to keep my mouth shut about it. Even today, the smell of hay reminds me of ol' Easter rubbing my face in the floor of the barn loft.

Sister, Gwen, and I also played "house" a lot, but Easter was not there all the time for that. Easter was known as a hard worker—and not without good reason. She did a good deal of the housework, water-drawing, and even some cooking at the Ward household. Gwen, being the baby, got out of doing much work at home, and, despite my water-carrying and hog-feeding duties, everybody knew me as pretty much do-less when it came to work. I talked myself out of every bit of effort I possibly could because, while I had an overabundance of energy for fun, I avoided any work that required exertion. It is true that I hoed corn, beans, and potatoes; gathered vegetables; strung beans; skinned beets and tomatoes; and helped around the house in any other way that I could not weasel out of. For all my involvement in the regular running of the household, I only performed those tasks when I had exhausted all methods to get out of them.

Easter was an altogether better soldier. Since a good bit of her time was consumed by chores, that usually left Gwen to play with me and Sister, who was too young even by mountain standards to be put to work. So the three of us played house on the side of a hill, with pots and pans made from empty tin cans and whatever other domestic objects our mothers could spare for us to use as props in our play. We made cakes and cookies out of dirt, hard-packing it in those pans and turning out perfect loaves. We used our dolls, and sometimes our pups or kittens, as our babies, and all of us planned to have a flock of kids—even Sister, who was only three or four years old. Many times I have heard my Aunt Exer tell the story of how my sister told her she was not going to have babies when she grew up; she was, instead, going to have kittens. Playing house was our way of preparing for what we were fairly certain would be our future as wives and mothers: cooking, straightening, "nussing" babies. It never occurred to me that I would ever do anything other than that or live anywhere other than on Two-Mile Creek. I was female; that was my future.

I got my first clue about males and females and their relative importance in God's great scheme shortly after Baby Sister was born, when I was six years old. On the snowy February day that my Daddy stuck his head in the door of Grandma Emmy's with the news that I had a new sister, both he and my grandma seemed delighted; so, of course, I was too. In the six years since I had made my entrance into the world, my family had made some economic and social progress. Once again there had been concern about my mother's health, so Sister was born in a hospital in Paintsville. Momma and Sister came home from the hospital six days later, and, in keeping with custom, a kind of perpetual open house ensued for the next week or two so that everybody in our little community could visit the new baby. The first afternoon that mother and child were home, some of our closest neighbors came by bearing gifts for Sister and declaring she was to a dot like her daddy. This is another of those rituals so common in our culture that it could be choreographed. Momma was propped up on pillows with Sister cradled in her arms, and I was stretched out across the foot of her bed, half wrapped in one of the new yellow crocheted baby blankets, when Roma Lou Ward, Maltie Preston, and Leonie Wallen came in the door. As everyone exclaimed over the baby's beauty, her robust health, and her striking resemblance to her father, Leonie said: "Poor old Lifie Jay. Looks like he ain't never gonna get him a boy." Everyone nodded agreement, and they continued to cluck over the new arrival.

Later I asked Grandma Emmy what Leonie had meant by the remark about the baby, and she said not to bother about such remarks because my daddy was "tickled to death with his two little girls." I did not worry about the comment, but I didn't forget it either. Even if I had not been privy to that particular remark, I could not have overlooked the widely held philosophy behind it because Leonie was only the first of many to remark on the unfortunate circumstance of an all-girl family. Our 'cross-the-road neighbors, Aunt Exer and Uncle Keenis Holbrook, had eight children (seven girls and one boy—their seventh child), and I frequently heard one or another community member tease Uncle Keenis by saying "took him seven tries to get his boy." Each time the subject came up, Aunt Exer would explain that it was her fault because she couldn't carry boys and had lost several to miscarriage. I never once heard anyone take issue with the underlying theme of such comments, and I surely never heard anybody suggest that an all-*boy* family was anything but a blessing.

Not only was this the case in my little community throughout my childhood, but such comments continued later on. In April 1960, when Brett Scott and I were engaged, a close friend of ours had her first baby. Her husband was a college classmate of ours, so we went by the hospital to visit her and the child. We encountered her young husband in the lobby, and he walked with us upstairs to the nursery, declaring, "It all went just great, over pretty quickly, JaneAnne's fine, the baby's fine, and it's a *goddamned* girl." He seemed to have no reservations about making such a remark, and neither of us took issue with him about it because that was the prevailing attitude.

A significant part of the decade between my seventh and seventeenth birthdays was spent in fairly close proximity to my 'cross-the-road neighbors and fairly close kin, Aunt Exer and Uncle Keenis Holbrook and their baby daughter, Gwen, who is my second cousin and oldest friend. Aunt Exer was a Ward, one of my paternal grandma's sisters, who had married Uncle Keenis when she was just a girl.

The only thing that can be said about my Aunt Exer Holbrook is that she was one truly admirable human being. I do not recall ever hearing her say an unkind word to or about anybody. Whenever Gwen and I would fight, she would caution, "Now, you girls don't be ugly." She was the youngest of the Ward sisters—Grandma Alk, Daddy's mother, being the oldest—and she and Uncle Keenis bought and moved into Pop Pop's house when Grandma Alk died. She sort of took Grandma Alk's place there on the creek, especially for Sister, who was only a baby when our grandma died. Uncle Keenis always said that the first time he laid eyes on Aunt Exer, he told all present that was the very girl he was going to marry, so after that it was all predestined.

Uncle Keenis Holbrook was a true character and formed the ground for many of the stories of my youth. Yes, his name was Keenis, pronounced just the way penis is pronounced, and no, as far as I know nobody ever alluded to the similarities between those two words. You have to remember that this was in the forties and fifties. As best I can recall, the "p" word was never spoken or written, so my neighbors and I were completely unaware of its existence. At least I was. I might also point out that in my home community, Penix—pronounced "pen (as in pig-pen) ix"—was a common name, and nobody ever made jest of that either. It was not that we did not make earthy allusions—boys named Dick and Peter, as well as the Titlow family, had a hard row to hoe—we just were not aware of "proper" names.

Uncle Keenis was a deacon in the United Baptist Church, and he took his religion seriously enough to refrain from cussing. However, a man had to have *something* to say in the face of adversity. "Dang" just did not cut it, so Uncle Keenis frequently used the term "Hell-o!" with the accent on the first syllable. On other occasions he would say "Hell-o Pete!" After he had put in his day's work, plowing or planting, Uncle Keenis was best known for lounging in one of the two front-porch swings and calling out to Aunt Exer in the kitchen, "Ek, brang me a drank o' water." When Gwen and I would get too het up over something, he would quiet us by saying "Hush Gwan. You're aworryin' me."

He worked sporadically at a number of different jobs, from mining coal to selling vacuum cleaners, and brought back stories from all of these excursions. Uncle Keenis was a remarkable storyteller, and his recounting of experiences enlivened my imagination and filled my childhood. He traveled more than most of the folks on Two-Mile and, through his big tales, painted for us a vivid picture of the world he saw. I think each of us who knew him came away with our personal favorite among Uncle Keenis's sayings. Among Sister's favorites is Uncle Keenis's oft-repeated description of traffic over on U.S. Route 23 ten miles west of us: he would surmise, "Hell-o, I bet she's bumper-to-bumper on twenty-three." Abiding forever in my memory is his recounting—on many occasions—of a visit with relatives in Nashville, when he attended the Grand

Ole Opry in Ryman Auditorium. As he spoke of country music stars Minnie Pearl, Roy Acuff, and Little Jimmy Dickens, he would pause dramatically for effect, give the listener a meaningful look, and declare: "Hell-o, I looked 'em right in the eye!" Uncle Keenis was a born raconteur and had a story to fit any occasion.

Most evenings in good weather, a number of us would gather on his big front porch to sing gospel songs and yell back and forth across the road to the group sitting in the opposite yard—ours. Such a practice was not considered at all inappropriate, since we were accustomed to shouting at each other in order to carry on conversations when we were working on different rows in the fields. In addition, one of the best things about having a house with a porch facing the main road was that it enabled us to talk with anybody who happened to walk up or down the road past our houses. We knew everybody who went by, and it would have been considered rude on the part of both parties not to shout greetings across the hundred yards or so that separated us. Even if we didn't know the person walking by, it would have been deemed impolite not to call out "Hidie" to him or her.

When I was going out with Billy Daniels, who lived over on Pigeon Roost, I would walk out in my yard all dressed up on a summer's eve to be greeted by Uncle Keenis's hollering, "I smell Bee Branch!" which predictably cracked up everybody on both sides of the road. I always yelled back to correct him about the Bee Branch/Pigeon Roost mix-up, but it did no good; he got the laugh anyway.

There was never any agreement about who would be included on which porch, since the entire evening ritual was never formalized, so I probably spent as much time on the Holbrook porch as I did on my own. The staple of such evenings was the telling of tall tales. Somebody always commented, "The first liar ain't got a chance," as everybody tried to outdo each other with their stories. It would be hard for me to exaggerate the importance of what got passed on at these little informal gatherings of friends and family of all ages, because virtually all the values that guided my early life were learned in that way.

One illustration of the respect for position (age and kinship) over book-learning happened when I was in the fifth grade. Uncle Keenis, for some reason, had been to Baltimore, a very unusual circumstance because, unless they worked away, most of our people hardly traveled outside the county, much less the state. Shortly after his return, several of us were sitting around on his front porch listening as he regaled us with descriptions of his adventures in the big city. As he was telling the story, he happened to mention that Baltimore was the capital of Maryland. I said I didn't think so; I thought the capital was Annapolis. He said I was wrong, and nobody else took a position either way. I was certain I was right; so I ran across the road to my house, found the information in my geography book, and carried it back with me to prove I was correct. I opened the book and showed everyone that it said the capital of Maryland was Annapolis. Uncle Keenis glanced at my book, said, "No, it's Baltimore," and continued with his tale. Everybody accepted his declaration as the final word, and that was the end of the story. Book-learning was not very credible on Two-Mile Creek.

Another of the characters in the evening gatherings was my grandfather Paris Preston, whom everybody called Uncle Pare—everybody, that is, but Sister and me. We called him Pop Pop. He was a skinny, dried-up little man who wore loosely fitting high-bib overalls and wore an old hat to cover his balding head. He had started out in life as a carpenter and in his old age worked sporadically building or repairing houses. In addition to that work, he did blacksmithing in "the shop," a weathered, board-and-batten building he and my daddy had put up between our two houses.

Pop Pop and Grandma Alk had lived at Bob's Branch when their children were growing up, but, shortly before Momma and Daddy were married, Pop Pop bought a house on a hundred fifty or so acres on Two-Mile Creek. It was a good-sized piece of ground, stretching on the north side of the road from Frank Ward's land east to Mitchell Wallen's property line, with the house sitting in the middle of the property and the barn directly to the west. The original house on that land, which Pop Pop, Grandma Alk, and my retarded Aunt Jo lived in—and which was later sold to Uncle Keenis Holbrook's family—was, for a number of years, the biggest and nicest house on Two-Mile. It had a big front porch that served as a gathering place for folks to while away summer evenings, lounging in one of the two swings, wooden straightback chairs, or old-fashioned rockers that faced the road. When my daddy got married, he and Pop Pop then built Momma and Daddy a house across the creek on the southernmost part of that property. Our house was directly across the road from Pop Pop's, and in the early evening that's where those crowds gathered so that we could carry on conversations by yelling back and forth across the road.

Pop Pop was thought to have done well financially, and he was pretty careful with his money. He had a big radio in the front room of his house where half the community came together to hear the war news, listen to University of Kentucky basketball, and, on Saturday nights, tune in to the Grand Ole Opry. Whenever anybody walked into his house, Pop Pop would repeat the line from the Little Jimmy Dickens song, "Pull off your coat and throw it in the corner," and we never failed to laugh at his cleverness. He never went to school past second grade, but he was a big UK Wildcat fan, as were we all—and not a high-school diploma in the crowd except for my momma. When Grandma Alk died in 1947, Pop Pop sold the big house to Uncle Keenis and Aunt Exer Holbrook as part of a deal to have Aunt Exer help take care of my Aunt Jo. Aunt Exer, Grandma Alk's youngest sister, cared for Jo and Pop Pop, who continued to live in the house for about a year until he built his own tiny place across the creek, right next door to us.

Pop Pop was not only close to me; he was close to all the kids in the community. He probably spent more time with us than any other adult in our lives. Although our mothers, aunts, cousins, and sometimes our fathers and uncles were within running distance, every one of us hung around Pop Pop. We would either go sit on the porch with him while he whittled something or sit in the shop while he worked on horseshoes and sharpened augers for the mines. When he was not busy in his shop, he could usually be counted on to take us on explorations through the hills. We were a curious little band: Easter, Gwen, Sister, me—and sometimes Hi John—led by my scrawny little Pop Pop. Pop Pop taught us how to tell if a 'simmon (persimmon) was ripe: "Don't try to taste first 'cause if it's green, it'll turn your mouth clear inside-out." And from him we learned the precise shade of brown the black walnut hulls had to turn before they were ready to be hulled, cracked, and eaten. He made us wooden swords so that we could play gladiators—whatever a gladiator was—in the weeds, and we were constantly calling on him to punch holes for a handle in our tin cans so that we could make water buckets for the playhouse. I can never recall a time when Pop Pop did not have time for us or even when he grew impatient with us. He would stop to show us what he was doing and even let us "help" him. Although we must have been a dreadful inconvenience, he was always patient and gentle with us. Pop Pop was not a demonstrative man—I do not recall his ever hugging anybody—but there is no doubt in my mind that he loved every one of us.

One other thing we learned from Pop Pop was that we could do anything we set our minds to and, if we didn't know how to do it initially, with a little help we could figure it out. He showed us how to whittle, then gave us a knife and some wood to try our hand at it, and he taught us all the moves in mumble peg. He said way too many folks just "set around" because they couldn't figure out what to do, when they should be "gettin' atter it." Although he voted in every election, Pop Pop showed little faith in local politics. He routinely signed petitions for opposing candidates because, as he put it, "Ain't none of 'em got much sense or they wouldn't be running for office." We were left to infer that some things were just more trouble than they were worth, and we ought to have sense enough to stay shy of them. I think all of us kids owe a debt of gratitude to my Grandma Alice "Alkie" Preston, who died and left Pop Pop to us kids.

I was never close to my Grandma Alk; she died of complications of diabetes when I was six years old. I remember her as fulfilling everybody's ideal image of a grandmother: white hair twisted back from her face, small silver-rimmed glasses, and always wearing a house dress covered by an apron. Whenever she was outside, she wore a big sunbonnet made out of the scraps of feed sacks. In those days, we bought hog feed in brightly printed, woven sacks, which the women sewed up into clothing for themselves and their children. Then they used the scraps to make aprons to cover their dresses and sunbonnets that shielded their faces and tied under their chins. Although she died early in my life, it has always been easy for me to remember what my Grandma Preston looked like because she had five sisters who lived for many years after her death. As everybody knows, the Ward women all look alike, right down to Sister, who is plime blank like that side of the family.

My Great-Grandma Ward—mother of Alkie, Exer, and a gaggle in between—lived with my grandparents and died just a year or so before her oldest daughter, Grandma Alk. All I remember of her is that she too wore huge aprons and sunbonnets and had a big lap to run to and climb on. She was a little different from most women in our community, however, in that she smoked a pipe and was rumored to have danced when she was a girl. I learned of these untoward behaviors in a whisper because such activities were considered more than a little scandalous. Her husband, Asbury "Azzie B." Ward, died before I was born, but I always gave him credit for being open-minded, since he did, after all, marry such an outlandish woman.

My daddy's oldest brother, Uncle Mitchell, a tall man with lots of curly, graying hair (he "took after" the Wards), was twelve years older than Daddy. Uncle Mitchell left home at fourteen when he married Aunt "Ogie" Fannin, who tried, unsuccessfully, her whole life to be called by her given name, Viola. Uncle Mitchell got a job doing carpentry work up in Pikeville and soon did well enough to go out on his own as a builder. He was the success story of the family because he got rich enough to buy a house in town and a new Cadillac every couple of years and to send every one of his five children to city schools.

Although Pikeville was only fifty miles away, in those days that meant a long journey over winding, often unpaved, mountain roads; so we saw Uncle Mitchell only every couple of months. When he came to see us, he was very seldom accompanied by Aunt Ogie or any of his children. It was that town-versus-country difference again. Since they lived in town, they thought they were a lot better than their country cousins, and I suspect they would never have acknowledged us if they hadn't had to. There was also bad blood between Aunt Ogie's family and ours because two of her big old sorry brothers had caught my retarded Aunt Jo outside the yard when she was thirteen years old and had taken advantage of her. (I don't know just exactly how much *advantage* they had taken because I'm lucky to have found out even this much.) Pop Pop went around to see Old Man Fannin to talk about it, and the brothers about beat him to death. This happened shortly before Pop Pop bought the land on Two-Mile, and there were those who thought that he moved his family to keep from having to kill the Fannin brothers. The attitude we adopted was that that bunch of Fannins was a wild and sorry lot and altogether not worth wasting good gunpowder on. They didn't come on Two-Mile, and that was just as well. Uncle Mitchell and Aunt Ogie were living in Prestonsburg at the time of the family trouble, and they chose to ignore it. But, like most family secrets, that story was just beneath the surface of every interaction any of us ever had with any of them.

Daddy's other brother, Uncle Glen, also became a carpenter; he and Aunt Ruth lived just north of Cincinnati, Ohio, with their only daughter, Glenna Lee, who was about five years older than I was. They didn't come home often, but we loved for them to visit because Uncle Glen was a great joker and often told funny stories on folks. I also recall his having brought the only firecrackers we ever had, so we were especially glad to see him on the Fourth of July holiday. He took after the Preston side of the family and was balding, dried-up, and pruny; he didn't look a thing like that strapping bunch of Wards.

Auntie Irene, Daddy's older sister, moved to Cleveland, Ohio, when she married Uncle Ernie Potts, who worked in the steel mills there. They had two boys, Robert Jay and Roby Lee, near in age to my sister and me, and the highlight of our year was when they would come home for a week in the summer when Uncle Ernie was on vacation from the mill. Their family seemed far more sophisticated than ours, and I recall thinking that their lives must be more like the people I read about in books. When I was about ten years old, Robert Jay was telling a story about something he had done "down the boulevard," and I had to stop him to ask what was a boulevard. I also learned the word "bored" when Uncle Ernie announced one summer afternoon that Robert Jay was bored. "Bob's bored," he declared in that affected accent. (The word was that his people had come from England fairly recently, but we just thought he was stuck up.) After that, anytime Sister or I would get all puffed up because Daddy wouldn't let us do something or another, he'd say, "*Bobe's* bored," which was usually enough to bring us around.

When the Potts family visited us, Uncle Ernie took lots of pictures and tried to fit in and have a good time with us. But he and Auntie Irene were just more sober than the rest of our family. The boys, however, were as wild as Sister and me, and we roamed the hills like mad dogs from beginning to end of their visits. In physique, Auntie Irene also took after the Wards—she was a big woman—but she favored Pop Pop in the face.

Daddy's younger sister, Jo, was the youngest of my grandparents' children, and, because she was severely retarded, she still lived at home. Family legend is that Jo was sharper'n ary tack until she was three years old, when she ran a high fever for days and her brain was just "burnt up." According to the official family story, Jo had "spinalmengitis."

I assume someone, sometime later in life, suggested a diagnosis of meningitis, but no physician was ever in attendance during Jo's bout with whatever disease the family held responsible for her condition. My daddy's people never were the kind of folks to do much doctoring. It could also be the case that Jo never had such an illness and was simply just not *right* from the time she was born. My Grandma and Grandpa Preston were first cousins. Pop Pop's mother and Great-Grandma Ward were sisters—both Prices—and sometimes tales like the *spinalmengitis* explanation are made up to cover the shame of having such a child. Just like all stories told over and over, after awhile everybody believes them for the truth, and it becomes impossible to separate fact from fiction.

Because of Jo's condition, my grandparents were very protective of her and shamed by her. My parents worried a lot that I was going to turn out to be "crazy as Jo." She would have "fits" where she would laugh wildly, stamp her feet, and bite her fist. The kids would mock her, and it sometimes seemed to me that Easter Ward made a career of acting-like-Jo. Since I never did have much control over my sense of humor, some of the problems I had growing up were due to my having fits of the giggles at the most inopportune times. These were often interpreted by my extended family as being "like Jo," and I know this worried both of my parents. I also think one of the reasons Momma and Daddy were so protective of me when it came to being alone with boys was because of Jo's encounter with the Fannin boys. Nobody ever specified exactly how that sexual assault took place, but it was made clear to me very early that I had to be careful around men and not put myself in a place where somebody could get me "in trouble." Since I was such a late bloomer, my parents spent a lot of time worrying needlessly about this sort of thing, since nobody seemed inspired to lust after me until I was well into adulthood.

I never knew my momma's daddy, Grandpa Lige Mollette, because he died five years before I was born. My momma always swore she loved her daddy, but even she said that he was just an "old rake." While he had a number of jobs, including some sort of ticket-taking job at the train station over at Kermit, West Virginia, as well as serving as high sheriff of Martin County, his propensity for strong drink apparently kept him from doing much of anything for very long. One thing he did do, however: he settled my Grandma Emmy on a small piece of land on the left-hand fork of Greasy Creek and was home just often enough to sow his seed in her twelve times. Three of those children were stillborn, one died in childhood, and eight lived to adulthood; the youngest was my mother.

My daddy once said that my Grandma Emmy was "the finest old woman who ever wore shoe-leather, but Lige Mollette was sorry as dirt." As a result, "not a goddamn one of those kids had a lick of sense." Although Daddy loved my mother's family, he sure didn't respect them much. He saw them as low-down drunks and lazy dreamers who talked big but didn't have a decent day's work in 'em. He said that they came by their low-bred sorriness naturally—got it from their daddy. Grandpa Lige's hips and legs were wasted—it was rumored that his affliction was caused by his getting hold of some bad 'shine—before his fortieth birthday. When he got down, Grandma Emmy took over the homeplace herself and worked the land, raised the animals, and nursed my grandpa ("waited on him hand and foot") until his death more than two decades later. Grandma Emmy Mollette was one of those skinny, withered old women with an olive-drab face that had seen more than its share of sunlight. She had a tiny little waist, and, unlike many hillbilly women who are hunched over from their years of childbearing and fieldwork, my grandma stood straight as an arrow until the day she died.

Since Momma was sickly and often unable to care for me, I spent quite a lot of my early life with Grandma Emmy. Perhaps the thing I best recall about my maternal grandmother is her attention to her person. Despite her daily burdens on the farm, she bathed and groomed herself every morning as if she were expecting a visit from the governor. Each evening she went through the same grooming ritual, as if, perhaps, she might invite the fortunate governor into her bedchamber. It didn't matter how many farm tasks awaited her; she made time in the morning for combing her waist-length black hair (which had not been cut since she was saved and went into the church as a thirteen-year-old), knotting it carefully into a bun at the nape of her neck, and taking a sponge bath out of a small washpan kept only for that purpose. Her first chores of the morning were to fire up the coal cookstove in the kitchen, put a fresh panful of water on one of the burners, and add coal to rekindle the fires in the front room and upper room fireplaces—or rebuild them if they had died over the night. She then headed for the barn to do the milking. When she returned from the barn, she brushed her teeth, washed what she considered critical areas, put on a clean dress, applied cream to her face, and started the waking-and-breakfast ritual that began the working day. The reason I describe this in such detail is because it was most unusual back then for anyone to go to that kind of trouble to groom herself, *especially* every day.

When I reached third grade, my teacher, Ellen Dutton, required every child in her class to bring a handkerchief to school. She also directed us to keep a record of washing our faces, combing our hair, and brushing our teeth—personal hygiene activities for which we were given stars. For many of my classmates, this was their first encounter with the face-washing and tooth-brushing ritual, but not for me. My Grandma Emmy had not only taught me to read, she had taught me that it was just as important to keep myself clean and attractive. As she helped me wash myself in preparation for bed, she told me that only sorry and lazy folks went to bed dirty. "You can always tell trash because it stinks," she would say as she supervised me scrubbing my face, underarms, privates, and feet.

Grandma Emmy was also generous enough to share with me the bottle of toilet water she kept to daub behind her ears and on her wrists, both morning and evening. Whether she was working the fields or going to church, she always carried a handkerchief scented with a bit of that toilet water in the bosom of her dress. These little vanities have been passed silently down through the generations, and my mother was fanatic about her personal grooming. When Momma died in her eightieth year, we found make-up and cologne in the glove compartment of her car and a new set of hot rollers in her bathroom cabinet.

Although Grandma Emmy never ventured more than a hundred miles from the homeplace, I know she visited many places in her head. When Uncle Burns returned from his Army stint in Europe, Grandma and I would sit by the fire in the evening and listen to him spin stories of the smells and sights and sounds of those faraway places he had visited. My first visions of Notre Dame Cathedral and bombed-out Dresden came from my Uncle Burns, interspersed with stories of eiderdown bed covers and other such wonders. My grandma had read enough about each place that often she would interrupt with questions, asking specifics about the people or the lay of the land or how long the journey would be from one place to another. She wanted to see Niagara Falls and the ocean and often told me of her dreams of seeing the Holy Land and the pyramids.

My husband teases me, saying that I want to stand on every patch of earth on this planet before I leave it. He is pretty close to right about that, a desire no doubt born on those long-ago evenings before my Granny's fireplace when we didn't feel the wind blowing through the cracks between the logs because we were standing at Stonehenge or marveling at summer snow on the Dolomites. Grandma Emmy never got to go much of anywhere, but she never let that kill her curiosity about other places and other people.

Folks who knew my grandmother often remarked that they never heard her complain about her lot in life and that if anybody else mentioned her burdens she just responded that life was not always good and there was no need worrying over things that could not be changed. I am sure, however, that she certainly would have changed things if she could have, since her husband was a notorious womanizer and her three surviving sons were low-down drunks. When Uncle Fred's first wife died, leaving him with three-year-old Leon, my uncle simply brought the backward little boy to Grandma Emmy's and left him there. Although Uncle Fred remarried and had another family, Leon was brought up by my grandma, who helped him with his studies until he finished high school and cared for him until she died.

Emmy Cline had married Lige Mollette when she was sixteen years old. She outlived him by more than two decades, but she never even came close to having a romantic or sexual relationship with another man. She was thought to be an attractive woman. Several little widowers let it be known that they were interested in keeping her company, but Grandma would have none of that.

When my Auntie Stella was widowed, she came for a time to live with my grandma, and I often heard her encourage Grandma Emmy to allow one widower or another to come to call. Grandma's answer was always the same, "I'm not living under any 'petticoat government' again. Never!" When I asked her to explain "petticoat government," she declared, "No matter whose house it is, when there's a man in the house, a woman's got no say." At the time I did not understand just what an astute observation that was.

Still, folk wisdom, independence, vanity, and a love of reading are not all I took from Grandma Emmy Mollette. When I was about eleven years old, I told her about a crush I was carrying around on Chadman Meade—who looked exceedingly desirable in his all-black outfit—when she imparted the only direct sexual advice she ever gave me. I can still see those green eyes looking very seriously into my own green eyes as she cautioned, "Now, Linda Sue, at night all cats are gray." I recall pondering—to whatever extent my eleven-year-old head was capable of deliberation—that statement for days, attempting to decipher its meaning. That bit of homespun philosophy may also have contributed to her refusal to be courted after her husband died, but I sometimes wonder on what grounds she was qualified to make such a declaration.

Like most churchgoing hill-country women, my Grandma Emmy never used four-letter words; the worst swear word I ever heard her use was "shucks." The story was told, however, that my grandma was hoeing corn when she got word that Grandpa Lige was up in the clearing with old Liz Necessary, only one of the women my grandpa was rumored to have fooled around with prior to his untimely paralysis. It was said that Grandma walked directly out of the cornfield and into the woods, thereupon discovering Grandpa and Liz in flagrante delicto. Aunt Mandy Walters was right behind my grandma and later recounted that Grandma Emmy confronted the guilty couple by drawing herself up, placing her hands on her hips, and staring them down. Ignoring Liz, she was said to have addressed Grandpa Lige directly by declaring, "Now, Lige, you don't shit where you eat!" She then turned on her heel and went back to the cornfield. I am told that was the only time anyone ever heard my grandma cuss.

Home is largely an idea, a place where we go and know that whatever changes we have made in our lives, we will still always belong right there. I always felt at home in Grandma Emmy's house. I was born there, and I lived there off and on for a good part of my early years. It lay to the left of the dirt road in a little clearing and came into view as you rounded the first blind curve going up Greasy Creek, about half a mile off the main road. It was sort of grayish, the color old wood turns when it is not painted but maybe whitewashed every couple of decades. It had a porch stretching all the way across the front of the structure and three chimneys, one on either side of the house and another, which you couldn't see from the road, off the lean-to kitchen out back. There were always two rocking chairs and a swing on the front porch, fronted by four spindly porch posts encircled by Grandma Emmy's profusion of morning glories. A door opened off either side of the porch, one leading to the front room and the other going into the upper room, where I was born. Grandma Emmy's house consisted of the front room, the upper room, the dining room, the kitchen, and the loft. The fireplace, with a grouping of wooden ladderback and rocking chairs gathered 'round it, was off to the left as you entered the front room. On the right were two quilt-topped iron beds, one in each corner—the footboards providing a pathway to the door to the upper room. Grandma Emmy never had a store-bought mattress, so her beds were always soft, for they consisted of two lower mattresses filled with corn shucks and two top mattresses packed with feathers. I loved to sleep in Grandma's feather beds because they snuggled up around me and hugged me right to sleep. Because there were no springs or store-bought mattresses, they were no fun to jump around on; there was no bounce.

On many nights, I went to sleep lying on my left side in my Grandma's bed—when I was little, I always slept with Grandma Emmy—watching the grown-ups sit by the fire and drink their last cup of coffee before turning in. Everybody in my family drank extremely strong coffee from sunup to sundown and experienced no sleep problems. I was an adult before I learned about the effects of caffeine on sleep patterns. As Loretta Lynn put it: "Th' work we done was hard. / At night we'd sleep 'cause we was tard." When Grandma Emmy and I were the only ones there, I would drift off to slumber as she sat in her rocking chair and read her Bible or Grit or some other book or magazine. I do not recall her ever sitting without something to read or something to work on in her lap. If someone was there with her, she would darn socks, do mending, string beans, or peel apples or potatoes; when alone, she always had something to read.

The upper room also had a fireplace, but there were no chairs around it. The only furniture in the room consisted of four more quilt-topped iron beds, placed end to end in each of the four corners of the room. A quilt horse hung from the ceiling of the room and was raised and lowered by heavy twine that stretched to each of the four corners of the room and was caught on small hooks placed in the ceiling corners and halfway down each corner. By the time I was born, Grandma Emmy lived alone or with Leon, who slept in the loft, so she would often leave the quilt horse down for months at a time; all of us would stitch whenever we had a few free minutes.

The loft consisted of one room, with no ceiling or insulation between the room and the roof. The room was filled with another four iron beds, placed exactly as were those in the upper room. Clothes hung from nails scattered about the walls. Only the good clothes were on hangers, sometimes two or three garments per hanger; work clothes drooped directly from the nails. Each family member had a nail and a hanger as well as a cardboard box for his or her personal garments, for there were no closets or chests in the house.

Grandma had a big trunk for keepsakes and another one for storing her quilts and linens. She kept both right up next to the pie safe in the dining room. In truth, she had no linens to speak of; all her sheets, pillowcases, and dishtowels were homemade from feedsacks. She owned one cream-colored damask tablecloth that had once been white and was pretty threadbare, which she put on the big wooden dining room table for Christmas and other special occasions. Her four towels, which she changed every two days, were also far from new; her washrags were made from old towels she had cut up when they had worn out. I spent a good while out of the hills before I learned to call that piece of fabric used for bathing a wash *cloth* rather than a wash *rag*. By the time Grandma Emmy dipped a piece of what had been terry cloth into her bath water, the term wash rag was a far more accurate description anyway.

The dining room, with the trunks, the pie safe, and the long, narrow table that could seat a dozen, was the center of the house, leading off the front room and on into the kitchen. It was the only room in the house that did not have either a stove or a fireplace, so it depended on the leftover heat from the coal stove in the kitchen and the front room fireplace. During the winter we preferred eating in the kitchen to keeping our coats and gloves on in order to eat in the dining room. We did use the dining room on Christmas Eve—even when we had to wear our headscarves and earmuffs, but I don't recall thinking that that was any big hardship.

Most of the winter we ate on the square wooden kitchen table—covered with brightly printed oilcloth—that sat by the back window next to the coal cookstove on which our food simmered. There was always some bit of teasing about whose plate was to go over the tennis-ball-sized round hole made by the ubiquitous food-grinder at one edge of the table. I do not recall anybody's kitchen table not so marked, since pimiento cheese and "ham" salad—made by chopping bologna and pickles and adding mayonnaise—were well-loved by all. I'm fairly sure that the only folks who did not have a hole for a food-grinder in their kitchen table were probably just too poor to buy one.

My Grandma Emmy had conceived and birthed twelve children in that little house. Although she did not have much in the way of material things, everything she owned was as clean as hard work could make it. Since Grandpa Lige was paralyzed before the Social Security Act was passed, Grandma Emmy, as far as I know, never had any cash income except what she got from selling a bushel or two of produce now and then. In many ways, I suppose she was poor by almost any standards then, but I never felt the least bit deprived when I was with her. She laughed often and well, and I never once heard her speak of wanting or wishing or longing for anything other than the safety of Uncle Burns when he was off in Europe during World War II. She wore out the knees of her long aprons from kneeling at the edge of the garden praying that her boys would stop drinking, but she didn't live to see that. From the time Grandpa Lige was paralyzed until he died twenty-four years later, my grandma took care of him, worked their land, and raised pigs, chickens, and all kinds of produce. She put up vegetables, milked the cows, killed and cured meat, and made her own butter and soap—all without electricity or indoor plumbing.

In addition, Grandma Emmy had one of the finest flower gardens in the community, with lots of different varieties all over both front and back yards. Each year when she dug up her iris rhizomes and separated them, she and her neighbor, Aunt Mandy Walters, would plant the extra rhizomes down along the creek bank across from the homeplace. Grandma Emmy lived pretty far upstream; so when the spring rains flooded the creek each year, some of those irises would wash out and down the stream. For many years after my grandma's death, we could visit the homeplace in the spring of the year and see Greasy Creek winding all the way to the main road past the yellow and purple descendants of my Grandma Emmy's irises.

Momma's oldest sister, Aunt Lizzie Colvin, was another strong woman. She was the only one of my mother's siblings whose overall attitude was steadfastly positive, and, physically, Auntie Lizzie was the only heavy person in Momma's family. While she probably had the hardest life of any of them, she was certainly the only one who consistently made folks feel good just to be around her. She was about five-foot-six, as round as a barrel, and she positively crowed with her ain't-the-world-just-wonderful demeanor. She was a devout Freewill Baptist. Without a lesson in her life, Auntie Lizzie regularly played piano in the church—the Freewills are one of the few small sects of rural Baptists that allow instrumental music in the house of the Lord—until she was in her nineties. She played by ear and with much gusto, as she would accompany her extraordinary contralto voice, leading the singing of the faithful at Thealka Freewill Baptist Church. After high school she had left the homeplace on Greasy Creek to marry Uncle Ray Colvin and given birth to five children, whom she appeared to adore without reservation. After four of the children were grown and gone, Uncle Ray came down with tuberculosis, died, and left Auntie Lizzie with a house in a coal camp and two children to support: Lois Ann, the baby of the family, and Tommy "Tucker" Daniel, her grandson, whose father was divorced from my cousin Francis and provided no financial support for his son. When Uncle Ray had become unable to work, Auntie Lizzie had taken the teacher's exam—at that time, teachers did not have to go to college in order to teach in the public schools—and gotten a job teaching third, fourth, and fifth grade at Thealka School on Muddy Branch, the coal camp where the Colvin family lived.

While Lois Ann and Tucker were the only ones who lived full-time with Auntie Lizzie, I can never recall going to her house when there was not a crowd, both drop-in company and staying-until-I-get-on-my-feet offspring, siblings, grandchildren, or house guests. If anybody in her extended family lost a job, a husband, or just ran out of money and needed a place to stay, Auntie Lizzie provided it. She did not seem to be the least disquieted by all the company. I continued to visit Auntie Lizzie occasionally until her death a few years ago, and I do not recall ever once being there alone with her in her little mining camp house.

Auntie Lizzie was perhaps the best cook I ever knew; she cooked skillfully, and she cooked a lot. Obviously she believed the Lord would provide, and I suppose He must have come through for her time and again. Otherwise, her ability to produce so much food had to be a loaves-and-fishes thing, since I cannot believe she could have had the income necessary to pay for all those vittles. Folks didn't just come to visit for the food, however, for Auntie Lizzie was an ace storyteller and always had some funny tale to tell, with herself as the dupe in the piece. She would roar with laughter at herself as she told of her gullibility or foolishness. One story I recall took place when Auntie Lizzie was just a girl and some suitor had come to call on her. Apparently they had been doing some serious sparking under the trees, down the path past the garden and toilet, when she returned to the house to get a pitcher of fresh water. On her way back, carrying the pitcher of water and two glasses, she walked past the toilet to find her young swain sitting therein doing his business, with the toilet door wide open. Now, most girls of that time would have run home in shame and never again been able to face the young man, but not my Auntie Lizzie! As she told it, she looked her suitor full in the face, said "Hidie," and marched on to the spot where she'd left him to await his return. For as long as she lived, my Auntie Lizzie gave definition to the term "unflappable."

She also must have been a good teacher, for throughout her life her former students continued to make regular pilgrimages to see her. I can recall their discussing how much fun it was to be in a classroom taught by Auntie Lizzie. "I'll whip the socks right off you," was said to be one of her best-remembered threats. Her zest for life in the face of hardship and disappointment suggests to me that our experiences do not so much shape our attitudes as our attitudes shape our experiences. In terms of attitude, Auntie Lizzie was far more similar in disposition to my daddy than to my momma or any of her other brothers and sisters. My daddy, who had little admiration for my mother's other siblings, always respected and enjoyed Auntie Lizzie, and they continued to swap stories until her death.

Grandma Emmy's second living daughter, Auntie Stella, was a tall, solemn-looking woman who, like her sister Lizzie before her, was widowed in middle age and became an elementary schoolteacher. Although none of Grandma Emmy's daughters were formally educated beyond high school, at some point in their lives, every one of them taught public elementary school. After she was widowed, Auntie Stella moved in with Grandma Emmy, but my aunt was so bossy and such a complainer that the arrangement did not work out as well as it might have. Thus, after a couple of years, Auntie Stella moved back to her own place. She had only one child, Veva, who was already grown and married when Uncle Tom died and left Auntie Stella far better off financially than her sister Lizzie. Unfortunately, she was not gifted with Auntie Lizzie's high spirits and was never nearly as satisfied with her lot in life. My Aunt Stella got along reasonably well with people, but she did not particularly enjoy them. Folks simply were not drawn to her the way they were to her older sister. Thus, with the exception of her daughter, sisters, and grandchildren, she spent her old age pretty much alone, complaining about small problems to all who came to call as the number of visitors steadily dwindled.

The third of Grandma Emmy's daughters, Auntie Amanda Holbrook, also left home at an early age in order to marry J. Kash Holbrook, a drummer or traveling salesman. Uncle Kash was on the road practically all the time, and, since she was unable to bear children, Auntie Amanda also took the teachers' exam and taught school for a time. In his early forties Uncle Kash developed severe diabetes, so Auntie Amanda quit teaching and spent the next thirty-some years of her life taking care of him. Fortunately, my uncle had made quite a bundle of money, so they were able to live in a fine house in town and spend their winters in Florida. Auntie Amanda probably gave Grandma Emmy a dollar or two on occasion, but she pretty much broke ranks with her family early on because her whole life was spent focusing on Uncle Kash's health needs. This largely unrecognized breach within the family was also partially brought about by Uncle Kash's tendency to brag, flash his money, and generally insist that the whole family agree that he was better than all the rest of the Cline Mollettes.

After Uncle Kash died in Florida in the mid-1970s, Auntie Amanda moved back to be with her family but was never able to get along with any of her sisters or brothers very well. She insisted upon saving both their souls—by bearing Christian witness—and their bodies—by attempting to get them to eat properly and quit smoking. She shuttled back and forth between Florida and Kentucky for several conflict-filled years before finally settling in central Kentucky near my sister, where she outlived all her siblings, a testimony to her diet and exercise routines. There can be no doubt that Auntie Amanda was right about the health habits of her siblings. But she never learned that she could not take back to them what she had discovered in the outside world and expect them to be anything but angry at her for pointing out their apparent tendencies toward self-destruction.

Uncle Fred, the oldest of my mother's brothers, looked very much like Grandpa Lige: tall, rangy, with a full head of dark-brown hair falling across his angular face. Portraits show both Uncle Fred and Grandpa Lige looking intensely into the camera as though lost in thought and unaware of their handsome countenance. As his father before him and his brothers after him, Uncle Fred was a drunk and a womanizer. His road back from the bottle began late in his life when he was saved by the Lord. He worked sporadically as a coal miner and fathered three sons, one by his first marriage and two by the second. I know less about Uncle Fred than I know about my mother's other siblings, but it is worth pointing out that he shared another characteristic with his two younger brothers: each of them was divorced from at least one woman—something practically unheard of in my home community.

I don't know what the initial stood for in Uncle John B. Mollette's name, but he always declared it to be short for "Bigfoot." Since nobody ever disputed him, I suppose I must report it as such. I should point out, however, that in the generation before Uncle John there were four local John Mollettes, differentiated by their middle initials: John B., John L., John G., and John C. Their middle names were Big-eye; Little-eye; Good-eye; and Cut-fly (it was said this nickname had something to do with his mastery of the whip), so it is quite possible that Uncle John B.'s middle initial stood for Big-eye. Called John B. by his family and friends, he was shorter than his two brothers and scrawny, with a little round, bald head and a tendency to poke fun at practically everything and everybody. He always claimed that he was bald because he had once laughed at a bald man and commented that "a man could polish a nickel on the shine from that feller's head." Immediately thereafter, according to Uncle John B., he began to lose his own hair. He would cackle with glee as he told that tale to folks to explain why he was the only one in his family who did not take a full head of hair to his grave. As a young man, he was elected to the Kentucky legislature, where, according to family lore, Uncle John B. learned to love alcohol. I suspect that to be a convenient excuse, however, since both his brothers apparently developed the same affinity without spending time at the statehouse.

Apparently the legislative process in the old Commonwealth was somewhat unrestrained during Uncle John's tenure downstate, and he added to that aura, at least to hear him tell it. According to Uncle John B., on one occasion as he was sponsoring legislation that would become the beginnings of Mayo State Vocational School in Paintsville, some citified scoundrel from over 'round Louisville suggested that spending money to try to educate those heathens from the hills was sheer waste. Uncle John, somewhat averse to being dubbed a "hethern," took exception to that opinion and challenged the gentleman from Jefferson County to step outside and say that to his face, close up. The flatlander sucker-punched my skinny little uncle and ran for the door, at which point Uncle John pulled his gun from his boot and fired at the retreating lawmaker. "Woulda got 'im too, hadn't a been fer them other boys a holdin' me back as I fired. As it was the bullet missed 'im—high—and went through th' door over his head. He 'bout messed his britches, though. Never did give me another breath o' trouble after that and nobody else did either, f'r that matter."

It was said that Uncle John B. could charm a bird out of a tree, and indeed he was able to parlay his command of language and negotiating skills into enough hard currency to support two wives and one child, although I do not recall his ever working steadily at anything over any lengthy period. Despite his uncomely physical appearance and well-known alcohol problem, Uncle John B. carried on the family tradition of philandering and was quite the rascal until his religious conversion in his old age.

Grandma Emmy's last boy, my Uncle Burns, had an abundance of charm and a lightning-quick mind but was just dirt-sorry. Everybody's favorite among the Cline Mollettes, he took his natural gifts and squandered them with abandon. He was Grandma Emmy's favorite child, which set the precedent for his relationships of the heart, for he loved many women and they loved him right back. Apparently as far back as high school he cut a fine figure, and all the girls were after him. After graduating from high school, he joined Roosevelt's Works Progress Administration (WPA), which took work crews all over eastern Kentucky, and he fell in love anew everywhere he worked, a girl-in-every-port pattern that followed him all the days of his life. From time to time when he was living with us, a strange woman would show up at the door, looking for my Romeo uncle. He always appeared happy to see them, and, since they did not leave in tears, I suppose the meeting must have seemed successful to both parties. Uncle Burns probably had more opportunities in every area than all the other men in my extended family put together, and he blew every one of them. He was married and divorced at a fairly young age; married and divorced again at forty-something. Then, when he was in his late fifties, he married a girl forty-some years his junior and lived with her until he died. I believe he loved every woman who ever loved him, but there was always a better one around the next corner. And he invariably returned to his one true love: alcohol. Uncle Burns was far too smart and charming for his own good. When faced with a myriad of choices, he wanted them all. He went into the army at the beginning of World War II and spent two years fighting in Europe, where he became fluent in Spanish, German, and French. The army then brought him back to the United States to work in a center for teaching languages, but—after paying for him to dry out twice—even they could not keep him sober for longer than six months, so he washed out of that.

Between jobs, Uncle Burns often lived with us or with Auntie Lizzie. When he was not drinking, he was just a great person to have around. Daddy financially supported him one way or another for most of his life. When he was not living off Daddy, you could almost always find him at Grandma Emmy's or Auntie Lizzie's. I really loved it when he lived with us because he would play cards with me, make the places in my geography book leap from the page, and field any questions I might have on history or literature. Before strong drink took away some of his recall, he knew a bit about everything, and he never lost his quick wit. He was working on the ceiling at our house when, as a teenager coming in from school, I read to him what appeared to me to be a not-so-poetic poem about facing death ("I Have a Rendezvous with Death"), and he explained that the word was pronounced ron-day-voo, not ren-dez-vo-us. That incident came a few days after my daddy had to get two stitches in his scalp after Uncle Burns dropped the hatchet on Daddy's head as he came in from work. My Uncle Burns was a study in strengths and weaknesses of character, but, in order to understand him or any of Momma's brothers, you have to have some insight into the way homefolks see the use of alcohol.

There is no such thing as social drinking on Two-Mile. What's more, I doubt that such a concept exists in any of the tiny rural communities that surround the small towns of Appalachian eastern Kentucky. This was the case when I was growing up, and so it remains today. This intolerant attitude toward alcohol probably came about due to the rigid fundamentalist religion pervasive in the area, but it is by no means confined to those who are formally religious. Many, perhaps most, of the folks (particularly the women) my age who have not yet been *saved*—affiliated with a church—still hold to an abstention from alcohol policy, most probably because of the way drinking is viewed by the community. While I would suggest that there is no social drinking in the creeks and hollers, I do not mean to imply that there is no drinking, period.

When I was a kid on Two-Mile I saw two approaches to alcohol: complete abstinence or recurrent sodden drunkenness; no in-between. Either you were one of those folks who eschewed the grape completely or, periodically, the grape got you. There was a particular pattern of drunkenness—as exemplified by my momma's three brothers and a few others in our community—that I saw during my years growing up on Two-Mile.

A man—always a man; women did not engage in such behavior—would go along for a period of time—weeks, months, or sometimes a full year—working steadily, treating his family well, passing for normal. Then, for some reason known only to him, he would take a drink and then another and another. The next thing he knew he would be rip-roaring drunk—and he would stay that way for some time, days or weeks.

I never heard anyone back home speak of someone drinking; they always said the person was "drinking and sworping." I have no better idea than you where the word "sworping" comes from, but I'll bet anybody from back home can define it for you with specificity. It means wildly running around, cussing and hollering, and in general acting in ways no good, sane, sober person would ever behave. That is frequently phase one of what folks back home would term "going on a drunk," which could last anywhere from twenty-four hours to a full week. Once the man had exhausted himself in the drinking and sworping phase, he would enter the "down" phase, meaning he literally could not stand up. Now, if he was lucky, somebody would find him and bring him home where he could live out this phase in the company of his immediate family. This stage could last as long as a month or for only a day or two, depending upon whether someone could sneak liquor to the besotted one. If liquor was not brought in, the drunk would surely manage to stand erect just long enough to get himself to the nearest bootlegger. While in the "down" phase of going on a drunk, the inebriate would not just lie quietly in his bed; he would moan and holler and sometimes lapse into praying for salvation till all the neighbors could hear.

Precisely what the drunk said during this time depended upon the range of his imagination—and here I must add that when he was down drunk, my Uncle Burns was a phenomenon. He was at the pinnacle of his intellectual powers for days, so long as his whiskey lasted. The trick was to *keep* him down by giving him less and less liquor each day until he could reach phase three, the "comin' out of it" stage. If he was not helped along with an ever-decreasing supply of alcohol daily, however, he would get right up from being down and go get enough liquor to put him to drinking and sworping again. Then, the process would begin all over— and the fear was always that this time he might not make it home before he got down.

One morning about two o'clock, we got a telephone call that Uncle Burns was "drunker'n a boiled owl and thumbing (hitchhiking)" up on the head of Two-Mile, just on our side of Two-Mile Hill. Although Daddy had to get up to go to work at four, he and Momma dragged Sister and me out of bed. All of us, with heavy coats over our pajamas, piled into the front seat of the old blue '49 Plymouth—which had succeeded the blue-black '41—and set out to retrieve our drunken uncle. We all had to go along because sometimes Uncle Burns would not go with anybody but Momma. Daddy wouldn't allow Momma to go by herself, and they would not leave Sister and me home alone; so the four of us set out. As it turned out, Daddy might as well have gone on alone; Uncle Burns didn't know a one of us anyway. When we picked him up, he just thought he had thumbed a ride with some tourists. As we drove him the two miles back to our house, he delivered himself of one of the most cogent lectures regarding the beauties of the area that I have ever heard. In an accent that drew upon his experiences abroad, he began, "You are entering the foothills of the Cumberlands." In the many years thereafter, all it took to send the four occupants of the front seat into gales of laughter was for one of us to refer to the "foothills of the Cumberlands."

The final comin'-out-of-it stage of drinking and sworping is characterized by nausea and physical debilitation, accompanied by much contrition and many promises that this will, indeed, be the very last time such a thing will ever happen. The remorse and the vows of this stage are as genuine as were the prayers of stage two, but the intentions of a drunk are not necessarily accompanied by any change in his behavior.

The current trend in treating alcoholism as a disease perplexes me, because all my uncles apparently suffered from it, yet they all were able to quit cold turkey—and remain sober for decades—when they got saved and joined the church. Shortly after I began teaching psychology, specifically addiction, I had an opportunity to ask Uncle Burns if he had any idea why he had drunk so much for so long. With a twinkle in his eyes, he lowered his voice and declared, "It was fun, little girl. When a man's young and got juice in him, he's got to have some way of getting it out of his system." When I asked why he never fell back into his old behaviors, he said that, after all he'd been through in his life, he knew God would "split Hell wide open" with him if he took another drink. In this case, then, the fear of God was apparently able to effect what two different detox centers, the U.S. Army, and a number of good women had failed to bring about.

Uncle Burns's full name was Burns Offutt Mollette, and he was called Burns by everybody—everybody, that is, except Uncle John. Uncle John also called him Burns when the two of them were sober, which, sad to say, was seldom, since one or the other of the brothers was drunk about half the time, and they did so love to get pig-eyed drunk together. When Uncle John was drunk, however, he called his baby brother Burn Offutt (pronounced burn-off-it).

Just a year or so before Grandma Emmy died, Momma, Auntie Lizzie, Auntie Stella, and a bunch of us kids were at the homeplace for a Fourth of July picnic. When Uncle Burns and Uncle John did not show up by noon, we just went on and ate without them, but we expected them shortly. The afternoon came and went and still no uncles. Around five

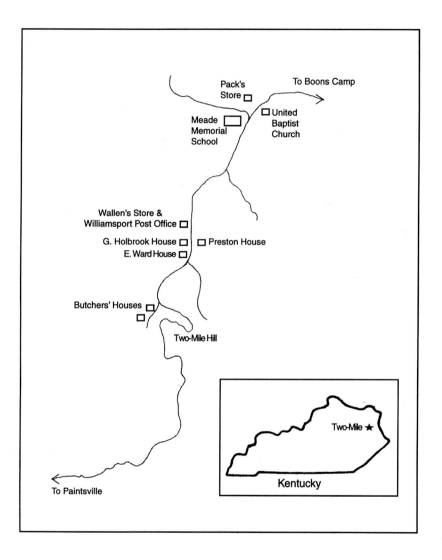

Pack's Store

To Boons Camp

Meade Memorial School

United Baptist Church

Wallen's Store & Williamsport Post Office

G. Holbrook House

Preston House

E. Ward House

Butchers' Houses

Two-Mile Hill

To Paintsville

Two-Mile ★

Kentucky

The Mollette Boys: (left to right) Grandpa Lige, Uncle Burns, John, and Fred.

Great-Grandpa Life Preston in a hat to die for.

My flapper Momma.

Grandpa Lige and Grandma Emmy
around 1930.

Daddy and Momma shortly after their
marriage in 1936.

With Momma in 1941 (top)
and ca. 1943 (bottom).

(Left to right) Aunt Exer, Ward Holbrook, Linda Sue Preston, Aunt Sally Ward Daniel, Great-Grandma Laura Belle Ward, Glenna Lee Preston, and Grandma Alice "Alk" Ward Preston, ca. 1943.

(Back) Great Grandma Laura Belle; (middle, left to right) Aunt Sally, Aunt Exer, Momma, Grandma Alk, Aunt Ruth; (front, left to right) Jo, Linda Sue, Cousin Glenna Lee, and Gwen.

Linda Sue, ca. 1944.

With Momma, ca. 1944.

Pop Pop's Barn, later bought by Uncle Keenis Holbrook, thereby becoming Gwen's Barn.

With Daddy (top) and Momma (bottom) in West Virginia, ca. 1945. The coal tipple where he worked can be seen in the background.

Pop Pop, in his best dress clothes, and Old Bessie.

With Grandma Alk, Robert Jay Potts, and assorted white leghorns near the wellbox, ca. 1945–46.

Pop Pop and Grandma Alk. Our old house can be seen across the road in the background.

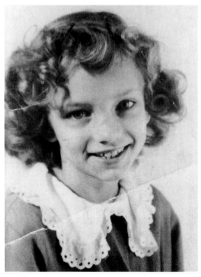

In third grade.

In fourth grade.

o'clock as our family was getting ready to leave, a strange car pulled up on the side of the bank out in front of Grandma Emmy's house and delivered what was left of my Uncle John. He staggered his way across the yard and up near the porch, where Auntie Stella, arms akimbo, drew herself up and demanded, "Just where is Burns?"

Attempting to focus his eyes properly, my Uncle John squinted sorrowfully at his sister, shook his head slowly from side to side, and said: "Burn Offutt, he fall by the wayside."

I know alcoholism is no laughing matter, but with my dear—but hopelessly sorry—uncles, there was not much else left to do. Everybody broke up but Auntie Stella. That's just the way it was in our family; we were always laughing when maybe crying might have been more appropriate.

I began my formal education in September 1947 at H.P. and L.G. Meade Memorial School in Johnson County, Kentucky. At that time the school consisted of five single-story wooden buildings spread out over an open field, bounded on one side by a dirt road and on the other side by a creek. The high-school building was the largest—one story, long, and slim, as I recall. One somewhat smaller building contained two classrooms, one for fifth and sixth grades and one for seventh and eighth. A still smaller building, with a little porch on the front, housed one classroom for primer, first, and second grades and another room for third and fourth grades.

The high-school building stretched along the edge of the creek at the confluence of Greasy and Two-Mile Creeks, while the two grade-school buildings perched on short stilts across the field next to the road and by the gymnasium, the one stone building in the group. The gym was by far the nicest building, having been built by the WPA during the Roosevelt years. Two other good-sized wooden buildings—the girls' toilet and the boys' toilet—sat in opposite corners of the field on either side of the makeshift baseball diamond. There was no running water in any of these buildings, but, unlike many of the students' homes, all the buildings except the toilets had electricity.

I do not recall how the largest school building was heated. When I was in fifth grade, we got a new two-story cinder-block building that housed all twelve grades, so I never spent much time in the old high-school building. The two-room grade schools, however, had a big pot-bellied stove in each classroom, where we left our galoshes and our wet socks to dry each day in the wintertime or when it rained.

Since many of us came from homes where we did not regularly brush our teeth, comb our hair, or wash our faces, one of the areas in which we were instructed was health and grooming. Thus, I particularly recall the porch of the first-grade classroom because Mrs. Mae Best, my first-grade teacher, sent me out there to comb my hair. In a school full of kids with straight, shiny hair, I was burdened with hair so curly you could hardly tell where it began or ended, and it was always impossibly tangled. Hence, on several occasions during my first year of school, I was sent to the porch to groom myself. I suppose that might have continued, but by the next year the teachers had grown accustomed to my bad-hair affliction, so Medusa-of-the-hills was never again publicly required to prove that her head had known the brush that very morning. My neighbor and nemesis, Easter Ward, also had curly hair, but hers was of the ringlet variety while mine was pure tangle. Easter's the one who christened me "Birdlegs," a name that stuck and colored a number of my experiences from first grade through high school.

Since there was no kindergarten in those days, it was customary for kids to take one year to complete the primer and first grades. There was no shame in taking two years, however, because we never had enough printed readers for everybody, and we could not move on to second grade without passing an oral reading test. I came from a family of voracious readers. My Grandma Emmy Mollette had taught me to read two years before I began school, so I was never required to read the little blue soft-cover primer but proceeded directly to the excitement of "Jerry saw toys and toys and toys!"

In the middle of my first year, Mrs. Best wanted to promote me to second grade, but my parents would not allow it since they thought I was a sickly child—spindly, you know—and they felt I would be out of place with the much-bigger second-graders. The truth is that I was healthy as a heifer, but because of my *whippoorwillness* everybody just figured I was not robust. I suspect Mrs. Best's motives may have had more to do with social than academic concerns, since I was probably not much fun to teach. I was something of a late-maturer, to say the least, and my unruly behavior never did endear me to teachers. Against the better judgment of my parents, however, Mrs. Best did not put up with me for the required two years. At the end of my first year of school, she double-promoted me to Mrs. Dutton's third grade.

Though kindly in appearance, Mrs. Ellen Dutton, a compact, gray-haired little woman, was a killer-of-snakes! Sister, who came along six years behind me, credits Mrs. Dutton with being one of the finest teachers she ever had. All I can say in explanation of Sister's opinion is that Mrs. Dutton must have undergone some sort of radical conversion during those six years, because that lady scared the pee outta me! She brought long willow switches to class—and, yes, folks, she used them to "wear us out." Although she did not often take her willow switch out specifically after me, she whipped Oneida Mae Wiley with regularity. I just happened to sit directly between Mrs. Dutton and Oneida Mae, so I got a welt or two with each whipping. Moreover, when I say Mrs. Dutton scared the pee out of me, I am not exaggerating. I wet my pants three times the year I was in her class because I was too afraid to ask to "be excused"—a euphemism used to request permission to leave class to go to the toilet. I do recall asking to "be excused" directly after the first incident of peeing in my pants and Mrs. Dutton chuckling as she asked if I didn't think it was "kinda late for that."

One drawback to going to school and living in the same place your whole life is that you are never able to get out from under your mistakes. I wet my pants three times in third grade, and I was still trying to live it down when I got out of high school. Easter Ward had a long memory for such things. I never did it before or after third grade, however, so I blame Ellen Dutton. Although I distinctly recall cowering before Mrs. Dutton's power, apparently my fear did not prevent me from holding the door to keep her from returning to our classroom one day when she had been "excused." I distinctly recall leaning back against that door, with Don Ed Pack on one side of me and Tilton Butcher on the other and the rest of the kids, big-eyed, staring at us from their seats. Finally Mrs. Dutton said, "I'm going to get Mr. Boyd (the principal)." As soon as she stepped away from the door, we three culprits scurried to our seats, and she came on in. At lunchtime two hours later, Ronalta Mae Pelphrey told on us; thus began my life of paying for my crimes by having to forgo recess.

And those classroom crimes were legion, including everything from holding the door on the teacher, talking in class, falling out of my chair, correcting teachers' grammar in class, sending a note to the teacher saying "Kiss my ass!" (I did that in fifth grade. I don't remember why I did it, but I *do* remember getting away with it), skipping and/or running in the classroom, making faces behind the teacher's back, emitting funny noises when the other class was being taught and the rest of us were supposed to be studying, and most of all laughing, laughing, and laughing in class. Nowadays I would probably be diagnosed ADD or ADHD or some such. Back then, they just kept me in at recess or whaled the tar out of me. One recommendation: If you ever have a choice between the switch or the paddle, take the paddle every time. Those willow switches cut. Trust me.

When I got to third grade, the only person from Mrs. Best's first-grade class to get there with me was my across-the-road neighbor, close friend, and second cousin, Gwen Holbrook. Her family had bought Pop Pop's house and moved to Two-Mile just before school was out the year before. I think she only attended the second grade for two weeks before being promoted. At seven years old, I was the youngest student in third grade, Gwen was second-youngest, and I think Ronalta Mae Pelphrey was also not quite eight years old. From there the range went all the way to age fourteen or fifteen. I know that sounds exaggerated, but in those days we simply were not promoted if we did not master the basic skills. Hence, there were two big old boys in third grade who were waiting to reach sixteen—the mandatory age for quitting school—and their academic train had ground to a halt in Ellen Dutton's class. During the few times I actually got to go out to recess, one or the other of these two young scholars always served as the "wolf" in the game of "big bad wolf." Clearly, school systems did not worry too much over the psyches or self-esteem of the students back then. I am not sure exactly what happened to one of the boys but, the last I heard, the other one has made a pretty good living following in the footsteps of his daddy, making moonshine and bootlegging hard liquor. Having listened to him do his sums more times than I would have liked during what was one of his last years of formal schooling makes me reluctant to purchase his product, since I cannot help but wonder how he figures the proportions he uses to make his 'shine.

Another third-grade experience stands out as having taught me a valuable lesson about cheating. Fairly early in my third-grade year, those who sat on either side of me and those behind and in front of me had recognized that I got pretty good scores on tests. Moreover, because there were so many kids in the class, Mrs. Dutton did not keep much of an eye out for cheating, so looking on others' papers was the order of the day. Then Mrs. D. gave us a "time-telling" test, using an illustration of eight big clocks. I had no notion of how to tell time; as best I could tell, those clock hands were all over the place, so I guessed wildly. Four of my classmates did not bother to guess but took their answers directly from my paper, and I brought them all down with me—each of us got two out of eight. Mrs. Dutton never questioned the way we had arrived at our answers, so the cheating continued—and I soon learned to tell time. But that experience made me realize that even the best students don't always have the right answers, so thereafter I always relied on my own judgment and was never tempted to copy from another student's paper.

During my fifth-grade year we had seven teachers; wore 'em out one after the other. My least favorite was Janis Carroll, a young woman who was the daughter of some city official in Paintsville and the recipient of my "kiss my ass" note. One of the reasons I never had to own up to authorship of that little memorandum was that she had so little control of us that, whatever happened, she'd just try to shame us and press on. She didn't last long as our teacher, but she was there long enough to get across the message that civilized behavior ended once you left the city limits of Paintsville. When things got just clear out of hand in the classroom, she would often burst into song, which might have been effective at calming us if she had sung something that was recognizable. In a class full of kids who could have sung every lyric to "I Saw the Light," "Sugar in the Gourd," or "Fair and Tender Ladies," Miss Carroll was given to bringing us light opera selections. She was as spindly as I was and would stand at the front of the classroom, swaying and gesticulating as she warbled:

Oooooh, a mother once she had a lovely daughterrrrr.
She was an actress on the stage.
Sheeeee traveled with some very well-trained lions.
And every night she went in the lion's cage.
The lion's caaaaage.
Oh!
Don't go in the cage tonight,
Oh mother darlin'
for the lions may be angry
And they'll bite!
. . . .

And when they bit the poor mother's head off,
These words came back to her so softly sang,
Sooooooo softly saaaaang.
Oh!
Don't go in the cage tonight,
Oh mother darlin'
for the lions may be angry
And they'll bite!

I do not know how many other pieces she chose to grace us with during her short tenure with the heathens from the hollers, but that one must have been her theme song. Although I have not heard that little aria before or since, I am able to recall that much of it today, almost fifty years after the fact. Another memory from Miss Carroll's tenure: Whenever one of us said we were *done* with a task, she would counter with "Nothing is *done* but a chicken." She encouraged us to respond to anyone using the term that way by asking, "Are you a chicken?" Miss Janis Carroll and her city ways were soon gone, but not before she taught us the difference between who she was and who we were.

Another academic lesson I learned at Meade Memorial came about in the eighth grade at the hands of Miss Billie Edyth Ward. Miss Ward was a very good teacher, but she tolerated no foolishness—and foolishness was ever my strong suit. By that time in my schooling, it was clear that, while I had no academic problems, I was a walking, talking, social misfit.

I was constantly being punished for some infraction of the rules, most often by not being allowed to go to the playground during break. By the time I reached eighth grade, recess was just a memory, but I had adapted so that by then I didn't really mind staying inside. What's more, I had discovered the library and pretty much preferred to spend the twenty minutes, morning and afternoon, reading anyway. Bear in mind here that I was not reading Euripides but something more along the lines of *Marcy Grows Up, Marcy Gets a Man. . . .* You get the picture—nothing with any redeeming value. Since it was a small school and the teachers had labeled me as smart, I had found that, if I did well on the tests, I got very little hassle if I skipped some of the homework.

Just a couple of weeks into Miss Ward's class, I had a series of math problems to work, and the evening before they were due I managed to get my right hand stuck in the wringer of Momma's washing machine. It wasn't on purpose, just a fortuitous incident that I planned to use to my advantage. I already knew how to do the assigned problems; with such a convenient excuse, I saw no reason to trudge through the homework. When in lieu of my math homework I presented my injured hand to Miss Ward the next morning, she was unamused. She not only kept me in at recess, but also made me use my poor injured hand to clean erasers and wash the blackboards instead of delving into the latest adventures of "Marcy." In my opinion, B.F. Skinner could not teach Billie Edyth Ward one thing about conditioning.

Although my peers thought I was smart, I would have given up that particular position in a minute for even a small degree of popularity. Popular, I was not. Part of popularity had to do with knowing how to act; I did not. Another part of it had to do with being pretty; I was not. But I will tell you who *was* and everybody knew it: Ronalta Mae Pelphrey. Not only was she pretty, I think she was born knowing how to act. She was everything an ideal girl ought to be: quiet, slow to smile, baby-fat-turned-full-figured, silky straight hair, blue eyes, regular features—namely, everything I was not! At any point in my life from age six to seventeen, I would have traded lives with Ronalta Mae Pelphrey and negotiated ten or so years off my piddly little existence for the privilege.

Every year, we had two big events at school: the Fall Carnival and the Spring Carnival. For these events, each class chose a candidate for Carnival Queen. Two times a year, with such regularity that I still do not know why we bothered to vote, my class elected Ronalta Mae Pelphrey. These carnivals were moneymaking ventures for the school, and part of the money was made by auctioning pies baked by the girls, who presumably became part of the pie package and shared said pie with the young swain who had bought it. This system created a real competition among the girls as to whose pie brought in the most money.

Practically every ritual I engaged in as I was growing up seemed calculated to let me know just where I ranked in the social order. As I reflect on it, they could have stopped this stuff fairly quickly, since it was pretty clear to me from early on that I was not going to succeed at any of the social competition. Okay, my pies went cheap! I now know that there are worse things than going through life with an unmarketable pie, but at that time it did not seem so. Clearly, in the social contests I was a repeated failure, but in the academic ones—well, thank God for those!

Now, you take spelling. Some of us are just hard-wired for spelling, and I always was one helluva speller. We had a county fair every autumn, and I once got to represent the whole school—my fifth-grade year, I believe—in the county fair spelling bee. I stood right there in my red-checked silk dress (we called it silk because it was *silky;* it was probably some form of rayon) looking out at Grandma Emmy in the front row in her brown-checked silk dress. Grandma Emmy had made both of our dresses from two bolts of cloth that she had bought at Ern Ward's store. While I did not win the spelling bee, I turned down about two dozen of Oil Springs' and Flat Gap's finest spellers until I was conquered by *accordion*—spelled it with a terminal A instead of an O. Do*d*doggit!

For a number of county-school students, just getting to and from school was a troublesome process. I was lucky that my family lived only about half a mile from Meade Memorial School, although nobody from Two-Mile walked to school. Since the school was located right in our community, ours was the last bus to get to school, which was a real convenience in terms of being able to get chores done both before and after school. Going to school was by no means the beginning of our day.

My typical morning involved getting out of bed; hauling the slop jar (chamber pot) to the toilet; cleaning myself up (taking a sponge bath in a washpan full of water that had been heated on the coal stove in the kitchen); going across the road and drawing—with a pulley chain—two buckets of fresh water and carrying them back to my house; preparing the pig slop of mash and table scraps and slopping the hogs; eating a breakfast of sausage, eggs, biscuits, and sawmill gravy (all prepared fresh daily by my mother—or the hired girl, when Momma was sick); and walking down to Leonie Wallen's store to sit on a carbide can or a pop case and wait for the school bus.

The pig pen was located parallel to the highway on the side of the hill, between our house and Pop Pop's. Since the school buses took that road, I always tried to time my morning pig feeding so that it fell between buses. It's not that everybody did not know that all of us had certain duties; it's just that I was not particularly eager to have everybody associate me with Moonbeam McSwine. One morning during my junior year, I was all dressed to go to school in my black tight skirt and a red banlon cardigan, worn backwards and buttoned up the back. As I sprinted along the narrow path to feed the pigs, I hit a patch of ice and, slop bucket flying, did a half gainer down about fifteen feet of slope, much to the enjoyment of every high-school kid from Concord, Buffalo, and Davis Branch. I think the school bus driver slowed down just so his passengers could view the entire spectacle.

Since there were no boys in the family and my daddy worked the mines some thirty miles away and had to leave for work before five every morning, I took on the water-carrying and pig-feeding chores when I was nine years old. It may sound like a lot to expect of a child, but I assure you my lot was much better than that of practically everybody I knew. Most people my age had many younger brothers and sisters. In addition to milking cows and working in the fields while still children themselves, they were very actively involved in child care. I am not quite sure why, but my mother was one of the few women in the community who did not turn a large portion of the household and cooking chores over to her children. When she was sick, we had a hired girl for the housework. My sister was too young to help out outside the house, so it fell to me to be the boy in the family. The work was done out of necessity, and it could not be put off or avoided. If I did not feed the pigs, they squealed and went hungry; if I did not get fresh water, my whole family was thirsty. There was a reason to do my work, and it had to be done on time. I think I was well into adulthood before I learned to procrastinate effectively.

Anyway, I had more time to get my chores finished—not *done;* I ain't no chicken—because ours was the last bus before school began. Some of those buses hauled kids from as far away as twenty miles across hills and dirt roads that were impassable when it rained, so it appears to me now that we were fortunate to have lived so close to the school. As I saw it then, however, the kids who had to ride over long distances were lucky because they had an increased opportunity to socialize on the bus before and after school. Since the buses took those of us who lived closest to the school home first too, that did not leave us much time to hang around each other either before or after school. I always thought that if I had a little more time to observe the popular girls, I would figure something out about what I needed to do to be more popular. I should note, however, that being on the last bus to school and the first bus out did not seem to bother Ronalta Mae Pelphrey or Easter Ward. They were certainly popular—and Easter Ward was also afflicted with curly hair. Of course, she was a full-figured girl, and that made up for a lot.

From about my fifth-grade year, when they began serving lunch at Meade Memorial, I ate lunch every day in the school cafeteria. It cost a dollar a week for a cafeteria meal ticket for five lunches, and I remember this well because eating there was never by my choice—my parents always insisted that I eat every meal there. I would have preferred to walk over to Walt Pack's store, where all the cool kids drank Pepsis with peanuts poured in them and ate Nabs cheese crackers and Moon Pies. The kids who ate at "The Store" were too sophisticated to have to eat meatloaf and macaroni-with-tomatoes and pinto beans and stuff just like we had at home every night of our lives. Although I made this argument to my parents at least twice a week, they never once relented. Every now and then, however, I'd get a quarter or so ahead in my personal finances and would just bag the pinto beans and macaroni and scurry for the heady atmosphere of "The Store," where I could revel in the ambiance and throw back Pepsi and peanuts with the best of them. Some kids brought their lunch from home, but not many, because that was even dopier than eating in the cafeteria.

The young sophisticates who went to "The Store" also often smoked a cigarette or two while they were there. Somehow the smoking thing was another of those customs that I couldn't quite take up. While it seemed like the worldly thing to do—I was in hot pursuit of worldliness—I just could not bring myself to do it. Let me tell you that in the fifties, in my little backwoods school, the only people who did not smoke were the basketball players—and even they smoked in the off season. My reasons for not smoking, like my reasons for any other commendable behaviors, were not pure. I am sure that had my parents not been smokers, I would have been a veritable chimney. However, my mother and daddy smoked three packs a day—apiece. Anytime we went somewhere and forgot to bring along cigarettes, we had to stop to buy them or go back home to get them, which made it hard for me to equate smoking with glamor. Sometime during my seventh-grade year, I took two puffs from a cigarette offered me in the girls' rest room during halftime of a basketball game, and that is the entire story of my history with cigarettes. I find it ironic that most of the virtuous behaviors in my life have been supported by grubby little reasons that I hate to admit.

Overall, I guess I would have to say that from elementary school through eighth grade, despite my social problems, I really liked school. For me everything was escapist, especially English and geography. The stories I read in popular teenage fiction of the day were as different from my own experiences as the literature I read in my English class. I never saw anyone even remotely like myself in anything I read—even the contemporary stuff. I believed those interesting people and places were out there, and I relished the time I spent with them. (I cried for three days over "The Soul of Ann Rutledge.") I never planned or hoped to go out there myself, however, for my dreams were formed of more ordinary stuff—that which should have been do-able for somebody like me.

Meade Memorial did not offer any classes in foreign language. My feeling, though, is that, for most of us from Appalachian rural areas, *English* is a second language. It is not just the accent or dialect problem; there is a difference in the ways words are used. Appalachian hillbilly, as spoken pre-television, is colorful, earthy, profane, and often devoid of subject-verb agreement. This is a very important part of our identity as hill folk, and our dialect is not something we should give up without a fight. In my experience, however, there has been little encouragement for carrying my heritage in my mouth. Outsiders use our dialect to peg or recognize us, while we use it to figure out and establish who we are.

Folks who study the different forms of speech used throughout the world term the various places of usage "speech communities."

Over the past twenty-five years, I have lived, visited, or worked for a time in a number of different countries and several different states, but I have not been involved in many speech communities at a level where I would notice major differences. When I have worked or traveled in Europe or Asia or South America, the people I talked with spoke English or we communicated with some combination of their more-than-adequate English and my dreadful attempts at Spanish (or, even worse, French). I have noticed that my native speech is often accorded more respect by my European or Asian colleagues than by my fellow professors in the United States. Perhaps to their ears I just sound like one more American, or maybe they see my work before they see (or listen to) me. I count myself lucky to have a good ear for languages; they come rather quickly when I am surrounded by native speakers. The down side to that facility is that when I am in their country my colleagues appear so pleased with my feeble attempts at their language (yes, even the French) that, much to my embarrassment, I must admit that I never bothered to learn any language in depth, and today I have trouble with a French menu unless I stick around for a week or so and talk to folks.

Here in the United States, however, I believe I have lived and worked in two very distinct speech communities: Appalachian hill country and the academic community. Although I have lived in several regions of the United States, I do not recall any marked contrast in the working vocabulary of the different areas. The people who play golf, go skiing, and read the best-seller list may have different accents, but they use the same words to signify membership in the same world. They may be a trifle more descriptive in Jackson, Mississippi, than in Boise, Idaho, but their language forms the boundary of worlds that are separated only by inflection.

Much the same thing may be said for the academic community. Although there are some differences in accent, the vocabulary is much the same. As for content, there are also topics that are unacceptable. In the culture of professors, while television may be considered an inappropriate pastime, we can discuss *Austin City Limits, Face the Nation,* March Madness, and even *Murphy Brown,* but we must feign ignorance if we happen to know the story line of *Roseanne, All My Children,* or *Murder She Wrote*; and woe be unto us if we should ever admit to knowledge of any of Oprah's latest guests.

In the hills of Appalachia, TV is ubiquitous, and soap opera characters are discussed by many women as if the characters exist. Other topics are also divided by gender, and members of one cannot discuss topics in the area of the other. For example, my husband routinely does housework, but I would be embarrassed if he discussed doing so with my family or members of my home community. By the same token, it would be quite all right for him to admit to partaking of alcohol every now and then, but I would never speak with members of my community about having a drink. While that may not sound like much of a restriction, it means exercising caution when discussing a number of social occasions. Champagne brunches, cocktail parties, and wine-and-cheese functions come immediately to mind as events that must be translated into something acceptable to the homefolks.

After Jim Bob Price got married to a girl he had met in Cincinnati, Ohio, and brought her back home to meet the family, we were all sitting in his Aunt LouAnne's kitchen one day getting to know each other. Sister remarked that she was planning to be in Cincinnati sometime the following month, and Jim Bob's new bride immediately said, "Oh, I'd love to show you our new place. You'll have to come by for a drink while you're there." The tale of that little faux pas long outlived that marriage—truth to tell, we haven't stopped talking about it yet. In the creeks and hollers, we don't issue specific invitations unless we're having a shower or something, and we definitely do not invite folks over for drinks. The men may take a little nip out behind the can house (the place where pickles, preserves, and other canned stuff is stored) or they may even be known for their drinking and sworping, but no decent woman takes even one alcoholic drink.

As to the accommodations I have made as I have moved between Appalachia and academia, I think my accent has changed very little, probably because my background is an important part of my identity. I have accommodated myself somewhat to the culture of academe through changing my vocabulary, which sometimes causes problems. Some years back, I was at a dinner-on-the-ground with about forty members of my extended family—folks who love me. We were sitting on the grass, eating Hazel Lee Johnson's cabbage rolls, when I used the word "atrocity." I don't even remember the context, but I do recall that it practically stopped the meal, mid-bite. Nobody said anything; there was just this pregnant pause where everybody stopped what they were doing to take note of what had been said. That one slip was as offensive as would have been bringing up the fact that I had returned from Japan the Friday before, which I would *never* have mentioned in that setting. That sort of glaring lapse has not happened often and never quite so blatantly. Usually, I am more careful, but it does require some degree of self-monitoring. I have found it easier to supervise the content of my speech, however, than to monitor the form—the way I phrase my comments, the words I use, and those terms that are common in my everyday life. For example, I can be tripped up on the most ordinary terms—like frequent-flier miles. If I should mention frequent-flier miles, it would likely be taken as a put-down by members of my home community. I would not want just anybody back home to know how much traveling I do because it would be considered unseemly for a woman to be going off all the time, especially when unaccompanied by her husband. While a few of the members of my extended family know that I have been outside the country, they also know enough to keep their mouths shut about it. Sometimes even they get me into trouble.

A few years ago, I stopped by to see Bonnie Sue Ratliff (we claim kin, but we're really just close friends). While she and I were sitting on her front porch kidding around with her ten-year-old grandson, Jacob, three women who had gone to school with Bonnie Sue and me joined our little party. Two of the women were in from Ohio visiting Vidie, the other one, who lives just down the road from Bonnie Sue. It was a typical backhome get-together; nobody had invited anybody anywhere, and we were gathered because each of us felt free to "come by" whenever. Now, Bonnie Sue's grandson is sharper'n ary tack and was holding his own in our conversation, when he suddenly looked at me and said, "Mammaw says you've been to China. Have you really been to China?"

"Mmm-hmm," I responded, and the conversation about how hard it was to grow cannas picked back up.

"Well, did you like it over there?" Jacob interrupted.

"Mmm-hmm," I echoed, hoping my short answers would signal to Jacob that this conversation was just too dull to pursue.

No luck there. Jacob came right back with, "What about Russia? Have you been to Russia?"

Another "Mmm-hmm."

"Did you like Russia?" he wanted to know.

"It was okay," I ventured. By this time, the canna discourse had been put on hold and everybody on the porch was giving us full attention.

"Well, have you been to England?"

With still another "Mmm-hmm," I owned up to having visited the mother country. Then, thinking there might be a way out of this, I immediately inquired, "Wasn't your pappaw stationed in Germany?"

"Was he, Mammaw?"

"Yeah, he was over there for two years," Bonnie Sue said, and I thought I was off the hook, without much destruction. Before I could even attempt to reconfigure the conversation, however, Jacob followed up. "Well, have *you* been to Germany?"

Not liking the turn this discussion was taking but with no earthly idea how it might be stopped, I confessed to having been to Germany. Do not believe anything you read about today's schools not teaching geography, because I have evidence to the contrary. Without once landing on any of the great majority of places on this planet I have never been, over the next several minutes—very long minutes—as I fervently prayed for some country, *any* country that I had not visited to surface, young Jacob hopscotched the globe. "Have you been to. . . ."

Until finally Vidie broke in, "Do you go on an airplane to get to all those places, Linda Sue?"

"Yes," I admitted.

"Why, Linda Sue! With all those planes crashing, don't you worry about getting on 'em?"

Fearing all was lost anyway, I launched into lecture number 347, the old song complete with statistics about how much safer it is to ride on an airplane than it is to ride in a car, when suddenly I knew exactly what to do. Abruptly, I said, "You know, Vidie, I figure if the Lord's gonna take me, he's gonna take me wherever I am, whatever I may be doing. So, I just don't worry about it."

Every adult head on the porch slowly nodded in agreement as, not to be deterred, Jacob said, "Have you ever been to India?"

"No, Jacob, I sure haven't. I never have been to India."

There is a God, and He helps with damage control in the most curious ways. I know the rules. It's those sudden shifts I have to watch out for.

I have also accommodated to the rules and expectations of the academic speech community in several ways, at least in terms of the content, topics discussed, and the form I use to discuss them. But I have retained a number of the expressions common to my home community and use them so often that some of my colleagues now regularly use terms they have picked up from me.

Although much of what I have read about language and culture suggests that working-class speakers are disadvantaged because they speak in restricted code, I doubt that such is true of native Appalachians. If restricted means the code is restricted to members of that culture, this is true of my people also. But if restricted means lacking in range, I do not think this is true for us. While my culture is working class, the working language, Hillbilly, is rich in its ability to describe all manner of things. Some examples are:

Suck-egg: Sneaky, sleazy, altogether bad form, as in: "That's a suck-egg thing to do."

Skylarking: Having a big time in a way that will not profit anyone: "He was out skylarkin' all night."

Sinkholing: A way of wasting time that involves laziness and worthlessness: "I've been out sinkholin' around."

Sparking: A synonym for flirting, dating, or courting: "I think Brenda Gail and Arkie Joe are sparkin.'"

Do-less: Not being worth much in the way of work. Country singer Loretta Lynn, who comes from Butcher Holler, approximately seven miles from my home on Two-Mile Creek, called her late husband, Mooney Lynn, "Do," which is short for Do-less. Mooney was known for doing a lot of sinkholin' *and* skylarkin.' "Mooney, you're just do-less."

Spot-on: Absolutely right—I also noticed "spot-on" used in England: "You're spot-on about that feller."

To a dot: Exactly; usually used to describe appearance: "He's to a dot like his daddy."

Plime blank: Synonymous with "to a dot" in describing appearance: "She's plime blank like her Aunt Suzie."

Smack dab: Also synonymous with exactly or precisely, but used to mark a spot rather than describe a person: "It was right smack dab at the starting line."

Take after: Appearance is somewhat but not exactly like another: "She sure takes after her daddy's people."

Favor: Synonymous with "takes after" in describing appearance: "That baby favors his uncle Johnny."

Get: Used to describe food preparation: "I've got to go home in time to get supper or Johnny'll be mad."

Cagged-up: Derisive term used to describe someone taking a nap or sleeping late in the morning; may have originated with "kegged-up" to mean drunk, but this is just conjecture since I have never heard it used that way in the hills: "He's all cagged-up in the bed."

Turn: A synonym for personality: "She sure is good turned" or "She's got a sour turn."

A'purpose: With intent, short for "on purpose": "Now, Jolene, you did that a'purpose and you know it."

Do-rag: A headscarf used to keep dust and dirt out of the hair, folded into a small triangle, wrapped around the head, and worn tied at the back of the neck—so-called, I suppose, because you *do* things in it, or it may be related to hair-do: "I need a do-rag 'fore I sweep this yard."

Hillbilly not only uses a range of *words;* there are a number of expressions that are commonly used that I have never heard anywhere else. Many of these expressions are so indelicate that I have not included them here. We use them so routinely, however, that they have lost their power to shock, and the people who use them would probably be surprised that they would be found offensive in polite society. Among the least improper of the expressions are:

Wouldn't strike a tap at a black snake: So worthless where work is concerned that he must be discounted. "That boy she's goin' with is pure sorry; he wouldn't strike a tap at a black snake."

Sharper'n ary tack: To be quick or intelligent, hence sharper than a tack: "Joe Bob traded Carl Dean that old bicycle for Carl Dean's new wagon. That Joe Bob's sharper'n ary tack."

Smart as a whip: Also to be quick or intelligent: "That Joe Bob's smart as a whip."

All his dogs don't bark: To be slow thinking or of low intelligence: "All

Carl Dean's dogs don't bark."

Fatter'n ary hog: Used to describe having gained weight. "Lord, honey, I'm fatter'n ary hog."

Can't see outta my eyes: Also used to describe a state of being overweight. "Lord, honey, I'm so fat I can't see outta my eyes."

Just like a little whippoorwill: Used to describe a state of being underweight, or "pore." "She must be sick. She looks just like a little whippoorwill."

Bring me a cat: Somewhat indelicate expression, used at table, based on the idea that the food is so unpalatable that one would have to lick a cat's behind to get the taste out of one's mouth; a compliment disguised as an insult and used only when the food is delicious beyond any doubt. After the first taste of Thanksgiving sweet potato soufflé, my daddy would say, "Bring me a cat."

Wild as a bottom hog: Used to describe acting-out or deviant behavior. As compared with a hog that has been penned up all its life, a "bottom hog," left to roam the field, or bottom, is much less manageable. "You'd better watch that Johnson girl. She's wild as a bottom hog."

Go to the closet: A euphemism used in polite company to describe the call of nature. We did not have indoor plumbing, and many families kept the chamber pot in the closet. In my house, at least the expression has lived on long past the arrival of indoor plumbing. "We gotta get home pretty soon because I have to go to the closet."

Four foot up a bull's ass in pokeberry time: A way of describing an exaggerated richness both in money and in food: "John B.'s richer'n four foot up a bull's ass in pokeberry time" or "This pudding is richer'n four foot up a bull's ass in pokeberry time."

Come out ag'in' you: To oppose or attempt to block an action: "I think I woulda had it but my brother come out ag'in' me and I lost th' race for sheriff."

As long as a rake handle: Describes the passing of gas under duress; used as a threat to prevail upon children to get to work. "I'll knock a fart outta you as long as a rake handle."

Sing like a wire nail: Also describes the passing of gas under duress; used as a threat to prevail upon children to get to work. "I'll knock a fart outta you that'll sing like a wire nail."

At the top of the stack: Describes the pinnacle of success: "Since John

Lee got that new job, his family's living right at the top of the stack."

By shit and forty miles from water: An expression indicating revulsion in regard to what one has been asked to do. "I'druther be by shit and forty miles from water than hoe out this cornfield."

Cleaned his plow: To beat up on some opponent pretty badly: "They had a fight and John B. just cleaned his plow for him."

Gimme s'm sugar: Come over here and kiss me: "It's good to see you, honey. Gimme s'm sugar."

Lived at the foot of the Cross: Used to describe a good Christian, a truly virtuous individual, about the destiny of whose soul there can be no question: "Law, that Vidie lives right at the foot of the cross."

I have always felt privileged to have had access to the speech of my childhood, for it has lent color to many otherwise difficult moments and supplemented so-called Standard English for me. I also believe I have been able to achieve full membership in both Appalachian and academic speech communities, although it certainly has taken some time and a sense of watchfulness. It takes time whenever I am introduced into a new community of scholars, and it takes watchfulness when I am in my home community. I suppose that when I first began teaching at a university more than three decades ago, I was much less likely to use the expressions of my "native" language freely. But over the years, as I have become more confident, I have exercised less restraint. Criteria for "full membership" are hard to outline, but I have had tenure at two universities and two liberal arts colleges and am ranked a full professor, so I suppose I am as fully a member of the academic speech community as anyone ever is.

As for my home speech community, that may be harder to define. Wherever I lived, I never went for more than two months without visiting my parents. During those visits, I continued to have quite a lot of interaction with folks who grew up with me, and I honestly believe that I sound pretty much as I did when I left there over forty years ago. Although I no longer strictly police my language when I am in academe, I do try to watch myself when I am home, so there may be some question of *full* membership. For my sake, I hope that is not the case, because much of my sense of who I am comes from my identity as a hillbilly woman, and I do not see that ever changing. Clearly, for me there is a lot at stake here. In order to maintain a sense of wholeness and of loyalty to the community that I was brought up in, I have held on to an accent that is too often mistakenly seen as an indication of lower intelligence than many other accents in the United States.

As I was growing up, I always hated it when somebody went off to Ohio or Michigan to get work and came home three weeks later speaking in an accent that was hardly recognizable. In the country, we almost always replaced the "ah" sound with the "ie" or "y" sound; Edna became Ednie, and Emma was pronounced Emmie. It often took less than a month up north somewhere for hill folk to forsake the "ie" or "y" sound forever. They not only said Edna and Emma, they also said spaghettah and Cincinnatah. Living outside my home community has meant that I come face to face with differences in dialect at odd times. Some years back at a picnic in Vienna, I was eating some small sausages and recognized their unique taste. Although it took me awhile to place the flavor, it came from one of the favorite lunches of my childhood—Vy-eeny and crackers. While I had asked Leonie Wallen to get me a can of Vy-eeny literally hundreds of times, I never stopped to read the label on the can—Vienna Sausage. Imagine.

I believe my speech is an advantage in the classroom because students tend to be willing to work pretty hard for me. They reason, perhaps, that if someone who sounds the way I do can master the material, they certainly should be able to understand it. With colleagues, retaining the accent of my childhood has not been without cost. For example, in one meeting, a fellow committee member once referred to me in my presence as Poke Sallet Annie. At such times, it is a good thing I have a sense of humor (and *sometimes* it's a good thing I'm unarmed). Some years ago, I presented a paper at an academic conference held in Boston. The following evening, I was having dinner with a group of people from the conference when one of the men, a professor from Ohio State University, expressing respect for my work, said: "I don't think I have ever heard an intelligent person talk the way you do"— and he thought he was paying me a compliment.

PURE MAGIC AND OLD FRIENDSHIP

New Year's Eve was hardly noticed in the hills, at least when I was there. I did not know anybody who stayed up that late, and I guess I was almost thirty before I ever actually rang in the New Year. I grew up going to bed with the chickens—that means early—and I still prefer to be asleep by nine o'clock unless there is some special reason for staying awake.

The first day of the year passed like any other back home, although folks tried to have cabbage with the ever-present pinto beans, since everybody said if you ate soup beans—our term for pinto beans—and cabbage on New Year's Day, you'd not go hungry the rest of the year. Daddy often worked on the first of January because he could get time and a half on holidays, so perhaps my family was the only one for whom the day held no special pleasures.

Valentine's Day was not a favorite of mine either. In my day, kids counted and compared the number of valentines received, and there was no school policy to save the feelings of those who did not get many valentines. Of course, my memories may be colored by my having spent ten long years sharing the classroom with Ronalta Mae Pelphrey; surprise, surprise. Even after I hit puberty and had a few gentleman callers, they did not make much of Valentine's Day. For the three boyfriends I had in high school—Brad, Johnny, and Billy, in that order—I bought, and received, some rococo Hallmark creation containing a sentiment that would have been embarrassing had it not been entirely expected. Flowers and candy were never part of the Valentine's Day tradition in my community—at least I do not recall anyone's ever receiving either. It remained for Brett Scott, who went on to become my husband, to buy my first flowers and candy. For Valentine's Day 1959, he brought me a pale-blue satin heart containing three pounds of Russell Stover chocolates. We broke up two days later.

But Memorial Day? *Now* we're talkin' holiday. Called Decoration Day by everybody back home, Memorial Day is quite a big deal in the hills; it has been ever since I can remember. We had an exceedingly special relationship with those who had gone before us, an attachment that often played itself out in frequent trips to the burial ground and the repeating of stories—perhaps apocryphal—about those who rested therein. It may be because my people never saw themselves in books, history, or fiction that makes it so important for us to tell and retell who was who and what was what in the graveyard. Or it may have to do with the fundamentalist belief that "the dead in Christ shall rise"—interpreted to mean that this very body will accompany me into eternity (which certainly puts a cap on any anticipation I might have of Heaven). All of the above make it important to visit the actual grave sites often. So, for one reason or another, where I come from, we spend considerably more time in graveyards than some folks might consider wise or healthy.

While our forebears built their houses in the valleys, they traditionally buried their dead on the top of the highest, hardest-to-get-to ridges they could find. At least it seemed so to this little girl who was dragged what appeared to be an inordinate number of times to stand over this or that relative who had passed before my time as well as those who were, at best, a dim memory. I could today recite to you all the important statistics and many, many stories of my Aunt Gladys Mollette, Momma's older sister, who died well before I made my entrance into this world. Placed in such a context, you can see the importance of Decoration Day.

Although the end of May finds a profusion of flowers growing in eastern Kentucky, a few weeks before Decoration Day, folks begin to create
crepe-paper flowers. Since crepe-paper flowers are longer lasting and will
remain after the live ones have wilted, almost everybody includes some
mixture of real and fake flowers in the baskets they carry to the various
cemeteries. Momma never had much use for flowers that had not grown
out of the ground, so, for the most part, I was only able to practice my
flower-making skills with crepe paper at the homes of my friends. At
least that is my excuse for never having become proficient at something
anybody over the age of four with a modicum of eye-hand coordination
could master. Sitting on the porch talking and teasing while we made
those flowers was a desirable activity in itself.

Early on, my family visited two graveyards. First we went to the
Mollette Graveyard, wherein rested the remains of my Grandpa Lige,
Aunt Gladys, and Little Jake (Grandma Emmy's son who had died at
age three). Little Jake was always very real to me because his sixteen-
by-twenty-inch sepia portrait hung in Grandma Emmy's upper room
(where, just incidentally, I was born and where I often napped when I
stayed with Grandma Emmy, since the upper room was cooler and qui-
eter than the front room). Uncle Jake was said to have been the very
sweetest of Grandma Emmy's kids until his untimely death from some
mysterious fever that three of the other Mollette children had endured
but survived. It seems he hung on for many days with Grandma Emmy
nursing him day and night before he was called home. The stories of his
suffering unto death grew more romanticized each year after Grandma
Emmy died as Momma and her sisters vied to see who could come up
with the most powerful memories of their long-dead brother.

While the Little Jake stories were always somewhat suspect, the tales
of Aunt Gladys rang true to me. She was the sister closest to Momma in
age—Aunt Gladys was three years older—and apparently they had been
very much alike. Together they had plucked each other's eyebrows until
they were both bald-faced, smoked corn shucks, traded boyfriends,
sampled Uncle John's private stash of moonshine, and *one* of them had
carved a bad word in the top of Grandma's butter brick on a Sunday
the preacher came to dinner. Though I pleaded mightily, I never found
out what the bad word was. Every time the tale was told, Momma denied that she had any part in the butter-brick caper, Auntie Stella re-

mained forever shocked by the action, and Grandma and Auntie Lizzie laughed till they lost their breath every time the subject came up. Whenever the Gladys tales were told, everyone agreed that she remained very spirited until the day she died. Grandma Emmy declared, "Gladys always had spunk. She had more gumption than any of my girls." "Of course," she allowed, "if the others had been like that I don't know how I'd have got 'em raised." The best I can make of it, Aunt Gladys died of tuberculosis or some other type of respiratory problem. Since there was no doctoring of any sort at that time, it is impossible to know precisely what killed her. Whatever the condition, it kept her bedfast and out of school so much that it took her two or three extra years to finish high school, so she was graduated with Momma's class. Although she died at age nineteen, my Aunt Gladys gave her family a whole lot more pleasure than pain while she was with them, if such can be judged by the stories of her relatively short life. And it probably should be mentioned that tales of her life injected merriment into many a graveyard visit too.

After going up on Greasy to visit the Mollette Graveyard, we went over to Bob's Branch to pay respects to the Ward-Preston Burial Ground. There we would decorate the graves of my Great-Grandpa Asbury "Azzie B." Ward and Great-Grandma Laura Belle Price Ward, as well as those of my Grandma Alk Preston and the three children she and Pop Pop had lost in childhood. Later, as other members of our extended family and friends died, our pilgrimage to their places of eternal rest took somewhat longer, but those two family cemeteries always formed the core of our trip.

This grave-visiting was not as heavyhearted or gruesome as it may sound, since frequently we were accompanied by other family members who had come in from distant places for the occasion. There was often much laughter in recalling deeds of the departed. Aunt Gladys is not the only one about whom tales were told. Most of the time there were two or more versions of the same story, and others would be called upon to support the veracity of one tale or another. After attending to the gravesites, we would all go home to a big dinner of fried chicken or chicken and dumplings, accompanied by every vegetable that was "in" in the garden.

What a wonderful holiday! I still try to go home on Memorial Day, both because I enjoy getting together with what is left of my family and because if I am absent they'll all tell tales on me and think I no longer love my parents and grandparents. Likewise, I do not completely discount the fact that "when the dead in Christ shall rise" my loved ones might well take me to task for not having been there on some long-past Decoration Day, and I surely don't want to be caught out.

July Fourth also used to be one of the most important holidays in eastern Kentucky, not just for the food or the fireworks (we never had fireworks unless Uncle Glen brought some) or even the fact that folks once again gathered home from all over. The Fourth of July fell during the biggest holiday in that place at that time—Miners' Vacation! All the mines closed down the first two weeks of July, so everybody's daddy was on holiday at the same time—and what a holiday! During the weekdays most of the men worked in the fields or around the house doing maintenance and repairs they did not have time to do the rest of the year. On the weekends and on the Fourth itself, it was one long meetin,' greetin,' eatin' frenzy as folks came in from all over and we just had ourselves a big-eyed time. We made homemade ice cream and had watermelon and lemonade and gooseberry pies—which have to "set" for a day before they're any good. Somewhere between the food and the laughter and the running-and-playing-till-I-was-sick, I developed a picture of what is meant by the term "festival." We never called them that, but festivals they were nonetheless. Late in the evening, as we kids were catching lightning bugs and fighting sleep, somebody would grab a banjo or a fiddle and then Daddy would get his guitar and they'd play music and everybody would sing—whether we could carry a tune or not—until I nodded off with little, round Baby Sister already asleep and sticky under my left arm.

Sister recalls when a couple of the older Ward boys, Easter's brothers, brought their instruments in from Detroit and were playing music with Daddy. That was the first time we had ever seen or heard a steel guitar up close, and it sounded like magic to us. It was just that: pure magic. Those festivals of my growing-up years were the kind of magic that bound me to a place and a people and a history.

There were other sorts of celebrations, too, occasions that had more to do with work than play, but celebrations still. Bean-stringings, for example, were created for the purpose of putting up beans for the winter, but they were always pleasurable occasions that, by joining work with play, made our lives more tolerable. One of the problems with raising vegetables is that it is not possible to know precisely when each crop is going to come in. Experience indicates that often several of the crops come in all at once, so the harvesting and canning and preserving often have to be done all at the same time, too. Folks who garden for fun find such circumstance inconvenient; for us it was more serious than that. We did not raise vegetables for pleasure; we lived out of our gardens. Since we were dependent upon that produce to feed us through the winter, we could not afford to lose any of it. One way to make the extra work less burdensome was to gather 'round and do it together.

When the last beans of the summer were harvested, people got together for a bean-stringing, an event that involved taking the ends and strings off the beans. I know that today green beans can be cooked with the ends just snapped off and with no special "stringing," but, I tell you, our beans had big old tough strings. After we had removed those strings from the beans, we used a needle and thread to put the beans on long lines, or strings; they first dried in the sun and later hung in the attic, thereby turning into what folks called "shuck-beans." When cooked with fatback or salt pork for a full day, shuck beans are larrupin' good. Working up the beans, however, was just the beginning of a bean-stringing, which included the same eating marathon as every other little celebration we had and ended with grown-ups singing and playing music and the kids running wild in the dark playing whatever games came to mind. I recall this part vividly, since I received my first kiss at a bean-stringing after several games of hide-and-go-seek—yeah, we put a "go" in there—when for some reason the boys just started catchin' and kissin' the girls at random.

I always tried to be present for that random stuff, since the criteria for participation seemed to be relaxed somewhat. In this particular case, Jimmy Butcher grabbed me and planted my first kiss squarely over my left eyebrow—thrilled the hell outta me, and I daydreamed about him for a while thereafter and sort of thought he might look at me funny and we might fall in love. Well, he never did, so the moment passed, unmarked except by me.

Hard on the heels of harvest time came Halloween, which was observed on Two-Mile much as it was in places I had read about–but with some variation. Although kids went trick-or-treating in small groups, there were no store-bought costumes. All of us just dressed in our parents' old clothes and went out with our little paper bags to get two or three gumdrops or chocolate drops at each house. Once we reached puberty, however, the dressing-up was over, and Halloween was a lot more fun. Then, those who were teenagers sort of got together about dusk and walked up and down Two-Mile in a pack, laughing and hanging out and pairing off and fooling around and acting like we were gonna do something really wicked, like set fire to a barn or put a cowpie on somebody's doorstep or something equally *bad*. In retrospect, the behavior seems a little like the youth gangs of today without the criminal exploits. For us, it only happened once a year, and, in all my seventeen years on Two-Mile, I never actually saw or heard of anything bad that happened at the hands of such a group. I can attest that, for me at least, Halloween was one of the most exciting times of the year, for it held out all the possibilities of camaraderie with the girls and perhaps romance—such as it was—with the boys.

Take, for example, Halloween 1955, during my sophomore year in high school. Carl Price, who was a junior, had passed me two notes in the hall at school, both of which I had answered in as welcoming a manner as I could muster, since I had little to no practice at such things. Then the day before Halloween, he passed me a note that asked if I would be "going out" on Halloween. I wrote back that I had plans to do just that. On Halloween day, just before fourth period, Carl again passed me a note in the hallway, and I was sure the big sort-of-date was at hand. As I completely tuned out my physics teacher and unfolded the note, I saw that Carl had passed to me the very note I had given him the day before. I found this particular little obstacle on the trail to true love more than a bit confusing, but, after puzzling on it and missing a truly engrossing lecture on levers, I figured it was still his move. (Today, I would probably say the ball was still in his court, but I didn't know about tennis in those days and thus had to make do with metaphors from checkers.)

When I passed him in the hall at lunch, Carl said nothing but just broke up laughing. I laughed too, since there seemed to be nothing else to do and it *was* sort of funny—at least it would have been if it had not been so desperately important to my young heart. The same behavior took place on the part of both of us three more times that day as we ran across each other in the hallway. No words were spoken, just more laughter. I can testify that, for my part, English and history classes passed in a blur of anxiety, anticipation, nausea, pleasure—all those physical manifestations that occurred when what I thought was my heart flat took over my entire ninety-pound corporeal being and turned it every which way. Perhaps there are folks who are prepared for the first time this happens to them, but let me tell you that Linda Sue Preston was not. I had all the symptoms—that falling-off-the-edge-of-the-world feeling where excitement and fear do battle, logic takes a holiday, and the rest of me is helpless to intervene. Fourteen-year-old Linda Sue Preston knew with precise exactitude what those feelings meant—love, oh, God, finally!!! Love—love—carved hearts on trees and love-to-stay, with Tim, Kim, Kay, and Buddy, my future children, just waiting in the wings.

I could hardly get through supper that evening before getting into my jeans with the checked cuffs. Jeans were not yet cool for the rest of the world, but we wore them to school nearly every day, cut off and rolled up to just below the knee, with bobby socks and dirty white bucks. My favorite pair had light-blue checked cuffs, and I wore them that evening with a pale-blue short-sleeved sweater and a big overshirt, the tails of which hung well past my less-than-ample hips and thighs. In those days, I wore big clothes, thinking that they would make me look heavier, while the heavier girls wore small clothes, thinking they would make them look smaller, both creating just the opposite effect. And I wrestled my crowning glory into submission. Summer's humidity had abated, making it less likely that my hair would "fur-up" on me over the course of the evening. On that wood-smoke-scented October evening, I set forth with high hopes and sorely in need of a Dramamine for my unsettled stomach. It has been the case over the course of my life that when the big "L" (love) strikes, I experience what feels like motion sickness; and it just plain puts me off my feed for a while.

Anyway, I joined Easter, Gwen, Libby, Ronalta Mae, and a number of older and younger teenagers from the Two-Mile contingent—guys were there, too, but they shall remain nameless, since they were invisible to me and I hadn't even heard "I Only Have Eyes for You"—as we ambled on down to Walt Pack's store to meet the Greasy group. It should be noted that "The Store," like the school, was considered much too far for anybody to walk—from Greasy or Two-Mile—except on Halloween, when it was expected that the two groups of teenagers would join up. It's unclear to me how, or why, that particular custom got started, but I surely was happy about it that night since Carl was from Bee Branch, making him part of the Greasy gang, and I was ready for love. I still do not know exactly what happened that night, but I know what did *not* happen; I never even spoke directly to Carl Price. Instead, I spent the whole evening largely in the company of Billie Jean Butcher—one of the older girls—attempting to position myself so that Carl Price could get a shot at me without appearing to take any overt action. But it just did not happen.

One thing, apparently, did happen on that All Hallows Eve. Somehow Ronalta Mae Pelphrey was just better at telepathy or something than I was, because she and Carl Price got together. Shortly thereafter, they began "going together," and the relationship culminated in their marriage after her junior year and his graduation from high school in the summer of 1957. As for me, it remained for Johnny McCoy to unleash the love-crazed being disguised by that twelve-year-old-boy's body in which Linda Sue was hiding out.

While we would not have termed it a celebration, another ritual we looked forward to in the hills was Rag'lar Meetin' Time. Probably the most influential social force in my early life and that of my peers was the Baptist church. In much the same way that the mores of Utah are shaped to a great extent by the presence of so many Mormons, rural eastern Kentucky, during my youth, was governed by the pervasive fundamentalist Baptist belief system. It did not really matter what sect of Baptists we belonged to; the ground was formed by reactionary religious doctrine, and we spent many hours discussing what we considered to be the moral issues of dancing, movies, instrumental music in the church, and other such trivia. It was not trivial to us, however, because we firmly believed that any one of these activities could send our souls to burn in Hell forever, and we approached such topics with absolute seriousness. The soul-burning-in-Hell issue was made all the more important to us because we also believed that on Judgment Day our physical flesh and bones would be restored to us. While we might have been willing to risk our immortal souls to hellfire and damnation, our bodies were a whole different matter. That would hurt! I know I worried about it just a whole lot. There were many activities I thought might be exciting to get into, but I have always been one who tries to figure out whether what I am getting is worth what it will cost me, and that burning business was hard to balance out.

The God I came to know in the hills was one tough hombre. He took no prisoners, and flexibility was not in His vocabulary. He was the one who made the rules, and we followed those rules without question or we were Hellbound and we knew it. Furthermore, we did not actually have to ask God, Himself, for clarification, since any number of good folks in the community were willing, some might say eager, to apprise us at any time as to the sinfulness of our behavior and—even more frightening—our thoughts. Let me caution again that what I am saying was true for churches in the creeks and hollers only. Town Baptists were about as worldly as Methodists and Presbyterians, and it has always appeared to me that when churches—and people—move to town, they lose their blood and guts (their color, if you will) and become white-bread kind of stuff. The dogma loses its edge when folks are at will to do anything they please in their daily living and still call themselves Christians. I know it may be hard to believe that the presence of a piano or an organ in the church could signify such a variance in creed, but it surely appeared that way to young Linda Sue. Before I go on here, I want to make it clear that I am in no way poking fun or throwing off on any group, anybody, or anybody's relationship with his Lord, mostly because that's none of my business. What's more, not the least of my concern is that the God with whom I regularly affiliate just might be almost as into payback as I was taught He was, in which case I approach this discussion with fear and trembling. With that in mind, let me explain, briefly, the structure of just one mountain church, United Baptist, the one with which I am most familiar. Ultimately, I became a Freewill, but that was later; the Uniteds were far more a part of my childhood.

Old Friendship United Baptist Church was the only church actually located on Two-Mile. It perched precariously on the hillside directly across from Walt Pack's store at the mouth of Two-Mile Creek. The aforementioned Uncle Keenis Holbrook served as a deacon. Little Nim Sturgill—Grandma Emmy's nephew, Aunt Liz Sturgill's boy—also was a deacon. His rendition of "Amazing Grace" could make the hair stand up on the back of any sinner's neck, as it did on mine more than a few times. Old Friendship was one of four churches that made up a United Baptist grouping called a conference. In addition to Old Friendship, that conference included Little Friendship United Baptist Church at Greasy, Concord United Baptist Church down near Muddy Branch, and Buffalo United Baptist Church at Buffalo. The service moved around from one church to another each weekend: first Saturday and Sunday of the month the preaching was at Buffalo, second Saturday and Sunday at Greasy, third Saturday and Sunday at Concord, and fourth Saturday and Sunday at Two-Mile. Thus, fourth Sunday in every month was what we called our "Rag'lar—as in regular—Meetin' Time." Particularly in summer, Rag'lar Meetin' Time was the high holiday social occasion of our month. It entailed three or four days devoted to preparing food, beds, and ourselves for a yet-to-be-known number of dinner guests, some of whom would stay the night.

Preachers from all four churches and beyond would begin the preaching around ten in the morning on Saturday, and the service concluded whenever the last preacher who felt called to witness finished having his say. Sometimes as many as six or eight preachers would be in attendance, but you never knew exactly how many would get the call to preach on any given day. Inside the church on wooden pews, we sat—women on the right side, men on the left (although we sat together during funerals)—slowly fanning ourselves with flat cardboard squares attached to the end of oversized tongue depressors. Gripping those tongue depressors, we cast our eyes on the languid motion of our own fans while one preacher after the next railed on about how very wretched we would be as we paid for our despicable behavior by spending eternity burning in Hell. Thoughtful examination revealed an advertisement for Preston Funeral Home on one side of the fan and a painting of the Last Supper or Christ in the Garden on the other, as we were implored by Brother So-and-so to avoid eternal damnation by coming to live at the foot of the cross. It could be that our concentration on the various preachers' supplications may well have been better in the winter when we did not have those fans to distract us.

In between preachers, we concentrated on our "Sweet Songsters" as the leader—usually Little Nim Sturgill, whose name was simply Nim but was called *Little* Nim to his grave—called out the words for us: "There's a call that rings, from the throne it springs," and we chanted after him, "There's a call" until the message was delivered that He would, indeed, "set [our] fields on fire if to sin is [our] desire." Then the next preacher picked up the theme that Jesus' return to earth was imminent, and, if we did not come to the altar to be saved right this minute, we would have only ourselves to blame when we spent eternity roasting in Hell. Sometimes the preaching was over by noon or so, but most often it was midafternoon before God had had enough of sending us the Word through his local messengers.

In the view of the young folks, the real fun began when church broke. That was when residents of the home community walked among the folks from the visiting communities, inviting them to come by the house for a bite of dinner. This particular repast had only been the focus of every female in each local household for three or more days, what with the baking, cooking, cleaning, and all manner of other domestic preparations. Most hosts would invite upwards of fifteen or twenty people to join them for the midday meal. It was not at all unusual for local families to put on a spread for twenty-five or more guests. Once we got them home, there was also a predetermined ritual for when and where each guest partook of that dinner. The first table was exclusively male, including the host, any preachers in attendance, and as many of the older males as could get around the table—seated pretty much in order of their age. Upon entering the dining room, there was always a flurry of activity as the host would try to give his seat to every male present and each male would try to defer to all other males over the age of about twenty, but the outcome was always the same, since everybody knew the game plan.

The women would then begin serving the meal, all of which would be spread out on the table and passed around until every man had his fill, at which time the men would leave the table, each gallantly giving up his seat to a female guest. As each man's plate and silverware were washed to be used again immediately, he retired to the porch to recap the day's activities with his former table companions. The second table, then, was made up of female guests and older teenage children and—if there were enough chairs—the hostess and younger children. The hostess and her daughters, however, were up and down constantly to refill bowls and platters and to make trips to the porch to see if the male guests needed anything to make them more comfortable, perhaps a glass of tea or ice water.

After everyone had eaten, the younger kids went out to play, and the women began the clean-up process. Since it was expected that all women and girls would take part in removing and washing the dishes, subtle sanctions were placed on those females who managed to opt out of this part of the experience by announcing their intent to leave early. A woman could get away with breast-feeding a young baby or going home, thus occasionally getting out of scullery duties, but woe be unto her if she made such practice routine. One of our frequent guests, Sophie Johnson, was termed "eat-and-run Sophie" for that very reason. Anybody who got up to go home early was told in jest, "Okay, eat-and-run Sophie!" I recall Gwen Holbrook's once saying those words to someone without realizing that Sophie's mother, Aunt Lucy, was in fact present at the table. Gwen's mother, Aunt Exer, a saint if ever there were one, countered with, "Now, Gwen, Sophie used to help with the dishes," the implication being that Sophie had grown less robust with the passing of time. Of course, all of us knew that Sophie was as strong and healthy as any of the rest of us. We suspected she was just bone-lazy.

As it began to get dark and the kids started catching lightning bugs and jarring them up, those who had decided not to spend the night would, one family at a time, begin to make go-to-the-house noises, inviting everyone to go home with them, being urged to stay over, and the like. This behavior was also highly ritualized and always carried out in the same way. Saying these good-byes could take up as much as an hour, with the leavetaker, wife, and children standing and making getaway conversation while being beseeched to stay, stay . . . stay. The ritual was over when the guest finally said, "Well, then, come, [Keenis]." And the host replied, "And you come, [Johnnie]." Until those words were uttered, the entire family of the host was expected to plead for the departing ones to stay while the leavetakers repeatedly demurred. The fact that sometimes as many as six or eight families had to act out this elaborate getaway ceremony could make for a very long evening.

In addition, everything described above as characterizing the Saturday ritual was also true for Sunday, with the exception that hardly ever did anyone stay over on Sunday night. Bear in mind that this was characteristic behavior of church members from all of the four small rural communities in that United Baptist Conference. Neither characters, roles, nor script changed one whit from one week to the next. Everyone rotated in and out of the host-guest position, depending on whose "rag'lar meetin' time" it happened to be.

Much of the above is true not only of the Uniteds but also of many of the small sects of Baptists who are in the business of saving the souls of rural eastern Kentucky sinners from the grasp of the inferno. Each group has some idiosyncrasy that is not true of all others, making that particular group most likely to succeed at getting past Saint Peter's screening process. I believe the Freewills are the only ones who acknowledge the possibility that members of other churches will make it to the golden streets. The Uniteds, Primitives, Pentecostals, and most others are dead certain that nobody has a chance of getting there but their membership; they will quote all kinds of Bible to support that position—as in "straight and narrow is the way and few there are who enter in" or something like that. When asked about all the Chinese or Africans who have never had the opportunity to hear the word of the Uniteds or Primitives and thus have been unable to join the Heaven-bound group, church members reply with a shake of the head and a "Law, ain't it sad [that whole continents of folks are going to Hell]?" An example of just how "sad" this narrowness of belief can be concerns my own family.

My Grandma Alk was a true Christian woman—lived right at the foot of the cross. She was a member of the Primitive Baptist Church, which, for lack of a permanent church house, met in the local one-room school building down on Bob's Branch. My grandpa, Pop Pop, was a carpenter and an unbeliever who, as far as I know, never darkened the door of any church house except maybe to go to funerals. In about 1920, Old Josh Ward, who owned the local sawmill, got saved in the tent revival and, in a fit of righteousness, cut and dressed enough timber to build a permanent church for that little group of Primitives. My grandpa took that lumber and single-handedly built the Bob's Branch Primitive Baptist Church. He then used the rest of the lumber to handmake every pew in that little church house. When my grandfather died in 1956, they had his funeral in that same church. Preacher Milroy Daniels—my grandpa's own brother-in-law—preached my wonderful Pop Pop into Hell. It became clear to me right then that you could not always trust claims made by folks who practice formal religion. Any god who would not want a man as fine as my Pop Pop is a sorry excuse for a man, much less a god!

My daddy carried on the tradition of not joining the church—or not much of anything else—while the other members of his family took after Grandma Alk and became good United or Primitive Baptists. When Daddy died four years ago, we had to get an out-of-town preacher to say the words over him and have his funeral at the funeral home, since using one of the country churches would have meant the resident pastor would have been called to preach Daddy into Hell. We couldn't even get any church people to sing. Anyone, family or friend, would tell you— and did—that my daddy was one of the finest moral men they ever knew—that he never cheated anyone and was always doing for other folks. Even his closest family members, however, did not believe he was going to be spending eternity anyplace other than Hell. Thus, they did not dare preach or sing at his funeral for fear that they too might put their souls in jeopardy by not holding fast to the teachings.

The biggest event of the year in the small fundamentalist Baptist churches that cling closely to the sides of the hills of eastern Kentucky is "foot-washin' meetin'"—the once-a-year occurrence of holy communion. Along with the partaking of the bread (broken-up saltines) and wine (grape juice), most of these churches also engage in foot-washing—hence, the term "foot-washing" Baptist. The rationale for this practice is grounded in Jesus' washing the feet of the disciples at the Last Supper. On this occasion, the deacons are charged with responsibility for bringing the washpans, crackers, and grape juice to church and passing out the same. I am not sure how it is done today, but in my childhood the broken saltines were passed from hand to hand on two small trays— one for the women, one for the men—followed by two cups of grape juice served in the same manner. That ritual was followed by water from a pitcher being poured into washpans—one pan per couple—and, without soap, each member of the pair washed the other's feet. This was a very moving occasion, accompanied by shouting, witnessing, and praying, as the spirit moved among the flock. These are good, sincere people who genuinely anticipate looking the Lord in the face when they have shuffled off this mortal coil, and the feeling of rapture that accompanies this ceremony is hard to describe to anyone whose belief system is not so strong—or so literal.

Religion was then and still is taken very seriously in the hills. I recall getting into some real trouble one day when Gwen Holbrook, Easter Ward, Baby Sister, and I took it upon ourselves to conduct a full-strength, high-holy funeral for a poor June bug that had met an untimely fate. We preached said bug into heaven, accompanied by abundant weeping, praying, singing—"I'll Fly Away," as I recall—shouting—many strategically placed "Well, well, well, Lord!"s—and considerable personal witnessing as to the religious commitment of ourselves and the bug, in whose loving memory all this was dedicated.

Some glad mornin' when this life is o'er
I'll fly away
To a land on God's celestial shore
I'll fly away.

IIII'll fly away, Oh Glory
III'll fly away—in th' mornin'
When I die
Hallelujah, by and by,
Yes, I'll fly away; Oh, fly awaaaaay.

As the four of us tucked into that first chorus of "IIII'll fly away, Oh Glory!" we could have graced any revival in the country and blown them right out of the tent—not one of us could carry a tune in a water bucket, but we were into a sendoff worthy of the best June bug of the summer. As I recall, the spirit filled us with ever more rapture as the funeral went on. When our little ritual got a bit noisy, our mothers took notice and were generally unamused by our display of fealty to the Lord or to said June bug.

I was saved by the good Lord, by way of Preacher Don Fraley, on a Thursday night in May 1957 at a revival meeting at the Thealka Freewill Baptist Church, and I was baptized into that very church the following Sunday. A whole gaggle of us went under the water about a quarter-mile up above the church in Muddy Branch, the stream that gave the community its real name. (Thealka was the name of the post office, but everybody called it Muddy Branch.) The creek was running high that Sunday, and, with Brother Don on one side of me and Irvin Castle on the other, I became one of God's children. As far as I know my name is still on the books of Thealka Church, but then the Freewills are not bad about turning folks out of the church, unlike the Hardshells (Primitive Baptists) or the United Baptists, who are far less liberal and more judgmental.

Although I knew a lot of folks who backslid, I only recall being present when one person was turned out of the church. At Little Friendship United Baptist Church, during the "business" part of the meeting, Deacon Orie Pack stood and announced that Sister Roma Lee Daniels had shamed herself before God and should no longer be considered part of the flock. He did not outline the manner or degree of the explicit sin itself, but then he did not have to because everybody knew she had been sleeping with that Eyetalian boy she brought home from somewhere over in West Virginia. You could pretty much expect that sort of behavior from Roma Lee because she was divorced, after all. Anyway, the men voted, and she was out. I do not believe Roma Lee was much torn up about the whole thing, because she went on to marry several times. The last I heard, she was living with some old man down in Tennessee and cooking at a grade school. Although Roma Lee was enough of an unabashed sinner to get herself turned out of the church, she got away with a lot—never had any kids by anybody, far as I know.

While the business of being "turned out" never seemed to have much of an effect on the above-named Roma Lee, it was taken very seriously by most of the folks who experienced it. I mean, it was not that easy to get *in* in the first place. The whole idea of a person just choosing to join the church, which was the way the town churches operated, never occurred to us. Just to offer your name to the rolls seemed to us to be making light of God's part in the process. I mean, who were *we* to choose to be with God? We put the power right where it belonged—with The Almighty! God had to choose us, and it just was not all that easy to get Him to make that choice. It went something like this.

You went to a revival and listened to the preacher tell you how God really wanted you to join him in Glory, thereby saving yourself from blazing in Hell forever. The more vile the preacher painted your imagined sins, the more concerned you became. Thus, when said sermonizer finally gave the altar call, you quickly hurried up to the altar, thereupon to fall down and ask God's forgiveness and repent the error of your ways. But wait. It did not end there. Repentance was not that easy. Once at the altar you were thought to have "come under conviction," a state that could last from a few minutes to a lifetime. While under conviction, you were expected to weep and pray for God's forgiveness for a lifetime of sinning.

Though some folks took longer than others to divest themselves of their burden of sins, I do not think the time it took had a lot to do with the extent of the sinning. After all, after a lifetime of transgression, my rascally Uncle Burns was saved in about half a minute. It had more to do, I believe, with the particular sect of Baptist from whom one was begging Grace. The Freewills pretty much got right on it, with salvation coming hard on the heels of conviction, while the United Baptists took awhile. Poor old Ferby Price probably never committed a sin in her life, except for marrying that sorry Joe Price—as notorious a drunk as Uncle Burns, any day—but she was a perpetual visitor at the altar. It took her more than twenty years to get saved, if I recall correctly.

As far as I could tell from watching, the time of petitioning for inclusion of the soul among the blessed was not spent by the postulant in a state of emotional agitation. There were a number of perpetual petitioners right on Two-Mile, and they all seemed to go about their lives pretty much the way everyone else did, with their salvation process being helped along, as it were, by the almost constant giving of Christian witness by all those whose souls were already included on God's great book. But, then, all of us were subjected to such incessant witnessing, which may have moved us onward to the altar a little earlier ourselves. Those known to be under conviction for many years maintained this state by going to the altar to pray for forgiveness at every rag'lar meetin' time, revival meeting, and funeral.

Funerals were special times of contrition for those known to be not yet among the chosen. Such services were as fervent as two or three preachers could make them and served as consummate occasions to bring lost souls to the Lord. I once took a sociology professor from the University of Kentucky home for Apple Day (the first Saturday in October), and our visit happened to coincide with the funeral of Zettie Price, a distant cousin of Momma's who was being laid to rest the next morning. Because Daddy wasn't feeling well and Momma did not want to go to the funeral alone, Sunday morning found me and one David Abramson, a New York nonbeliever, sophisticates both—or so we thought—sitting on the end of the very back row of the church, funeral-home fans clutched in one hand and a good white handkerchief in the other. We had entered the church and walked past the pink plastic telephone, with receiver off the hook, that rested on a pink-bordered, white-crepe-paper square announcing "Jesus called." We joined in the singing of "Never Grow Old" as the Price family came in and took their place in the front row. The eulogy was read—"Zettie Carol Price was born in the year of our Lord . . ."—and the first preacher commenced to preaching. He outlined both the past and expected future of Zettie as she walked upon the streets paved with gold to take her place at God's right hand, for she had been a good and faithful servant of the Lord. When he concluded some fifty minutes later, three of Zettie's fellow parishioners sang "I'm Going to Stroll over Heaven with You." By this time my urbane friend wore a perplexed look.

Then Preacher Milroy Johnson took the pulpit and began, "Sister Zettie was a faithful Christian and many's the time I have seen her right there in that very pew (where her children were sitting) praying 'Oooooooh Lord! Oooooooooooh Lord, please save my children. Don't let them go to the fiery furnace where they will never return . . . never see their dear mother again.' Well, well, well, Lord! Brother Bad (Zettie's husband, Ballard) is up there with her and on this day he has welcomed her to the house of the Lord foreverrrrrr. They are together in death as they were in life, Ooooooh Lord, waiting and hoping that they will one day see their beloved children in the land where we'll never grow old. And you children, Ooooooh you children have lost Mommy. Ooooooh Lord, now you will go home today and you'll look at that picture of Mommy on the mantel and wooooooooooooooh Mommy's gone. She's gone forevermore. Wooooooooh, you'll look in the pie safe and Mommy's butter mold will be there, but Mommy won't be there to make butter. And in the can house are Mommy's pickles, but Mommy will make no more. And Ooooooh, without redemption you will never see Mommy again."

Brother Milroy went on like that as he was wont to do. When he gave the floor to Little Nim Sturgill, who delivered a chilling rendition of "Amazing Grace," I noticed that, as I was wiping tears, so was the esteemed Dr. Abramson. A good funeral of true believers is enough to bring more than a few of us who fancy ourselves worldly ones right to the foot of the cross.

Lest you think that the good Dr. Abramson and I were making light of the rituals and beliefs of my youth, let me assure you that nothing could be farther from the truth. If anything, he came away from that funeral service with an increased respect for the customs of my people. I believe he found the experience very moving; I know I did—always do. Sister and I had a virtual replica of the Zettie Price funeral for Momma just a few years ago, and I expect something quite similar for the both of us when it's our time to be laid to rest amid the Wards and Prestons on top of the hill in Bob's Branch.

Christmas was, of course, our biggest holiday, and even today my husband marvels at how excited I get over the whole Thanksgiving-Christmas season. As far as I am concerned, they cannot commercialize it enough. In July, I am already thinking about Christmas, so why should the stores not decorate come September?

One of the events that was a part of Christmas at my elementary school was the dissemination of barrels of toys that came from big cities in the East through a little mission in the hills. The toys were things like colored macaroni bracelets for the girls—in third grade I got a red and green and yellow one—wooden wheel toys for the boys, and construction-paper ornaments. Each present had a child's name on it, and some included the names of the people who made them. I was always thrilled to get my toy of the year—sent by somebody who wanted to buy his way into Heaven or to pay us back for the coal rights we sat on. No doubt his astute grandpa had come into our hills and bought those coal rights from our illiterate granddaddies for ten cents per acre, and they were mined by our daddies for a dollar a load until so much of the coal dust filled their lungs that they choked on it. My macaroni bracelet fell apart before Christmas Eve, but I've never forgotten it.

Each classroom at school had its own Christmas tree, put up and decorated by teachers and students the week after Thanksgiving. We customarily sang at least one Christmas song every school day between Thanksgiving and Christmas break. At home, my family usually put up our tree about two weeks before Christmas Day, not nearly early enough for me. Since the time was never set in stone, our tree got set up and decorated as soon as I could politic to get it done, and I always began negotiations at the Thanksgiving dinner table. I would begin by suggesting, "We oughta go after the tree before the weather gets bad," and Sister would chime in her support.

The first step was for Daddy, Sister (as soon as she was big enough to walk), Leon (Uncle Fred's boy who was raised by Grandma Emmy), and me to go up on the hill across from Grandma Emmy's house and pick out and cut two little cedar trees—one for us and one for Grandma Emmy. There was some bargaining involved here too, because I perennially wanted the biggest tree the four of us seemed capable of dragging back to the house, while my parents had much more modest expectations. Ordinarily, our trees were of the five- to six-foot variety and shaped more like a torch than a traditional triangular-shaped Christmas tree. Cedars that grow wild in eastern Kentucky are fairly skinny, bell-bottomed little fellers, but they decorate up well.

Then we would help Grandma Emmy decorate her tree, which was also one of my favorite times. She told stories about her childhood when Santa left an orange, Brazil nuts, or a colored comb in her stocking. She forever teased me by declaring that she would hang up one of her thigh-high cotton stockings, thus causing Santa to be without any goodies left in his sack by the time he got to my house on Two-Mile. We always opened presents at Grandma Emmy's place on Christmas Eve, while Santa did not come to our house until Christmas morning, so it was clear that Santa made the Greasy Creek stop on his way to Two-Mile.

I loved my Grandma's dried-apple stack cakes and pies, so she was sure to have baked both especially for me. Christmas was the only time of year we had tangerines or chocolate-covered cherries or mixed nuts, to be savored once they were liberated from their various shells. We were also rewarded at Christmastime for our yellow-stained hands and the extra work that had gone into gathering, shelling, and meticulously extracting the black walnuts that now flavored our fudge. Although they are now available much of the winter, tangerines will always smell like Christmas to me.

After being tucked into one of my grandma's big feather beds in the front room, I would luxuriate in the promise of Christmas traced by the newly decorated tree in the firelight as Momma, Daddy, and Grandma Emmy sat by the fire and shared their last cup of coffee of the evening. Even in the days before electricity, we never used candles on the tree for fear of fire. But the fireplace and the coal-oil lamps cast enticing shadows on our little tree, its shining ornaments, and presents. We customarily decorated our own tree the day after we had "helped" Grandma Emmy with hers. Most often she, Leon, and Pop Pop were there for our little decorating festivity. Much the same ritual went on as the night before at Grandma Emmy's, complete with rich food and treats and memories of past Christmases. Although all of us loved Christmas carols, early on our laughter was the only music accompanying those occasions, since, with the exception of Auntie Lizzie, nobody on Momma's side of the family could carry a tune under any circumstances, Daddy only sang when he played the guitar, and Pop Pop was not the type to burst into song. Once we got electricity, however, strains of "Silent Night" and "God Rest Ye Merry Gentlemen" as well as strings of glittering Christmas tree lights augmented our little celebration.

Christmas promises have always come true for me, and I cannot think of a time that Santa did not bring me precisely the toy or sweater or bracelet I was longing for. That did not change as I grew up, either, for I have never had a Christmas that did not exceed my expectations. One of the values my family passed along to Sister and me (and that we have tried, in turn, to hand on down) is the ability to take delight in being together and sharing food and laughter and memories at Christmas. Although I have often found myself in faraway places, Christmas is comin'-home time. Over the years, Sister and I have explained to our friends that "Santa Claus only comes to our Momma's house on Two-Mile," which is our way of saying we are not available for any engagement that would keep us from home over this most important holiday. Wherever I have lived, my tree goes up the day after Thanksgiving and stays up until New Year's Day. But it watches over an empty house Christmas week, when my nuclear family returns to the Kentucky hills and once again becomes part of my family of origin. When Sister and I first moved to central Kentucky, we tried mightily to persuade Momma and Daddy to spend Christmas with us, offering to drive up and fetch them and return them to the homeplace on any schedule they preferred. They steadfastly refused. For thirty-some years we dragged bicycles and Barbies round-trip from wherever we were living back to Two-Mile. The difficulty of gathering at the homeplace on Christmas escalated as our children grew and all of us scattered, which can best be illustrated, I think, by excerpts from two of my Christmas letters sent to close friends.

I write this letter while sitting in the Salt Lake City Airport (Silent Night is *not* the same over Muzak), either going to or coming from Kentucky. I have made the trip so many times recently, my body no longer recognizes the direction.

Momma is gravely ill, Daddy is also failing and it is not fair to put all the burden on Sister just because I chose to move so far from the homeplace. Thus, my frequent flyer miles mount as my bank account diminishes—at some level we all pay, both financially and emotionally, for our mobility.

We are looking forward to still another Christmas in Kentucky where we hope good health and good weather will enable all the family to gather again at the homeplace to make Christmas magic happen once more.

What is left out of this account is that my sister had driven a three-hundred-mile round-trip to the hills almost every week of November 1991, supplemented during that period with my frequent weekend visits, but we had reached the end of our collective rope. The second week of December found Momma still hospitalized and Daddy too confused by Alzheimer's to stay at home alone. Sister had teenage children and commitments she could not avoid, and I had to get back to Montana for final exam week, so I was frantically calling friends and relatives trying to hire somebody to stay with my daddy.

My son, Brett Preston, who was then twenty-eight years old, listened to my plight and volunteered to take a week—half of the two weeks of annual leave he accumulated as a lawyer for the Justice Department— and come home to stay with his grandpa. This solution had not occurred to me, for I knew how he hoarded his precious few days of leave as well as how much he—a young bachelor—was looking forward to the pre-Christmas parties in Washington. The fact that he offered to—and ultimately *did*—come and stay with his grandpa was one of the best Christmas gifts I ever received. As I eased into the rental car to head to the airport and back to Montana for four days, my son stood with his arm around his grandfather on the porch of the house my daddy built. He pointed to his little red convertible parked in front of me on the drive-way and said, "Wish you'd get on out of here, Mom. Grandpa and I are going to put the top back and go lookin' for hot babes. Right, Grandpa?" I left my daddy laughing for the first time in days.

And then, from the letter I wrote Christmas 1994:

Well, here I sit on Thanksgiving Day—the German chocolate cake is on the sideboard, alongside the sweet potato soufflé, my brother-in-law Michael's cherry-surprise cake is in the oven and I am watching the Macy's Parade so it must be "the season." Although the world changes, there is still much we can count on. For me, one of those things that never changes is Christmas.

Many of you have heard me say that Santa Claus only comes to my mother's house, as I explained that I never spent Christmas anywhere but the homeplace, with many of the people I know and love around me. I look upon my Christmas routine and see it as my way of making the world stand still—at least for a while.

Whatever happened during the year, at Christmas, I could be sure that I was safe again, sheltered from the suffering of the world by the first people who watched over me—Momma and Daddy. As I sit here, I am aware of how very much I have taken for granted for fifty-four Christmas seasons— that there were enough resources to go around (both physical and emotional), that those I loved would love me back, that whatever losses the world could extract from me and mine, Christmas would come and we could make it right again. At this point, however, I am facing my first Christmas ever away from home.

If you have been on my Christmas list for a while, you are aware that both Momma and Daddy have not been well for the past three years. The first weekend in October, they took a turn for the worst and, at this point, my daddy is in very poor condition and my mother died on November 11. We checked them both out of the hospital four days earlier and brought them home.

Over the past few years, Momma suffered a great deal (as folks say, it was a blessing) and she is with her God. My daddy does not know about my mother's death, as he spends his days building houses with Cap and Spud and others of his work buddies; and I think this too is a blessing since the years he spent building houses were the happiest of his life.

The only sadness in this whole affair is on the part of my sister and me, who find ourselves orphaned at Christmas. I realize how ridiculous that sounds for two grown women, one well over half-a-century old, the other almost to that mark, to feel as if they have lost their compass in deep woods.

The truth is that physically it will be much easier on all of us. My parents lived in deep eastern Kentucky which, over the years, entailed carrying everything from rocking horses to bicycles to stereos to bread machines (as kids got older) three hours east of the nearest airport over roads that, while improved over the last thirty-some years, are still none-too-good.

And there were the first two years in Idaho, when Arthur and I drove home at Christmastime and our camera froze overnight, at eleven degrees below zero just west of Kansas City—but we saved the onions and the other things we thought would be perishable. There was also the time we were trapped in Gillette, Wyoming, when they closed the road and the kid at the service station advised us to spend the rest of the night across the street at Husky restaurant/service station because there were no rooms in town.

What is it that Maya Angelou says: "Wouldn't take nothin' for my journey now"?

We will make the pilgrimage again this year but right now the destination does not appear to hold much Christmas joy. We hope the holiday season finds you in good places and fills you with hope for all life's possibilities.

My daddy died 12/5/94.

Daddy died after the letter was written but not sent, so I included that last statement at the bottom of the letter. In many ways I am glad my parents died just prior to the holidays, because I never feel their presence in my life as powerfully as I do during the Christmas season when Sister and I continue to go through the rituals that come so naturally to us and as we watch our children take up the self-same customs. Since Momma and Daddy died, Sister and her family have spent Thanksgiving in Montana with me, and I and mine have spent Christmas at her house in Frankfort. Since my children live in Tennessee, North Carolina, South Carolina, and the District of Columbia and Sister's are in Kentucky and Virginia, these gatherings are difficult to arrange, expensive, inconvenient, and time-consuming. My kids and my sister's children did not grow up in eastern Kentucky and thus do not feel guilt or emptiness for having moved "away from home." They missed out on a lot of Decoration Days, and they may not ever be able to understand the enchantment of anticipating Miners' Vacation. But for as long as Sister and I are around, I 'spect we'll be keeping the creek in Christmas.

FROM NATURE'S GRACES
TO GATHERING PLACES

*N*ature was hard to miss in my home country. What with the floods, the humid heat, and the paucity of bottomland, I often viewed her as somewhat less than kind. But she sent flowers to take the edge off. The summers of my youth were filled with a remarkable array of flowers, both indigenous and cultivated, that seemed to surround every house in my community. The scent of honeysuckle always takes me home because it grew wild every- where in my home county. On the bank directly across from my house, Aunt Exer fought the dread honeysuckle—which we called "the weeds"—with her climbing roses, but it was pretty much a losing battle. Wild honeysuckle is the kudzu of eastern Kentucky. As children, we loved to chase each other through the honeysuckle thicket by the creek. Some adult, usually Pop Pop, would always check for snakes in the weeds before we were allowed to cavort in there.

At the edge of the weeds across the creek in front of our house, a huge stand of immense orange tiger lilies multiplied each year and held their ground in the face of the honeysuckle onslaught, while purple flags proliferated every which way on the side of the hill that bordered our backyard. Momma planted red and white gladioli in her bed in the side yard, along with sweet williams, peonies, spiderlegs, and cannas, but she was never able to get a climbing rose to do a thing, even though she routinely put in new ones every year. Along the walk by the well box, Aunt Exer had the healthiest stand of sweet williams and spiderlegs you ever saw, and they coaxed a smile every time I passed, carrying my fresh buckets of water.

Nobody back home could tell me the proper name for spiderlegs, and I could never get any to grow from the seeds Momma gave me; so that was one favorite I was unable to carry with me from the hills. Then about five years ago I saw some spiderlegs blooming in a nursery and learned their proper name (cleome). Since I have been able to name them, I have bought cleome plants each year and have raised a few of my own. Most of the ones I have raised have not felt particularly welcome in Montana's cool, dry, and short growing season and have refused to grow tall or to return on their own. A good part of my heritage is in my flower bulbs and seeds that I have carried with me as I have moved around the country. Two deep-purple irises and a white peony—homegrown, all— grace my desk even as I write this piece.

It has been interesting to watch the descendants of the flowers of my homeplace adapt themselves to the soil and climate of a new land while I also have been learning to deal with the different environment. I think sometimes that I am much more tolerant and flexible about my expectations of my flowers than I am of my expectations of myself and other human beings. After I moved to Montana in 1988, it took seven years for my peonies to bloom. I continued to feed them and neither cursed them, spat at them, nor displayed any other signs of impatience or disappointment. I wish I could be as patient with human nature as I am with my physical environment.

As we learned to appreciate different aspects of nature—from floods to flowers—we also had to learn how to harness nature to our own ends. In most families, women learned one set of accomplishments, men another. Since my daddy had no sons, I was required to master some skills clearly in the male realm. Growing up as a country-wife-in-training and as Daddy's "boy," I learned many skills that would serve me well if I should ever need to breed, raise, kill, and cure my own meat; or grub, plow, and otherwise prepare a field for planting; or sow, hoe out, and harvest vegetables; or cook, can, and preserve those fruits of my labors. With small variations, we shared an unwritten calendar that marked the proper time to put in one crop or another. For me, Valentine's Day is far more likely to bring back memories of sowing lettuce and planting onions than remembrances of romance. In case you ever need to know, you always put in your lettuce and onions on February 14.

Some of the times I felt closest to Momma were when we would take small knives and go looking for the first mess of sallet greens in the springtime. I learned very early how to pick sallet—to get just the right combination of plantain and dandelion, with a bit of poke thrown in. There was always much discussion on the part of the women as to the poke question—whether to include it and, if so, how much. Most folks could agree about the combination of other greens, but each spring brought another argument about poke. I am not sure just why it was that the disagreement always concerned poke and not the others, but it was important enough to be discussed over and over. Some said poke was poisonous unless it was cooked; some swore by its healing properties; still others warned that if you rubbed raw poke stalks over your chest it would cause your heart to clear run away with you. Momma was perhaps the strongest poke partisan; she liked more poke in her greens than most. But then, my momma always did like to live dangerously.

Although back then I may not have been the most willing worker in the world, I feel a lot stronger now in the knowledge that I can take care of myself because of having taken part in all those life-preserving duties. Let me admit that I have not done most of those very basic tasks since I left home at age seventeen, and I hope I never have to do them again. In the sixties and seventies, when many of my academic friends and colleagues longed to return to the land, my suggestion was that if they had ever lived on the land, they might not have been quite so nostalgic for it. Trying to keep a coal fire banked so that it will last the night and not burn dangerously high, as well as having to break the ice frozen on the top of the water bucket in the morning, instills a powerful appreciation for central heating; and just a few times of carrying last night's full chamber pot to the outdoor toilet as day breaks makes indoor plumbing most welcome.

While nature brought us much-needed water, she also delivered the predictable spring floods. Though we could predict that it would rain in the springtime, we had no idea when or how much water the good Lord would visit upon us. We needed that rain to grow the crops, but sometimes the heavens' generosity was just too abundant. At such times, we were forced to get out of our houses and to the high ground—fast! My family lived on the "flood" side of the road, but Daddy had built our house up high so, although we had a few close calls, we never got flooded out. The old school building used to flood regularly, spring after spring, but when they built the new school in the early fifties, they put it up by the road and I only saw it flooded twice. You might question why people would build in a flood plain, but to understand the answer to that you need to get the lay of the land back home.

We do not have mountains in Appalachia; we have steep hills and ridges, nestled very close to each other with very little room in between them. In the early days when folks were building on that land they had no heavy equipment, so they built in the hollers (hollows) between those ridges. They also often built near a creek to be able to dig shallow wells for water. In the house I grew up in, I could look out the front windows and see a hillside or look out the back windows and see a hillside. In order to catch a glimpse of the sky, I had to walk out into the yard and look straight up. It was late in the morning before the sun burnt off the mist and erased the shadows over our house seat. We lived close in those Kentucky hills and built on the land that was left after we used the bottomland for our crops. Thus, we dealt with the floods as we dealt with other inauspicious visits from Mother Nature, such as forest fires. Since my family lived right on the side of the hill and the timberline came within three yards of our wooden house, we were always concerned when the woods caught fire. I recall once being awakened in the middle of the night to carry water as a half-dozen men from the community helped my daddy dig a trench at the edge of the trees while the women carried water from the creek to fill the trench. The fire got close that time, but we saved the house.

Growing up as I did gave me a unique perspective on nature because we had to deal with all manner of nature's creations for dominance over that land. In the summertime, it was not wise to walk across the yard after dark without a flashlight, since we wanted to see the creatures before they saw us, particularly copperhead snakes. Some said there were rattlers too, but I never actually saw a rattlesnake, while copperheads were regular visitors to our property. The summer I was eight years old, a seven-year-old boy who lived around the bend from me was leaning up against a tree in his yard when a copperhead struck him in the back. He lay in bed for three days before he died. He was not the only person I knew who got snake-bitten, but he was the only one who died from it. A few years ago one of my academic brethren from the university system in Kentucky began a movement to save the copperhead. At such times, I find it hard to empathize and just have to wonder where the fellow grew up.

After folks saw the movie *Deliverance,* I was often asked if it was safe to be outside after dark in my home community. The answer is yes and no. When I did social work in Appalachia in the early sixties, I was never afraid of being up the most isolated holler as darkness fell, because there was little threat of random violence. In my experience you actually have to do something to somebody before he'll come out after you. Although I have never felt any real danger from human beings back home, I was always careful to look where I stepped because snakes—and cowpies— lurked.

For a number of years I used to buy fruits and berries and make my own jam, but I stopped doing that once my son, Brett Preston, began kindergarten. Instead I began to buy my jam at the summer community fairs held in rural areas. When he was in law school, Brett Preston brought some fellow students home with him for fall break. The first morning, I baked them some biscuits, fried up sausage, and made sawmill gravy— my son's favorite breakfast. One of the boys commented on the delicious strawberry jam. Brett Preston responded, "Yeah, Mom makes it every summer, and we stick to the floor for about two weeks after every batch." At that time it had been almost two decades since my son had seen me make jam. I did not rush to tell the boys those strawberries were picked and worked up by a little widow in Adrian, Oregon. In fact, for once, I just kept my mouth shut.

My family had the first flush toilet on Two-Mile. Daddy installed it when he put water in our house when I was in fourth grade. At that time he also replaced the sink in the kitchen with a bigger one and put a small sink in the bathroom, but we did not get a bathtub. Then in the summer of 1955, Daddy was laid off from the mines for a couple of weeks, and he used the time to build an extension on the back of our house, making a breakfast room and another small bedroom and putting a bathtub in the bathroom. Momma then refinished Grandma Emmy's old pie safe and table and a bedroom set she had bought at a roadside "antique" sale. Finally, at age fourteen, I no longer had to sleep with my sister. Our old house had originally been built in a square. From the left side of the porch, you entered the living room, where we had a maroon-and-gray plush couch and chair, a small TV set, and a coal heater. Just inside the front door on the right was a door to the front bedroom, heated by an open fireplace, where Momma's bed and dresser took up most of the space, but by then we had Grandma Emmy's porch rocking chair sitting at the edge of the hearth facing the fireplace. If you walked straight through the living room, about five good steps brought you to the kitchen door, where we had a yellow-and-gray quilt-printed plastic-and-chrome dinette set, a sink with a built-in cabinet, and Momma's new gas cookstove. The bedroom I shared with Sister—the girls' room—evened out the square. It was positioned directly behind our parents' bedroom and to the right of the kitchen and could be entered from either room. Although our room had no heat source, in the winter we left all the doors inside the house open. It was not too uncomfortable except during the very coldest spells, when Sister and I would take our quilts and bed down on either end of the couch in the living room. Daddy tucked the bathroom in between the two bedrooms by partitioning off about a quarter of what was now Sister's room, added my new bedroom behind Sister's, and put the breakfast room just to the back of the kitchen. At summer's end, instead of four rooms, we had six.

Despite the additional plumbing, I still had to carry water because our water tasted awful and turned anything washed in it varying shades of orange. I did, however, begin my sophomore year of high school in September 1955 with my own room and my own things in my own chest of drawers and my own dresser with my own mirror. It appeared to me that life for Linda Sue Preston was looking up.

The first Saturday in December 1955, we went to the company store at David to do some Christmas shopping. I bought Brad Williamson—my first boyfriend—a canary-yellow banlon V-necked sweater, and Momma bought a bunch of stuff she secreted away the moment we got home. My family was big on Christmas surprises. On Tuesday next, I was standing in the hall at school just after the last bell had rung to dismiss us, when Clifford Butcher ran up and said, "You better stop laughing, Linda Sue. Your house is burning down." The school-bus driver had seen the house burning as he was on his way to pick us up. He had then told somebody, who informed Clifford Butcher, who duly reported it to me. By the time our bus got me and Sister home, a crowd, including Momma, had gathered on Aunt Exer's porch. What had been our house was a smoldering ruin.

Momma had left around ten that morning to go to Paintsville to pay bills and buy ingredients for a fruitcake. Someone saw smoke coming from the house around noon and called the Paintsville Fire Department— some folks did have telephones by then—but the fire truck would not come outside the city limits, so our house was a total loss. They never did determine exactly what was responsible for the fire, but, when you heat with coal in open fireplaces, losing a house to fire is not that unusual. People in our circumstances did not have insurance. When my Daddy pulled in on the driveway some half hour later, he saw everything he owned—or was owing for—in blackened embers. He got out of his car, walked slowly up to it, shook his head slowly, and muttered "Aye, boys."

Pop Pop had died the previous summer, so we moved into his little house next door until Daddy could build back. It was a one-bedroom house with no indoor plumbing. Momma and Daddy slept in a bed in the living room, and Sister and I were together again in Pop Pop's little four-by-six bedroom, where the bed took up so much space that both of us could not stand up in the room at the same time. What's more, I once again had to take on slop-jar duty every morning. Pop Pop's toilet was quite a trek from the house, so, when I had to take the pot out before daylight, I just poured the damned thing in the creek and neglected to tell anybody (until now, that is).

My dear husband, the original tree-hugger, will probably shoot me when he sees this account, but he has no idea how very close to nature some of us were forced to be. He grew up in a small town in Connecticut. If he wanted to commune with nature, his family drove to the shore or to the Berkshires. Therefore he is concerned for every snail darter and tree owl on the planet. Although it is not true that I would lay four lanes of blacktop across Yellowstone Park and call it progress, I am not too far away from that position. Town folk live in places where nature has been so long domesticated that they don't know her for what she is. Living close to the land taught me that nature can be—indeed, usually is—a mean mother.

Although we lived in a natural setting, there were centers of commerce in the form of country stores. We had two stores in our community: Mitchell and Leona Wallen's—which everybody called Leonie's—and Walter Pack's, otherwise known as "The Store." Leonie's store also served as the Williamsport Post Office, where we got the mail delivered twice a day.

Hershel Ray, from east over the mountain at Tomahawk, drove the mail truck. In the morning, he met the train in Paintsville, picked up the mail from all parts, and brought it to a half-dozen or so little communities along the twenty miles of main road between Paintsville and Inez, Kentucky. The mail arrived at our little Williamsport Post Office around ten o'clock and was sorted by Leonie, who called out the names of those receiving letters.

After leaving our morning mail and picking up any letters to go east toward Inez, Hershel would head out. We would see him again around three in the afternoon when he brought mail from Inez and environs and picked up outgoing messages for the big world beyond eastern Kentucky. Not many people gathered for the afternoon mail because it only brought letters from twenty miles east. I hardly even knew about Hershel's afternoon run until I had a brief but intense correspondence with one Johnny McCoy from Inez, during which time I 'bout drove ol' Hershel and Leonie both crazy trying to pin down to a dot when the afternoon mail would "run."

When somebody would walk up the road from the direction of Leonie's store around ten o'clock, folks would call out to the traveler, "Has the mail run?" If he answered in the affirmative, that called for a trip to the store and a peanut-filled Pepsi as we checked to see if anybody from "away" had remembered us. People in my community genuinely looked forward to getting mail. Mail meant news and gossip and catalogs and, if you were really lucky, a punchboard! Oh, joy, a punchboard!

Punchboards—along with a list of prizes to be won on that board—

were sent to folks, with instructions to collect a certain amount of money for each punch or letter on the front of the board. Then, for five, twenty-five, or fifty cents per punch, folks would select the letter of their choice. The person's money was taken and his name duly noted next to his chosen letter on the back of the punchboard. Once all the letters were sold, the punches or tops were pulled off the punchboard in order to find out the prizes they had won. The money and information were sent to the original sender of the punchboard so that the prizes could be mailed out. Another variation of punchboard was that there were simply dollar amounts underneath the numbers, so folks got greater or lesser amounts for their punches. Except for the occasional poker game—which most folks would not even acknowledge went on because playing cards was thought to be a sin whether or not money exchanged hands—punchboards were about as near to gambling as we ever got. As far as I know, nobody ever pointed out that playing punchboards was gambling, so we just enjoyed the heck out of them—at least I did. Punchboards taught me early on to anticipate surprises that might come my way. It is true that sometimes the outcome was not so positive, but the fun was in taking a chance with my nickel, in high hopes of the unknown prize hidden under that tab.

In those days, it was more fun to receive mail than it is now because people did not get bills by postal delivery. First of all, there was little credit advanced, except at the local country stores like Leonie's. Even if there *had* been, few merchants would have been foolish enough to advance it to those of us out in the hills and hollers. On occasion, somebody would buy a sewing machine or a bedroom suit—we said suit as in "suit of clothes," not suite as in "sweetheart"—on time, but they would go to town once a month or on payday to pay the merchant in person.

Any form of posted paper reminder was considered a "dun"—a mark of disrespect indicating that the person was not fulfilling his responsibilities to the merchant. Believe me, *nobody* wanted his friends and neighbors to see him getting mail like that! That whole scene left an indelible mark on me in that, although I buy everything by credit card today, my home mortgage is the only thing that I do not pay off each month. I cannot sleep well if I am "owin'" somebody, so I try never to live beyond my means. I suspect that Gwen, Easter, and the rest of the kids who hung around the post office at that time don't do much business on credit either, although they probably run an account at Leonie's or Walt Pack's.

During the summer months, Leonie's store–post office served as the gathering place for the community, where one or more members of every household would congregate, Pepsi or Royal Crown Cola in hand, to swap tales and wait for the mail. Most families got up and about quite early in the summer because it was far more pleasant to do the plowing, planting, hoeing, weeding, and gathering chores in the garden before the oppressive heat and humidity of a Kentucky summer day. Thus, by mid-morning, the early chores were finished, and we could get out from under our mother's (or wife's) footsteps while she prepared dinner—the big midday meal—to be served at noon, sharp. What better way to spend an hour or so than sittin' on pop cases or carbide cans at Leonie's and listening to everybody blow?

I am going to change some names here, but this is a true story that did indeed happen at an unnamed post office sometime in the fifties. I promise. Leroy Travis was this little dried-up feller out of the head of the creek who wouldn't strike a tap at a black snake, but he was sharper'n ary tack. Leroy was a regular at the post office, waiting for the mail to run because he was right sorry. Since his family could hardly get a decent day's work out of him, they felt like he could at least pick up the mail. Our other protagonist was one Don Ed Butcher, who was a big ol' boy, built like Li'l Abner; as they say, you could smell holler rat all over him. A pretty good worker, Don Ed had been shell-shocked in the big war, and it had slowed him down somewhat above his eyes—all his dogs didn't bark. Every day those two would come to pick up their mail, and every day Leroy would taunt Don Ed unmercifully—just funnin,' everybody said. This would go on for a couple of days until finally Don Ed's patience would wear thin, and he would just flat clean Leroy's plow. That in itself would not have been worth reporting, since fights broke out and were broken up now and again. However, it was Leroy's habitual response that made the interaction so fascinating. While Don Ed was on top of him pounding his head into the dirt, Leroy always uttered the same cry, "Pull 'im off me 'fore I kill 'im! Pull 'im off me 'fore I kill 'im!"—a quote that has come in handy more often than I would like.

Walt Pack owned the other store on Two-Mile, but, since it was actually located at the mouth of the creek—where Two-Mile Creek joined up with Greasy Creek—it was considered too far to walk for day-to-day things. Walt sold a lot of items that Leonie did not, so Daddy and Momma would often take the car and go to Walt Pack's on a Saturday to get supplies for the week.

We bought on credit at both places, and Daddy settled up the bill on payday. Everybody in the community ran up credit at both stores; we would go in, open the pop case, where the cold drinks rested in frigid water up to their necks, pull out a frosty Pepsi, and say, "Onie, I got me a Pepsi," whereupon Leonie would draw out our family's little book of slips and write "Pepsi—5¢." Then when Daddy paid the bill, he would bring home the slips showing what we had charged.

The same procedure was employed at Walt Pack's store, but I never felt at home there the way I did at Leonie's. Perhaps it was because Pack's was "The Store" used by the cool kids at school, and I was not often among them. Or maybe it was just proximity, since Leonie's was only about two hundred yards from my house, while we had to get in the car to go to Walt Pack's. It may also have been something of a social thing, since Leonie and Mitchell Wallen were common people, just like the rest of us, while many of the Packs were rich folks—some even had businesses in town or worked there.

Town was/is Paintsville, Kentucky, population forty-five hundred, located across Two-Mile Hill, eight miles from our little community but eons away in terms of class, values, expectations, and anything else that counted for much. For some reason, Walt Pack's store, while located half a mile farther from town than Leonie's, was more upscale just because it was owned by Walt Pack. That was another of those givens.

I recall one experience centered around Walt Pack's store that happened repeatedly from the time I was eight or so until I became a teenager. The Preston family headed to Pack's on a Saturday to buy groceries for the upcoming week, pulling up in the old blue-black '41 Plymouth with Daddy driving, Momma in the front, and Sister and me bickering in the back seat. We would drive onto the gravel and up to the gas pump out in front of the store. After Walt filled up the gas tank, Daddy would pull over to the side, and he and Momma would go into the store.

I always wanted to go in with them because, once inside, I could politic for a Pepsi and a treat. But every single time, as they exited the car, they gave me the same explicit instructions: "Stay in the car and mind your sister." The very moment the screen door closed on their behinds, I would open the car door and put my chunk of a baby sister out with instructions to "run, run, run." Once she got a head start, I would rush into the store after her and exclaim: "She got away and I couldn't catch her!" My parents never called me on it, and Baby Sister got me inside Walt Pack's store every time! Until she was twenty-some years old, I recall this recurring little scene as the only time I found it advantageous to have a sister.

The thing I remember most about country stores, be it Leonie Wallen's, Walt Pack's, or Ern Ward's (which was on Greasy Creek), is that they all had a distinctive, rather pleasant aroma. It was somewhat sweet, like tobacco as it hangs in the barn to cure, but softened by some combination of linseed oil on old timber flooring, chocolate drops in gallon jars, burlap bags full of potatoes, oatmeal cake sandwiches, and Moon Pies. If you mixed all that together and let it steep for several decades, it would be instantly recognizable as country-store perfume—unforgettable. Although I have recognized that fragrance many times in my life, I have never smelled it within the city limits of any town, large or small.

The life we lived may appear to outsiders to have been somewhat discouraging, but we also had our pleasures as we found ways of transcending the day-to-day struggles. One of those ways was through religion. Another was through basketball—the University of Kentucky Wildcats. We gathered 'round the Wildcats. Yes, we *did*.

Some of my earliest and most pleasant memories are of Daddy carrying me into my Grandpa Preston's house, where everybody encircled the taller-than-I-was, arch-shaped brown wooden radio to cheer on the Wildcats. Even if we had had the money to buy our own radio, we were staying with Grandma Emmy, who did not have electricity until the REA brought it to the more remote areas when I was in the second grade. By that time we were accustomed to enjoying the game at Pop Pop's, cheering on the Cats with half the community.

In those days in Appalachia, we may not have felt we had a lot to invest in or be proud of, but we always had our Wildcats. We never missed a game broadcast, and as the team took the floor to the strains of "My Old Kentucky Home," there was not a dry eye in the house. For us, Kentucky basketball was transcendence. It took us outside our lives—removed the boundaries and made us all one—and I'll wager there was not a child in the whole commonwealth who did not dream of someday playing basketball for Kentucky. This preceded the institution of women's varsity basketball at the University of Kentucky, so today feminists might inquire why I, as a female, did not question the ubiquitous basketball programs for boys while none existed for girls. I must admit that it never occurred to me that I was not represented by those male gods who played for Adolph Rupp. All I aspired to was to feel myself a part of that tradition through hearing and cheering and, later, watching them play. Although there were no formal girls' programs at that time, every house on the creek had some sort of makeshift basket nailed up to regulation height, and boys and girls played pickup and one-on-one. I cannot recall a time when any of us, male or female, could not run a passable fast break—the trademark of Kentucky teams. This is another area where Ronalta Mae Pelphrey excelled; every playground pickup team wanted her. At Meade School, we put our all into basketball because we did not have football at the county schools.

There was and still is a fairly rigid class system between the folks who lived in towns and did white-collar work and those who lived in the country and mined coal, worked at unskilled labor, or scratched out a livelihood from the unforgiving land we inhabited. Most of the country folks I knew did all those things in order to support their families, and, to a person, they were all basketball fanatics. People who lived in town had football teams that played each other's small-town schools. But in basketball, they had to face us, their country counterparts. There was a cheer the town schools used when they played against us: "Two bits, four bits, / Six bits, a dollar; / Send those creekers / Back up the holler!"

That cheer was made bearable by our certain knowledge that they could not conquer us in basketball. I would suggest that we were tough in this sport because we had little else to dream about and because we considered ourselves part of the great Kentucky basketball tradition. One of the reasons we formed such a bond with "our team" may have had something to do with a sense of personal powerlessness that existed in the creeks and hollers of eastern Kentucky. We did not have television then—many of us did not even have electricity—which made it hard for us to find heroes; God and the Wildcats had to do. I think that goes a long way toward explaining the emotional bond some of us have to sports.

Although there were no organized sports in my elementary school, we played games regularly. Since those games were largely unsupervised, problems were pervasive: the most athletic kids were always chosen first (like Easter Ward and Ronalta Mae Pelphrey); the kids with little talent or skill were perpetually chosen last (like me and Gwen Holbrook—think Jack Spratt and his wife); the makeup of teams changed from day to day, so there was little, if any, opportunity for team-building or cooperation; whenever there were problems between two kids, the more popular one was chosen and the other shunned by both teams; since there was no formal organization, there was never any time for skill-building or practice; and, although basketball was played daily, team makeup changed based on who was playing on any given day. Given those factors, it is hard to make the case for sport as a character-builder or even as a desirable physical activity. None of that made one whit of difference in our dreams; someday each of us would *be* a Kentucky Wildcat. I certainly thought that way, and I'll bet every other little kid on the creek did too. It never occurred to me that being a girl excluded me from that dream; it still does not.

IMPLICATIONS OF FOREVER

Adolescence such as we know it today did not exist in my community. Folks went directly from childhood to adulthood, and the date of passage was more likely governed by onset of puberty than by any particular age. If a boy got his growth early, he dropped out of school as soon as he could and went into the mines. If he could not get a mining job immediately, he took off for one of the cities to the north—Dayton, *De*troit, Columbus, or sometimes Akron—and moved in with family already there until he drew his first paycheck. Once he got himself a job in a factory, he came back to the hills to marry his girl and take her back with him. Sometimes the steps were arranged a little differently. At such times, the boy and girl would drop out of school simultaneously, get married, go north together, move in with family, and the rest of the pattern remained the same. At such times, the baby usually came early. I was surprised every time that happened.

When I reached adolescence, my dreams were filled with the first scenario, with me as a major player. I had it all worked out in my head very early, well before my teenage years. I wanted somebody to care enough about me to take me away to Ohio, where we would have four kids named Tim, Kim, Kay, and Buddy. (I have no idea where those names came from, but I had those babies named by my twelfth birthday.) The only problem was that I could hardly get a date, much less a mate. It is easy to be flippant about that from where I sit now, but at the time there was a lot of adolescent angst involved in not having anybody who thought I was pretty enough, or special enough, to spend time with.

I had a lot of unformed, confused thoughts about sex and boys and myself. Since we bred hogs, I had some idea as to what went on in the sex act, but that was another of those mysteries I could not seem to figure out—and the reading material of that day was so vague about the whole thing that there was really no way for me even to attempt to satisfy my curiosity. I really envied the popular girls—Easter Ward and Ronalta Mae Pelphrey come to mind—who seemed so sure of themselves with the opposite sex, while I could never seem to come up with the right thing to say and was always making jokes nobody thought were funny or could understand. I also experienced considerable embarrassment because my body was just not acceptable. It's hard to say what troubled me most: the possibility that I *ever* would have sex or the fear that I *never* would have sex. In the fifties, on Two-Mile, big breasts sure looked to me like the ticket to love and sex and adulthood and popularity. I just didn't have the currency to gain entry into any of those places I wanted to go. I wanted desperately to be a woman rather than a little girl, but, in order to do that, I needed a man.

Because the water on our side of the creek was bad and because I was the older child and had no brothers, the job of going to the well across the road from my house and carrying fresh water back home fell to me (Daddy's boy, remember?). This usually required two buckets in the morning before school, one in the afternoon after school, and another in the evening just before dark. The exception was each Sunday evening, when I drew and carried thirty buckets of water home from the well, a distance of approximately a quarter-mile. This Sunday chore was necessary in order for Momma to wash our clothes on Monday. One of my most vivid memories of adolescence is of walking back and forth along that footpath in the twilight and wishing on the first star of the evening that somebody, anybody, would fall in love with me.

To this day, more than forty years hence, I am incapable of seeing the first star of the evening without making a wish. As my life has progressed, I have wished for a number of different things (sometimes I have even wished on an airplane, which I mistook to be a star). Over the years, my wishes have changed, sometimes from day to day; but I recall only one wish throughout my teens—a wish for intimacy, for belonging to another person who would make my life meaningful. As a young girl in that community, I commanded about as little respect as could be imagined, and I saw only one avenue open for me to gain any respect—to affiliate myself with a man. Doing so would automatically grant access to all the perks of adulthood—credibility, for example. Nobody would dare tell an adult to sit down, shut up, or stop acting crazy, admonishments I got all the time. In addition to instant maturity, the act of getting married would make me a wife, a position implying much more power through my husband than a single woman could ever hope for.

Since I was always trying to avoid physical labor, I found that I could sometimes escape such chores by claiming schoolwork. Although nobody in my culture had much respect for education as such, my family wanted me to finish high school, so some time spent with the books was allowed. I found out rather early that homework itself took relatively little time, so I would quickly finish my schoolwork and dive into whatever book I was reading. It is important for me to set down here that, however much I loved to read, I would have given up reading in a flash if I had found a girlfriend to talk with or a boyfriend to pay attention to me. Despite all my reading about relationships, however, I just could not seem to convert the things I learned from the printed page for use in my own life. Although it seemed to me that I was living by all the stated rules, I was never able to connect in human relationships. I didn't look grown-up; I was too thin and underdeveloped. I didn't act grown-up; I was far too reluctant to take on my share of day-to-day work. My biggest problem, however, had to do with my general unwillingness to be serious, which was perceived by members of my community as immaturity.

When I reached puberty, I was expected to give up all the activities I had enjoyed as a child because adolescents were considered adults (grown-up) and made to feel ashamed if they did not act mature. This meant that at age twelve I could no longer swing from tree limbs, laugh at all sorts of inappropriate times, talk out of turn, or practice "cheerleading" motions as I walked around. Walked around, indeed! I never just walked around—I skipped, hopped, swung, and swayed, snapping my fingers as I gyrated down the road. Although this behavior was not much appreciated in a child, it was completely unacceptable in an adolescent. I laughed too much, talked too much, sang and danced, and just plain acted-out too much. Clearly, I met all the criteria for immaturity, especially in a place where seriousness about the hardships of life and the necessity of accepting one's responsible place in the scheme of things was a God-given duty. Both the body I was born into and the mind I developed conspired to keep me in childhood long after everybody thought I should be putting away childish things.

My first recollections of living in my body are fairly positive. I loved to run and tumble and play, and I was in motion almost constantly. Since I grew up before television came to Appalachia and there were often more people than there was space in the houses, kids spent most of their time outside whenever possible. A lot of time was occupied exploring in the hills or playing hide-and-seek, follow-the-leader, and other such kids' games, supplemented with whatever work we were required to do.

I recall having my first doubts about my body when Easter Ward told me that every girl on Two-Mile (except me, of course) had "got her period." I must have been about eleven years old—it was more than four decades ago—yet that moment comes vividly to me today. I was wearing faded red shorts and a shirt with tiny pink-and-tan rosebuds that Momma had made from a feed sack; Easter and I sat under the coal bank across from her house. I even recall my blatant lie in response. I didn't think twice before I told Easter that I, too, had "got my period," but that I had not yet told anyone. She was not fooled, of course. Invention I might get away with, but outright falsifying I did not carry off well. Easter may not have been a great speller, but she was far enough ahead of me in the book of daily reality that she was always able to read me. Besides, I came late to puberty and at the time of my big lie to Easter I probably did not weigh eighty pounds. It took no genius to guess correctly as to my level of sexual development.

The other kids had always teased me about being skinny, calling me

Pop Pop and Cousin Robert Jay in front of Pop Pop's shop. Blacksmith equipment can be seen in background.

With Sister, 1947.

Momma and Sister, 1947.

With Sister and Daddy, ca. 1949–50.

Momma, ca. 1954.

Sister's third-grade picture, 1956.

Momma in her red shorts in our living room at Two-Mile.
(We got a television in 1954, so the picture was taken
after that.)

Sister's tenth birthday party. Gwen Holbrook and Linda Sue (upper left corner); Sister (seated third from right).

Easter Ward.   Linda Sue Preston.

Sister.

Sister and Cousin Jimmie Gambill. Across the road in the background is the Holbrook house; everyone used to gather on their porch in the evening.

With Daddy, Momma, and Brett Dorse, August 7, 1960.

The Scott family, summer, 1967.

Daddy at one of his construction sites in the early '70s.

Daddy relaxing, 1975.

"Birdlegs," but I had never really minded before because, except for basketball, my body had pretty much performed as I expected it to. What's more, I was the only one of my age group who could do a backbend and the splits and could lock my legs around my neck and roll around like a ball. Upon hearing this new information, however, I was heartbroken to find that this body that had previously served me well apparently could not bleed on Easter Ward's schedule—and that was just the beginning. Although I did, in fact, start my period a few months later, my lack of confidence in my body and its ability to pass for normal continued for many years and became much worse before it got better.

My recollections of my body and my love life—or lack of same—in high school are pretty negative. Often I recall my teenage years as one long, lonely walk, wishing fervently that somebody would come along and love me. In truth, there was a somebody or two who succumbed to my meager charms. The first was Brad Williamson.

It took me years of consciously drawing myself up to correct the slouch I developed as a result of my relationship with Brad Williamson. Although he claimed to be five feet, eight inches tall and I claimed to be five feet, five and a half, he was probably five-six to my five-seven, which resulted in some major-league stooping on my part. Brad was from Butcher Holler, around the bend from Loretta Lynn's family—which was no big thing back then, since Loretta hadn't even been heard from and was just beginning having babies and taking care of Mooney. I met Brad in our freshman year when the Van Lear Junction kids were fed into Meade Memorial High School. Although he was not traditionally handsome, Brad was cute, with his little crew cut and his good teeth. In 1954 good teeth were not taken for granted because there was little to no dental care, and many a smile was ruined by decayed or missing teeth. Despite the impediment that our height disparity presented to my skeletal development, I thought Brad was just perfect for me. We went together from about Thanksgiving of our sophomore year until we were juniors, but I suspect that the relationship had more to do with neither of us being much pursued by anyone else than because we had great feelings for each other.

I was out of that relationship in a flash the moment I met Johnny McCoy, and Brad was so broken up over my abandonment that he took up with another girl immediately. Apparently those feelings did not run very deeply either way. Although we had considered ourselves sweethearts, we were never once alone together because my parents would not allow me to go out in cars. Even if they had, Brad did not have a driver's license or access to a car. Thus our dates consisted of my meeting him at the movies some Sundays, his hitchhiking over to my house for a Sunday afternoon, or our meeting briefly after basketball games—he played on the junior varsity basketball team, all five foot, six of him—before we caught our separate buses home. These big dates were supplemented by our lounging in the halls at school during lunch hour, which is where I developed my posture problem by curling my spine into various corners, while Brad stood perfectly straight in order to tower over me by a quarter of an inch, as we spoke words of love. I still have Brad's school picture, taken in our sophomore year, inscribed "To my sweetheart for life I hope. Love, Brad." I do recall that we talked about getting married someday, which suggests that Brad's imagination must have been nearly as vacant as my own. Any thoughts of a future as Mrs. Williamson were blown away, however, when in January 1957 I met Johnny McCoy—a name that shall live in infamy, at least for me.

My cousin, Barbara Ann Allen, lived in Inez and was a year behind me in school. Her parents were as strict with her as mine were with me, so, about one weekend a month, Momma and Daddy allowed me to exchange visits with Barbara. I loved going to Inez, population five hundred, because it was a town; that meant that we could hang out in the Sweet Shop and jitterbug and talk to guys. Although technically Inez was a *town*, it was without the condescending attitude so prevalent in Paintsville. Perhaps because Inez High School served both town and country, Creeker was spoken there. My trips to Inez confirmed my belief that, if you could get past the smugness on the part of the residents, towns held out all sorts of opportunities that my rural community lacked, and I was always happy to take full advantage of same. Furthermore, I had found that I was a somewhat more attractive commodity in Inez than I was at home—the Inez boys seemed to find me more charming than the guys at Meade Memorial. It took me twenty-odd years of reframing that experience for me to deduce that guys hung around us because my cousin Barbara Ann was a pure doll. Go figure. Then, in January 1957, while I was visiting with Barbara Ann, she introduced me to Johnny McCoy.

Johnny had just moved back from Ohio to live with his grandparents and had transferred into Inez High School.

Any feelings I had ever had for a male person paled before the emotion I experienced when I met Johnny McCoy. Now, there was a pure doll! He was about the prettiest thing I had ever seen, standing a bit over six feet tall—took the kinks outta my spine right there; straightened right up, I did—with blond, curly hair and a beautiful smile. He was a great dancer and a good basketball player, and he could sing. Most impressive of all, he told me I was beautiful! It was certainly the first time in my life anyone had ever used that "b" word in relation to me. We met at the Sweet Shop after the basketball game on Friday night, and he took me to the movies the following night; as the song says, "Speaking strictly for me, we both could have died then and there." He went to church with Barbara Ann and me on Sunday morning, and, by the time Daddy and Momma came to take me home, Johnny had told me he loved me. He had also given me an eight-by-ten framed picture of him as well as his silver basketball to wear on a chain around my neck. It's a grand wonder my family got my head deflated enough to get me in the car and carry me home.

Thus began my first correspondence with a guy. We wrote each other every day, five- to ten-page letters pledging eternal devotion with every hackneyed image that could be conjured in our young imaginations. Then he hitchhiked to my house every Sunday to reiterate those written promises. I was fifteen years old and believed him; he was sixteen and may have meant what he said. This intense and heated exchange went on for five weeks until one Sunday when Johnny just did not show up. No appearance, no phone call, nothing. So I waited. On Monday there was no letter when I returned from school. Three more days passed, and I still had not heard anything from him. Finally, Ronalta Mae Pelphrey, secure in her affianced state—she and Carl Price had already set the wedding date—turned around in her desk in front of me before English class and said, "Are you still going with Johnny?" When I responded affirmatively, she said, "Well, he was over in Paintsville with Nancy Daniel on Sunday." Now, why is it that the worst possible news comes from just the perfect messenger? I said that Johnny and I had been "having some trouble."

I have been afflicted with lupus for nearly four decades, and a few years ago I had such a severe attack that my physician called my husband and son to the hospital and told them he was not sure I would survive. Speaking from where I sit, I want you to know that I was in much worse shape when good old Ronalta Mae gave me the word about Johnny McCoy than I ever was in any hospital with any life-threatening disease. I did, however, survive until school turned out that day, and I did not bleed publicly.

I had been dying to call Cousin Barbara ever since Sunday to see if she had any idea what was going on, but I kept hoping Johnny had a plausible explanation—like amnesia or a broken neck—and we could just pretend nothing had happened and no one would have to know. Meanwhile I had read and re-read the letters I had received on the last Friday and Saturday, looking for any possible clues to his behavior and had found none. As soon as I got home from school on the Thursday of Ronalta Mae's report, I called Barbara, who said she had been wanting to call me, but her mother wouldn't let her. Barbara said that Johnny had told her on Monday that he no longer loved me. He added that I was "just not pretty enough" for him and asked Barbara to retrieve his eight-by-ten picture and his silver basketball, items he now wished to bestow on Nancy Daniel. I wish I could tell you that I called Mr. McCoy immediately and suggested what he could do with both his picture and his basketball. I wish I could say that I salted his fields and burned his house down or at least that I put a potato in his tailpipe. At the time, however, I had no desire to do any of the above; I was just sick. I thought I would never stop hurting. At the time, I knew not the word fickle, but Johnny McCoy burned that definition into my heart and mind.

That incident pretty much killed Inez as a desirable weekend destination because I felt more than a twinge of sadness every time I thought of my Johnny McCoy period. Our paths crossed a few times over the next couple of years, and we were cordial; but every single time I saw him I had to fight the urge to throw myself at him and promise anything if he would give me just one more chance to make him happy.

Then I went to college, and Johnny joined the air force. In November of my freshman year, I called home to let Momma know my Christmas schedule. She told me Johnny McCoy had telephoned and wanted to see me over the Christmas holidays. The lone telephone for Derriana Hall was located on the first floor, and I took the stairs three at a time on my way back to my third-floor room as I envisioned how wonderful it was going to be once Johnny saw that I had finally become "pretty enough" for him. Ever-hopeful, I once again had dreams of our riding off into the sunset together.

I returned to Two-Mile on a mid-December Saturday afternoon, and Johnny came over the same evening. He recited the script I had written in my heart for almost two years as he apologized for having been a fool in not recognizing true love when he saw it. He further declared that he now realized that I was the one with whom he wanted to spend his life and that we could get married the next summer, then I could join him in Salina, Kansas, where he was stationed. He said and did everything I had dreamed of his saying and doing. He looked the same (still gorgeous); he sounded the same (beautiful promises); whether he was the same, I'll never know, because I had changed. The moment he walked up on my porch, I realized that I no longer felt anything for Johnny McCoy. Now, that is not exactly true. I *did* feel something for him: fury.

Thus it was that I returned his affection in kind and told him that I had indeed loved him all along. I agreed that we would marry in the summer but suggested that we could tell no one because I wanted to finish my freshman year before announcing that I would not return to college. He returned to Kansas a few days later. Once again we corresponded regularly, letters full of plans and promises. In March he brought me an engagement ring. It was then I told him that, as far as I was concerned, there was nothing between us, never had been, and that, unfortunately, he just was not "pretty enough" for me.

If anybody expects me to say I regret having handled Johnny McCoy in such a cold-blooded way, let me suggest that I do not regret one minute of it. It was as close as I have ever come to salting anybody's fields, and it felt good! The last I heard of Johnny, he was preaching the gospel on TV somewhere in Ohio. May he go in peace.

Between the Johnny-in-high-school and Johnny-in-college periods, I began going out pretty steadily with Billy Daniel during my senior year in high school. The relationship never went very far because, while Billy might well have been ready to marry, he certainly was not ready to marry me. The relationship was not very satisfactory to either of us because we wanted from it very different things: he wanted to have sex; I wanted to get married. Since by that time I had pretty much internalized the idea that I had little to offer in the marriage marketplace, it was pretty certain that I was not going to lose my only currency, virginity, to somebody who clearly had no intention of making me his wife.

Maybe it was because we were all held in thrall by Primitive Baptist dogma, perhaps it was because there was no reliable way of preventing pregnancy, or maybe the penalties for transgressing were inordinately severe. But I honestly believe that, as an unmarried teenager, I would not have "gone all the way" even with Elvis Presley. My college students today refuse to believe that most young women of the fifties actually remained virginal until their wedding night because there are just enough examples of folks "having" to get married to make a convincing argument that they did not. I would contend that during my growing-up years—shotgun weddings and early babies to the contrary—the belief that women should remain virginal until they married was pervasive in every part of the world I knew about. It may well be that my experience is unique, but then I am the only woman I know who was actually *certified* as a virgin.

In the fall of 1958, two months into my first semester in college, I received an urgent telephone call from my mother. The call itself signaled a crisis, since, in those days, a long-distance call was a significant expense and was reserved only for emergencies—and this was indeed an emergency. Momma directed me to take the next train home. She did not indicate the cause of the trouble, but she was very upset. Being the good girl I thought I was, I did as I was told. I walked straightaway down Pikeville College's "ninety-nine steps to success" to the railroad station, caught the next train from Pikeville to Paintsville, and two hours later was facing an extremely concerned Momma. She met me at the train station and took me immediately to the office of Dr. F.M. Picklesimer, the same physician who had delivered me a little more than seventeen years earlier. Thereupon it was left for him to deliver me once more.

The reason for this command performance was a rumor that had finally reached my mother. The story was going around back home that I was not only away at college—something already unusual enough for a girl from my background—but that I was also pregnant by the aforementioned Billy Daniel. My mother was justly concerned; and, after my first vaginal exam, we departed his office with a letter certifying that I was, in fact, a virgin. We then took this letter and paid a call on a girl I had considered one of my closest friends, who was responsible for originating the rumor. We showed her the letter and told her that, if the gossip did not cease, we were prepared to go to court. My mother then returned me to the station, where I caught the train back to Pikeville College. To everyone involved in the situation—my mother, my former friend, the doctor, and me—the examination and certification constituted a perfectly logical response to the rumor. The whole affair became a family secret never to be acknowledged. Both Momma and Daddy died without ever discussing it with me.

The whole question of virginity—or lack of same—so completely permeated all male-female negotiations in those days that it is difficult to explore decisions I made without treating that question first. Sexual fulfillment, emotional intimacy, social credibility, adulthood, freedom from parental control—resolution of all of those goals seemed to me to hinge on my getting married. This gave my inability to bring about a union immediately a significance that is difficult to describe to anyone who was not around before the cultural shifts of the past thirty years. When I say I wanted to get married, I mean that I truly thought of nothing else. But I did not get married then; I went to college. While that looks like a good decision from where I'm sitting now, I want to make it clear that going to college was not even on the B, C, D, or E list of routes I wanted to take with my life. College was a detour, at best, and I detoured by way of Pikeville College.

Pikeville College was not my *first* choice among those schools that offered me scholarships; it was my *only* choice. I did not even consider the offers from schools in the East or state universities, including Morehead State. It was not that I did not want to go a long way from home. I tossed all those offers of free education in the nearest trash can in hopes that Billy—who was studying drafting at Mayo State Vocational School in Paintsville—would decide to marry me if I stayed close to home and continued to see him. I was not worried about going a long way from *home*; I just did not want to go a long way from Billy Daniel. Billy and I had been going together for a little over a year; he had asked me to the Junior-Senior Banquet in April of my junior year, two short months after the Johnny McCoy debacle. I was as crazy about him as I could be about somebody who was not Johnny McCoy, and I think he liked me too. He was, however, constantly saying that we might ought to back away from our relationship since we did not have the financial means to get married and therefore should not tie each other up quite yet. Translated, that meant whenever Ann Duty came to see her grandparents down on White House, Billy wanted to be free to go out with her. In addition, he also wanted to continue to see me regularly, in hopes that someday we'd just get clear out of control and actually have sex. His vacillation on the Linda Sue Preston/Ann Duty question broke my heart several times over the year or so we went together. Although I decided to go to Pikeville College, Billy could have stopped it at any time literally right up to my moving into my dormitory room. All I was waiting for was some sort of declaration of purpose, with implications of forever.

MARRYING UP

*F*ormal education was never included in the list of things I expected of myself. I grew into it randomly, precisely the way I did practically everything else in my life, without priority, plan, or sequence. I went to school for a long time and earned at least two of my degrees before I managed to get any real education of the life-changing kind. Had it not been for the rigid formal structure of the education system when I was growing up, I am convinced that I would have finished high school and spent my life cooking, cleaning, and watching soap operas, believing that whatever was missing in my life could be bought with money or found in the shelter of some man. In short, I would have become my mother. Coupled with the era's inflexible educational requirements and a set of expectations about the meaning of a high-school diploma, I had some excellent teachers who gave me a shot at achieving goals I would never have had sense enough to have set for myself.

Ellen Dutton's insistence that I learn my multiplication tables so that I would not have to spend another year in her classroom, Billie Edyth Ward's requirement that my homework be finished completely and on time, Helen Elam's repeated correcting of my grammar, and the entire school system's dedication to rote memorization of what was considered essential to know in order to receive a high-school diploma assured that I was about as well equipped to face down a standardized test as my cohorts at Choate and Foxcroft. I am not suggesting that the playing field was level in the forties and fifties, but at least folks from my background had a shot at getting a real education along with their diploma. Today, I wonder if that is the case.

All my years in elementary school, high school, and undergraduate school were spent memorizing stuff, *getting ready* for education. As I see it, the memorization was learning the language so that, when I was ready to use that language, it was there for me. The academic world could not use the language requirement—standardized tests—to screen my people out. If that sounds like an exaggeration, I do not think it is. I never expected to go to college; I neither wished nor wanted to go. Until I was graduated from high school, I did not have many teachers who had been to college in the traditional sense of going away, living on a college campus, making new friends, dating other students, and taking four or five courses per semester for four years. From the first grade through high school at Meade Memorial School, many of my teachers were folks whose college experience was practically all gained by taking Saturday classes at Pikeville College or Morehead State College.

Because of the lack of qualified teachers in Appalachian rural areas, a number of people were hired on so-called "emergency certificates" that allowed the person to teach with a high-school diploma so long as he or she continued to work toward a college degree. Momma and her sisters all acquired teaching certificates this way, but I believe Auntie Stella was the only one who ever took college classes. Both Pikeville College and Morehead State offered classes on Saturday, so the teachers formed car pools, sharing rides on Saturdays, with each teacher taking two three-credit courses per semester. Then, if the teacher could afford it, sometimes he or she also attended summer school at one of those institutions. This plan meant it often took a number of years to obtain a bachelor's degree; many were never graduated, because their jobs were safe so long as they took one or two classes per year. While their college work was not done in traditional ways, they were required to teach a curriculum that was standard throughout the state and the country. Most went about their teaching rigidly and without much creativity, which meant a very literal interpretation of academic material, much emphasis on rote memorization, and an unyielding attitude toward standards.

I do not recall ever wanting to become a teacher—but then, I do not remember ever wanting to *become* anything in particular, other than a wife and mother. I was certain of what I wanted to do—be the wife of somebody and the mother of Tim, Kim, Kay, and Buddy. During the first seventeen years of my life, it did not occur to me that I might ever *have* to work outside the home; *wanting* to work was certainly beyond my realm of comprehension. Moreover, if I had planned someday to work, I doubt that I would have chosen teaching. I always saw teaching as a job that was best done by someone rather humorless and "sour-turned," but I suppose whipping our little backwoods heads into shape cannot have been much fun.

Aspiration was another area that separated Appalachian children who lived in town from those who grew up in the country. A majority of the graduates from Paintsville High School went on to college, while most of the graduates of Meade Memorial High School did not. When the Johnson County schools consolidated in the early sixties, Paintsville city schools did not join in, even though the new county high school was sure to have better facilities and equipment. At the time, nobody publicly stated that the city schools were better, but it was whispered that the children from town would not be able to make as much progress if they had to be in classes with those from the creeks and hollers. That theme ran throughout every activity that brought the county students together with those from Paintsville. Schoolteachers were among the most respected folks in Paintsville, while, in the rural communities surrounding Paintsville, that was just not the case.

In my community, teachers were to be respected in the same way any adult was to be respected, but there was little, if any, respect for book-learning in itself—remember the capital-of-Maryland experience. I slid through elementary school and high school exactly the way everybody else did—as completely without thought as possible. I earned good grades, but that was because I could memorize quickly and well. I certainly did not think about what I was memorizing or whether the material had any meaning beyond something to be recalled for examinations. If my mind was troubled by anything in those days, it was that I could not seem to learn to drive.

We were the only family on the creek to have two cars, and, although I obtained numerous learner's permits, I could not seem to master the act of driving. Meanwhile, Ronalta Mae Pelphrey got her license at the first possible moment and flaunted it by driving that turquoise-and-white '56 Bel Air Chevrolet past my house two or three times a week. In truth, that is only one of the many Ronalta Mae situations that gave me far more cause to doubt the existence of God than any blasphemy against the scriptures I might have heard or read. Driving was very important to me—it was a major goal—but, just as I was incapable of acting grown-up, I was also completely inept behind the wheel. As for the learner's permits: well, thank God for standardized tests, since they were responsible for practically every positive thing that happened to me during the first two decades of my life.

A very small percentage of freshmen entering Meade Memorial High School made it through to graduation. Fewer still went on to college, most often on basketball scholarships. I attended college not by choice but because of a combination of factors over which I had little or no control. Although I really wanted to get married immediately and get started on Tim, Kim, Kay, and Buddy, in the fifties, in Appalachia, a girl was unmarketable if she could see the ground (think Jayne Mansfield).

At that time, Kentucky administered standardized tests to all high-school seniors, and some combination of my not missing anything on that test and the fact that I had a very clear view of the toes of my shoes was responsible for my finding myself in college. I received scholarship offers from a number of schools, but, since I didn't know the difference between Smith College and Smith Junior College of Knoxville, I applied the only standard I knew—distance—and chose Pikeville College, which was only fifty miles from home.

Pikeville College was by such a gigantic margin the right choice for me that I am ever thankful I chose old PC. Considering my lack of sound judgment and paltry social skills, I honestly believe that any other place would have chewed me up and spit me right back up Two-Mile Creek, never to be heard from again. If I had landed at a school that allowed me to choose from an array of courses or from a number of extracurricular opportunities or that even provided a lot of free time or lax policies about curfew or . . . or. . . . The list is long and includes almost anything that would have allowed me to exercise my woefully underdeveloped judgment. As it was, Pikeville College took over where my parents had left off, and they granted social sovereignty bit by tiny bit.

Despite my teachers' lack of credentials and the limited offerings at Meade Memorial High School, I was academically well prepared for any college. Educational policy at that time mandated that no student pass any course unless he or she proved mastery of specific subject matter. My high-school math and English teachers were superb, and I had done what was required—memorizing everything, understanding nothing. I not only knew the basics; I was not afraid to try *anything*, if the first step called for pencil and paper. Although I think I could have handled the academic work anywhere, Pikeville College was every bit as far as I could have stretched socially and emotionally. While it may well have been close to home in distance, Pikeville College was light years away in all the things that nobody talks about but are critical to know—such as how to pass for normal, how to fit in, and, most of all, how to keep folks from knowing I had no idea what I was doing while I figured out how to do it—the very things that had given me such problems the first seventeen years of my life. While I had always been able to fulfill expectations on paper, doing so in other areas of my life had been somewhat more problematic. Over the years, I think I have made progress on reading others' expectations up front, and Pikeville College provided precisely the structure I needed as well as a clarity of requirements necessary for me at that time.

Technically, I moved out of Appalachia when I was thirty-nine years old. But I submit to you that I really left Appalachia and the comfort and pain of shared values that early September Sunday when my daddy loaded up our black-and-yellow '57 Chevrolet and hauled all bad-haired ninety-four pounds—not counting my three new sweater sets—of Linda Sue to Pikeville College. That was the end of Linda Sue Preston right there, and I think my daddy knew it.

Daddy was never a demonstrative man, and I saw him cry only two times in my life. Pop Pop had died when I was fifteen years old, and, although all of us were pretty broken up over it, my daddy showed no emotion whatsoever until just prior to our leaving the house to go to the funeral, when he walked out into the backyard, leaned on the can house, and wept huge, racking sobs that frightened me. I had never seen a man cry, and it was the very last thing I would have expected from my daddy. He repeated the very same behavior on that September afternoon directly before he got into the car to carry me to Pikeville College. At the time, I found it somewhat confusing because by then I was well into denial about my failure to attract a husband and was rather looking forward to the new college experience. But I think my daddy envisioned the fork in the road right there. Education, if it takes, changes the inside of our heads so that we do not see the same world we previously saw.

I have been out in the world long enough to realize that all my talk about the time and energy I wasted trying to get a man and *thinking* about trying to get a man and *dreaming* about trying to get a man will set the feminists' teeth on edge, as well it should. I wish I could claim that when I went off to college I was taken by philosophy or transformed by British literature or even inspired to delve into the history of southern women during the Civil War. I also recognize that it would be more acceptable for me to say that I got very involved in the social and political movements on the campus—there was much debate about Castro and the meaning of same—or even that I discovered a blinding ambition to become somebody in my own right, to change the world by teaching or practicing social work or to become a captain of industry (back then we probably would have called it a *captainess* or *captainette*).

Sadly, none of that would be even close to the truth; the years of conditioning had taken. I was the perfect product of my background, with an IQ to die for and a head full of nothing. What can I say? The turnstile in my head that led to any sort of complex thought was just way down the road, well past the man-and-love-and-marriage detour. Even when I look back, I do not think I could have arrived at that passage any other way. I did not "get it" for a long, long time, but I think it is significant that I finally did.

I guess that is why I find it so appalling that we often are quick to write off folks who are struggling with their issues where *they* are rather than where we would *like* for them to be, which is, of course, where *we* are. I, for one, have not always been where I was supposed to be, and much of the time I was not even close. My education did not take for a long, long time. Yet during all that time, good teachers kept beating my doors down to make certain that when and if I ever reached the above-named turnstile, I had the ticket to cross it.

It concerns me that, as professors, we are so quick to squander the future of the students because, when they come to us, they do not appear to be committed to scholarship or have not read Shakespeare or cannot write proper English sentences. If we recognize that they are products of the culture they grew up in and the lives they have forged out of that, then I think we are much more likely to take the time to make certain that they master those things they lack by the time they leave us. I repeat: Education, if it takes, changes the inside of our heads so that we do not see the same world we previously saw. Before I could experience that world, however, there were some things I had to get out of the way.

I met Brett Scott, who would become my first husband, during the second week of classes at Pikeville College. He was wearing faded Levis and a red plaid shirt with the sleeves rolled up to his elbows. The man had the most beautiful arms on the planet; damn near took my breath away. I was not really interested in going out with him, however. He was a senior—five years and a lot of experience older than I was—and I had the good sense to stay away from older guys. Besides, at the time I had already sort of hooked up with another freshman, one Thurmas Gail Reynolds, and we were sparkin' a bit. Today, years later, it is still difficult for me to believe all this happened only a few weeks into my first semester of college.

While *Linda Sue* Preston could not have attracted a man if her life depended on it, let me tell you, *Lee* Preston had to beat 'em off with a stick. I have always claimed that one of the reasons I got such a different reaction from peers in college was because I gained some weight. In truth, I was only a coed for a few days before good things began to happen for me in the areas of friendship and romance. I walked through the gates of Pikeville College, and, almost immediately, my stock—in the areas of friendship and romance, as it were—took off. Like a full moon on a werewolf, Pikeville College effected a metamorphosis in me that nobody would have predicted. I recall looking at my image in my dorm-room mirror about two weeks into the semester and thinking, "Lord, girl, how much you've changed!" It is pretty remarkable to think such a major change could come about overnight. In fact, the transformation took a bit longer than that.

Probably the first step toward changing my life began when I changed my name. Although I had taken Pikeville College up on their scholarship offer early in the spring, I did not really believe that I was going to go away to college until sometime after my class returned from our senior trip in May. Once I accepted that Billy was not going to come through and marry me, I began thinking on what my plan would be so as not to repeat my miserable high-school experience, my social failure. I had never particularly liked or disliked my name; but I knew a bunch of Linda Sues, and every one of them seemed to fit into that name better than I did. As I pictured it, the birth of a whole new character would begin with the creation of "Lee" Preston. I wanted to be different somehow: sexier, prettier, more confident, more popular—all the descriptive adjectives that had never been used about me in high school. Please don't ask how I thought a simple name change could accomplish such a miracle, because I had no idea; maybe I was just ready for a leap of faith. I recall trying on a number of different names—to myself, of course. (I was certainly not stupid enough to let anybody else know what I was doing.) I figured that the name had to be close enough to my own that I could get away with claiming it as a valid nickname, but I also knew I did not want to be identified with anybody I had ever known before. In addition to the Linda Sues, I knew many Lindas and lots of Sues. I even tried on both Susan and Suzanne, but neither seemed to fit.

When, finally, at midsummer, I hit upon Lee, it seemed positively inspired. It began with an L, just like Linda; it could easily have been a middle name. Even though I knew a few Linda Lees, I knew no one named simply Lee. The name could be either male or female, though that did not occur to me until much later. Most important of all, Lee sounded to my ears like someone who was popular, beautiful, sexy, and fun—everything Linda Sue wanted to be but was not.

In retrospect, I am sure I merely found a name that seemed plausible as a nickname for Linda and attributed to it every characteristic I desperately wanted to embody. Given the times today, I would probably have become just (L) Elle, as in McPherson; but back then I had never heard of such a name, and creating Lee taxed my poor imagination to the limit. As for the dreams I had for Lee Preston, let me say that for some reason they all worked out. Lee was everything Linda Sue had not been, and the transition began in my head as soon as I settled on the name. Whenever I was called upon to think about something or act on something, I would think: "Lee says" or "Lee thinks." Okay, so now it sounds pathological, but it worked. Thus, in the summer of 1958, through the simplistic process of picking a new identity and channeling that new person on every occasion, Linda Sue Preston, social misfit, became Lee Preston, everybody's sweetheart.

I never once spoke of my plans to anybody, and if the homefolks—my parents, Billy, Gwen, or Easter—noticed that I was becoming a whole different person, they certainly did not let on to me. Actually, by that time, I had already become a closet coed because I didn't want anybody to know I was sort of looking forward to college for fear they'd think I was getting above my raisin.' (Lee Preston did just that for awhile.) When I arrived at Pikeville College, I introduced myself to everyone as Lee, and I kept that name for two decades before I was ready to become Linda again. Changing my name was my first attempt at taking control of any part of my life; considering my goals—or lack thereof—the plan was wildly successful.

Between the competing goals of getting married—or even engaged—and going on to school, there was never any doubt in my mind which was more important to me. So, while I did not even consider another school in order to give old Billy time to get in touch with and announce his intentions, Billy never had a chance after I spent the first night in my narrow bed on the third floor of Derriana Hall. He was so far out of the loop so quickly that, a few months later when the pregnancy rumor was spread around back home, I never even discussed it with him. We continued to go out together occasionally when I was home on the weekends, but neither of us was very serious about the relationship. I am sure he was not too heartbroken over the shift in my attentions, what with the Ann Duty thing and all. I later heard that Billy finally did ask Ann Duty to marry him, but she refused. Billy was a handsome young man—great teeth and hair—and I hear he has done very well for himself financially, parlaying his drafting credentials from Mayo State Vocational School to where he now is quite a successful builder of condominiums somewhere near Columbus. Changing my mind about Billy is another one of those quick decisions I made that, upon reflection, was absolutely inspired—missed the bullet by that much.

Much to my delight, I found that Pikeville College was just full of young men who were captivated by me. Most will remain nameless because I recall that one of my more enchanting characteristics was my complete lack of any ideas, opinions, or thoughtful consideration of issues, which pretty much tells you that the guys could not have been very serious scholars either. I had retained my sense of humor but, in conversation, was much more likely to listen to what other folks said than I was to offer up any ideas of my own. As I saw it then, Linda Sue Preston had been just full of ideas and opinions, and that had gotten her exactly nowhere socially. Therefore, *Lee* Preston knew when to keep her mouth shut.

I began the year taking my classes very seriously. After all, those were the days when, in the first freshman assembly, the dean told us to look on either side of us and warned that next year one of the three of us would have failed out of school. I received four A's and a B at midterm, but I told everybody that I had "done okay" because it was the highest set of grades I had heard about in the dorm. I had learned in high school that admitting I made good grades created a barrier to the kind of popularity I was aiming for. What's more, for the first time in my seventeen years, I seemed to be on the right social track. Since I was doing so well socially, after midterm I allowed the academic side of things to slide unconscionably. I stopped showing up for any class where the professor did not take roll and only attended when an exam or quiz was scheduled. At the end of the semester, my grades had fallen so much that I barely got above a C average. Since my parents had not gone to college, they assumed it was simply much more difficult than high school and gave me no static about goofing off. I earned that C average despite having an A in my English class. I was one of the few freshmen who were not required to take the remedial English course—termed "Bonehead" by the students. Since I could conjugate verbs with the best of them, I landed in an English class with interesting content and a professor who was funny. I managed to do all the reading, make it to that class without an absence, and earn a decent grade.

I also succeeded in getting my only D—down from an A at midterm—in trigonometry. By midterm, I had determined that trig was my easiest class—no math phobia here—so after midterm I only attended when there was an exam or an announced quiz. I did not bother to study for the final exam, which consisted of nine problems, and I left the final convinced that I had done well. Imagine my surprise when I received my semester grades and saw that big old D in trigonometry, the lowest grade I ever received—before or since! Convinced there had been some error, I went to see the professor, one Ms. Wilson, and asked if there had been a mistake.

She replied, "If I made any mistake, it was in giving you a D, rather than an F." She went on to say that I was the only person in the class who scored 100 percent on the final, which was her reason for giving me the D rather than flunking me. She suggested, however, that I had not learned anything in her class and had not had enough respect for the discipline even to bother to attend the class. In addition, she said she would not allow me to re-take the class and attempt to improve the grade because she wanted that D to serve as a permanent reminder to me that class attendance is important, if for no other reason, as a matter of courtesy.

For all my playing dumb, I was not thrilled by this turn of events. Visits to all authorities, including the president of Pikeville College, were in vain. Today that big, glaring D is the very first grade on my undergraduate transcript. Although I was not on academic probation, for me it amounted to the same thing because my scholarship required me to maintain a B average. I wish I could report that, beginning with the D, my abominable set of first-semester grades turned me around where school was concerned—but, remember, I *said* that in many ways I was a slow learner. Despite having been brought up short by my trigonometry teacher, I did not see the error of my ways for quite a long time thereafter. I did get better about class attendance, however, and found that when I attended regularly I usually managed to learn something I might not have known otherwise. Ms. Wilson's lesson, therefore, was not a total loss.

Though it pains me to relive it, until I got the intimacy thing out of the way, I was virtually ineducable. As you may have guessed, though, that intimacy thing was coming right along. I went out with more guys during my first semester at Pikeville College than in all my teenage years up until then, and, let me tell you, the experience really turned my naive little head. So much so that by the Christmas break of 1958, I was thinking myself much like Sweet Georgia Brown, as in "fellows she can't get are fellows she ain't met." Hey, I was seventeen years old; what did I know? I will not bore you with tales of romantic exploits with my gentleman callers during that most interesting semester except to recount one that I just cannot resist. I will call the young man Jack because I do not believe I ever went out with a Jack. My best recollection of the incident was of one evening at the Pikeville Drive-in Theater when, I guess to old Jack's way of thinking, we'd had one kiss too many. I swear we were not even necking, honest to goodness. In mid-embrace, he tore himself from my arms and began fervently to pray! At that point, I was unsure of what to do, since I had never experienced any behavior even remotely like this. Not wanting to appear the harlot, I just bowed my head as if I too were remorseful for having succumbed to temptation, such as it was. As I recall, Jack and I did not last long after that—and just as well, I suppose. I probably would have sucked sorrow living with someone so righteous over the long term.

Somewhere near the end of the first semester, I relaxed my no-older-guy rule and began dating Brett Dorse Scott, whom I ultimately married. The road to forever-after with Brett Dorse was not, however, smooth, and it took a little while for us to negotiate it. Again, there goes that slow-learner thing. I had some fairly critical growing up to do.

One of the major bumps in that road was a young hunk who entered Pikeville College at the beginning of the second semester of my freshman year. I did not meet him right away because I was back home and out of school for an extra week recuperating from an emergency appendectomy. However, two of my friends—who later served as my bridesmaids—excitedly announced upon my return to the dorm: "The new guy, Buck Johnson, is gorgeous. Wait till you see him!"

I, of course, thought myself committed to Brett Dorse at the time, but I distinctly recall thinking, "Wait till ol' Buck sees *me*!" Let's just say that, at that point, modesty was not one of my more endearing characteristics. I would very much like to excise this little recollection, both from my memory and from this account, because I am quite well aware of the unfavorable light it casts on me. Still and all, if I'm going to begin hedging now, I may as well just quit telling the story right here. Unfortunately, this incident is a pretty accurate reflection of the person

I was at that time. I would prefer to believe I would have been less self-centered and impressed with myself had I not been such a social pariah for the first seventeen years of my life, thus holding those earlier experiences of rejection accountable for my coming to see myself as some sort of seventeen-year-old femme fatale. Anyway, I can give rationale for my thoughts and behavior only if I admit to them, so here goes.

And so it came to pass that I did meet Mr. Johnson, the attraction was mutual, and I suggested to Brett Dorse that we might want to give each other some space, which in 1959 meant the same thing it means today: I wanted to continue to keep Brett Dorse around while I auditioned Buck Johnson for Brett Dorse's role in my life. It ain't pretty, but it's the truth. Brett Dorse was smart enough to know that old cliché. He said, in effect, that I could go to hell and disappeared from my life. Actually, he did not tell me to go to hell. His exact words were, "Lee, I like you enough so I will put up with a lot from you, but I will *not* be shit upon."

I was disturbed by that turn of events, but, figuring there were plenty of guys where he came from and anxious to give those guys a chance at old am-I-not-the-prettiest-thing-you-ever-saw Lee, I hastened to take Buck Johnson up on his proffered invitations. We went out together for about a month, but the truth of it was, I think, that both of us were serving as trophies for each other. When the new wore off the pretty picture I thought we made together, I called Brett Dorse, did a full grovel, and that was the end of my playing the field in college. I can only say I give thanks every day for whatever remnant of intelligence that made me fall in love with Brett Scott.

I married the first time when I was nineteen years old. Lee Preston married Brett Scott. The marriage lasted long enough for us to complete our respective educations and to give birth to a son we both adore; long enough for us to become adults, separately and together. I loved him when I married him, I loved him when I divorced him, and I love him today. I think he would say the same about me. At the beginning, the marriage was pretty good; at the end it was better. Marrying Brett Dorse Scott was one of the best things that ever happened in my life, and, despite my Baptist guilt over being divorced, I think choosing to split up the marriage may have been the best joint decision we ever made. We used the same divorce lawyer, a kid who practiced law part-time in addition to his real job with the State of Kentucky. He charged us two hundred dollars to draw up the papers, and we have never had even one disagreement about the terms of the divorce. I am not even sure what the terms of the divorce were or are because neither of us has ever had occasion to question the document.

Although I have the best, most amicable divorce possible, it was probably the most painful event of my life. Brett Dorse and I rode together to the courthouse for the final decree, and both of us cried all the way there and all the way back. I don't believe I will ever stop loving Brett Dorse Scott. He is as much a part of my family as my husband, my son, and my sister, and he remains very much a part of my life. I think I am a far better human being because of having married and lived with Brett Dorse, and I also think he benefited from being married to me. The nineteen-year-old Lee Preston who married Brett Scott was hardly a beginning on the Lee Scott who left him. That Lee Scott was to a great extent shaped by the man she had spent those years with, the experiences they had shared, and the life they had created together.

It is difficult, if not impossible, to show change taking place as it happens. I lived my history, as everyone else does, face-fomus—as they say in the hills—or heads-up, straight into it. It seems to me that my life has progressed much the way the hands of a clock travel from 6:00 A.M. to noon—I can witness that the clock face has changed but, from moment to moment, I could not see it happen. I think my values changed much as a pie bakes: The edges bake first, while the center stays mushy for much longer, and you can't always tell from looking at the crust what is going on in the mushy middle of that pie. It was like that with my first marriage. I believed early on that a big part of marriage was having somebody take care of me. Then, as I grew up, I *thought* I changed my mind about that—I certainly changed my philosophical position on it—but I am not sure my needs ever caught up with my creeds when it came to the love business. However, I am getting ahead of myself here, so let's get back to age nineteen and my wedding.

What can I say? My wedding was better than anything I had ever dreamed of, but, then, it was supposed to be the high point of my life. I got married in the summer after my sophomore year. The date was negotiated right down to the last minute. Brett Dorse gave me an engagement ring at Christmastime, and the original date was in June. Then he began to hedge. I cried a lot and finally pinned him down to August. This was a scenario that was not too unusual in those days when, as the song said, "A man chases a girl until she catches him." I must say that everybody I knew, including me, thought that marriage was much more desirable for a female than a male; that was another one of those "givens" that I certainly never thought to question.

Somehow, when she was younger, my momma had become acquainted with Gena Frail, whose husband's family owned one of the fanciest little clothing stores in Paintsville. When Sister or I needed some really nice outfit, Momma would carry us over to Frail's and pay way too much for it. Clearly, then, when it was time for her daughter to marry a fancy young man from "Town," the whole affair called for the attention of Gena Frail. Thus, in January 1960, by the time Momma and I were through at Frail's, my poor old daddy was financially obligated in a big way.

First, there were the bridal magazines, where I selected from among 736 expensive constructions of pristine satin and lace a dress guaranteed to present me to my life's companion as the greatest package he'd ever happened upon. Certainly that much was truth-in-advertising; otherwise, he would not have been marrying me in the first place. The wedding dress was, indeed, a vision and cost my daddy roughly what he would have paid for one semester's tuition at Pikeville College (if he had been paying my tuition, which he was not—scholarship, remember).

While I never would have asked my family to spend so much money on higher education, the fact that I was marrying so well made it seem a sensible investment to send me off properly. Let me say right here that I had picked up the idea of a "proper" wedding from magazines, television, and a few weddings of my college friends. I am fairly certain that no Two-Mile girl before me had ever had such an elaborate wedding. I mean, I even wore little lace gloves—with the third finger, left hand, slit so that the wedding ring could be slipped on, rendering said gloves useless for any later occasion. (But, then, how many places was I going to be expected to wear white lace gloves?) I recall questioning the necessity of spending so much money on gloves, but Gena Frail assured me that "a lady doesn't go to the outhouse without her gloves." And Lord knows, I was in training to be a lady!

I had three bridesmaids and a maid of honor, all clad in pastel chiffon. I was attended by my sister and three of my college friends. Nobody from Two-Mile or my high school was in the wedding. I just never thought to ask them. Many of them did not come to the ceremony where "the gracious custom of open church was observed"—which is another way of saying that we did not have to spend money on invitations. While they may not have attended the wedding, folks from Two-Mile bought and brought stuff to my local shower—given by my bridesmaids but held at my house because all the bridesmaids were from out of town. Those gifts were pretty well expected, however, since Momma and I had bought and brought stuff to showers for all of them when they had married. I suppose that folks on Two-Mile might well have thought that such a wedding was more than a little pretentious, and I guess it was, but by then I was movin' on: no more creek and holler, no more drawin' water from the well, no more skinnin' beets, no more of any of the above! 'Y God, I was movin' to town—success with a capital "S."

It seems rather bizarre to me today that it has taken me almost four decades to see any of those things. At that time, I gave no thought to what any of my activities *meant*. I knew only that I had met a man, fallen in love, and chosen to cast my lot with him forever. It was natural, it was meant, and I would have fought anybody who tried to enlighten me as to any of the meanings that appear so evident to me now. At the time, like a trailer in a tornado, I was caught up right in the middle of my life.

I married Brett Dorse Scott on Sunday, August 7, 1960, and we left Thealka (Muddy Branch) Freewill Baptist Church for what we had planned to be a week-long honeymoon, touring Kentucky. I had taken much the same trip with my high-school graduating class two years earlier as our "Senior Trip." Brett Dorse had traveled much more than I had; he had ridden a motorcycle to visit his brother Larry when Larry was stationed near St. Louis, Missouri. My new husband had not, however, visited Mammoth Cave or Kentucky Lake, so our itinerary included those places. We left the church around four o'clock, and it took us nearly four hours to drive out of the mountains.

While the roads in eastern Kentucky are winding, narrow, and ill-kempt, a transformation occurs as the multi-treed hills and ridges give way to bluegrass and the road becomes an asphalt ribbon, bordered on either side by the white fences of horse farms. Winchester is the eastern-most town of the Bluegrass Region of Kentucky, and we stopped for our wedding dinner at the Hi-Hat Drive-in, right at the edge of town. Yes, Brett Dorse was more sophisticated than I was, but he stopped for supper where I said to stop for supper. We pulled up to the curb, told the little carhop in the red shorts what we wanted, and ate our deep-fried catfish from little yellow plastic baskets before driving the remaining thirty miles to Lexington, where we spent our wedding night in the Catalina Motel on the bypass. The next day, when I asked my new husband the price of the motel room, I was appalled at what I considered the exorbitant cost—$10.30 for the night—while Brett Dorse thought the expense perfectly reasonable. In retrospect, that conversation was a harbinger of many future discussions reflecting our incompatible views of money.

From my present perspective, the four-day tour of our home state does not sound much like a romantic adventure, but in 1960 I honestly did not know anybody who had been on a more elaborate honeymoon. Most folks I knew went only about fifteen miles the other side of Paintsville to Chandler Cabins—the only local motel—or just went directly to housekeeping, skipping the wedding trip entirely. Thus, I was thrilled to be going on a honeymoon. After all, Brett Dorse was from Pikeville, and expectations were very different for folks from town. Let me emphasize here that when I married Brett Dorse Scott there was no doubt in anyone's mind but that I was marrying "up" by every standard known to us at that time. The fact that we had a wedding trip at all was one more indication that I was marrying *up*.

There are few positive adjectives that did not apply to my young groom. He was smart, funny, and good-looking; he was from "town" rather than the creek or the holler; he was an honors college graduate; he had a full-time job and a brighter future than any young man I had met or was likely ever to meet. I brought a few things to the match, too. I was pretty; I was pure, as in virginal; and I was smart enough to make a man a good wife—or so I thought.

I should have sensed trouble, however, when only three days into our "tour of Kentucky," my young groom suggested we cut the honeymoon short and drive on back to Pikeville. I saw no reason to disagree, so we headed for the hills on Wednesday morning and arrived at our new apartment late that night. On Thursday morning, Brett Dorse announced that, since we were home anyway, he thought he would play in a local golf tournament that just happened to begin that day. A precedent was thereby set for our married life. Over the course of our marriage, I do not recall our having one holiday that did not in some way revolve around golf.

Our new home, on the second floor over Pauley Lumber Company, consisted of a twenty-foot hallway with three rooms—kitchen, living room, and bedroom, in that order—opening off the hallway to the left and a bathroom, directly across from the kitchen, on the right. Although the apartment was quite small, had no air conditioning, and was perhaps thirty feet off the major highway out of Pikeville, I loved it. As far as I was concerned, this was the pinnacle of success. True, it was not a trailer, which many of my high-school friends bought when they married and went to housekeeping, but I figured we would get there someday. Meanwhile, I was married, living in town—well, just on the edge, but close—and finally, I was a mature adult. Although I did not have everything I had ever wanted, I felt that I certainly had a good start on it.

When I married Brett Dorse, I did not see living in a trailer as the class marker that it appears to be today because, for one thing, a trailer park was not part of the scenario. When a young couple bought a trailer, they moved one step up on the independence hierarchy, since that meant they no longer had to live with one or the other set of in-laws. They were at last on their own. Often they were not completely independent, however, because the trailer was customarily set up on a piece of ground owned by the in-laws and within hollerin' distance of the homeplace. Still and all, they were no longer sleeping under the same roof as their parents, so they had to be taken more seriously as an autonomous unit. Folks often joked that their kids didn't marry *off*, they married *on*. Getting a trailer got the young couple from on to off as far as family and neighbors were concerned, and that was a big step. I don't recall anybody else ever getting married and renting an apartment, but I'm not sure why. It may be because apartments were in town and were owned by folks from town or it could be general distrust of living that near at hand to somebody who wasn't close kin. It occurs to me that I may have cleared new ground by moving into an apartment with my new husband, but, then, just about everything I was doing in those days was unlike anything I had expected myself to do. Although my new in-laws loved me and my mother-in-law was especially welcoming, Brett Dorse and I never even considered moving in with them. But, then, he was from town, and I sure was trying to be.

Although Brett Dorse and I "went together" for a year and were engaged for eight months, we entered our union with a diverse set of expectations of ourselves and of each other. We had certainly talked endlessly about our future, but, from those intense conversations, we had apparently retained quite different things. Since Brett Dorse was a very good student—easily the smartest boy I had ever met—he had been encouraged to go on to graduate school by his professors at Pikeville College and, not incidentally, by me. I had been pretty impressed by the whole faculty-wife-serving-tea routine that I had been privy to at Pikeville College. Those faculty wives stood around all dressed-up and looking good, pouring tea to the strains of Chopin. To young Linda Sue, that sure looked like an easy life—beat hell out of hoeing corn, skinning beets, or canning tomatoes. Meanwhile, Brett Dorse was teaching history at John's Creek High School and working part-time in the meat department at the A&P Grocery, half a block from our new apartment.

I thought the result of our premarital discussions had been an agreement that after we married I would work while he went back to school for his Ph.D. When he received his doctorate, I could quit work—except for cooking, home-decorating, and the occasional tea-serving—and we would set about having Tim, Kim, Kay, and Buddy. Okay, I had not been explicit about the four children, but the rest had been pretty clearly outlined, or so I thought. Consequently, as soon as we returned from the honeymoon, I put my application in for a job at all three local banks. Since I had never taken typing and had few useful skills, I was pretty much limited to teller-type jobs.

Even though Brett Dorse had his bachelor's degree when we married, I had completed only two years of college. As I saw things, my having become a wife sort of disqualified me from going back to school and finishing the degree; I felt quite grown-up—or *finished*—at this point. Although it was not something the two of us had discussed explicitly, to me it was another of those givens: I was a married woman and had no need for further schooling. Inasmuch as I had gone to college only because I had no offers of marriage, now that I was married I saw no point in continuing. After all, we two had become one and *he* was the one, so it was *his* education we needed to attend to. Therefore, in mid-September, when Brett Dorse asked if it wasn't time for me to return to school, I replied that I thought I might just stay out of school for awhile until I heard about those jobs I had applied for and until I got this wife role under control. He was simply incredulous, since at the time I had a full scholarship and generated some extra income as a student. He asserted that, because I actually made money by going to school and I only needed two years to finish, it would be foolish for me to drop out. I pointed out that Pikeville College was about a mile, straight uphill from our new apartment. My argument that I could not drive and he would be unable to carry me to and from school since his job was at John's Creek, ten miles away, fell on deaf ears.

My notion of wifedom centered around home and family, and working hard did not mean engaging in any more physical activity than would have been necessary working in a bank. I could easily envision myself putting on dyed-to-match sweaters and skirts, with color-coordinated high heels, and going down to the bank every morning. I could *not* feature carrying a load of books and slogging through the weather, over the river, through the edge of town, and up Pikeville College's famous ninety-nine steps to success every damn day of my life for two long years. This was just not my idea of proper wifely behavior.

I maintained that, two years earlier, Brett Dorse's sister-in-law, Sally, had left college after her first semester to marry his brother Phill and had not returned to school or worked outside the home since their marriage. He pointed out that I had married Brett Scott, not Phill Scott. Although I mounted what seemed to me at the time to be a brilliant defense of my position, my husband was simply better at the words than I was; my days as a student continued.

There have been several points in my history that, when viewed in the light of later understandings, clearly changed the whole direction of my life. In most cases, these turning points came about pretty much after I had fought against them with all the forces I possessed at the time. Going to college rather than getting married was one of those turning points, undertaken because, try as I might, I could not get any male—specifically Billy Daniel—to marry me. I see my returning to college at Brett Dorse's behest as another of those points. He forced me to revise my whole view of myself as a part of a couple, as well as my definition of what it meant to be a wife. I honestly thought I wanted to be Lee Scott, but step by step—beginning with the decision to pursue my degree—Brett Dorse compelled me to give up the dreams of the person who ultimately would have become Linda Sue Scott, whatever I might have called myself.

The disagreement about my returning to school was only the first of many conflicts between my young husband and me in our attempts to come to terms with what it meant to be married. I can still hear him saying, over and over, "Lee, I won't hold your hand while you go to the bathroom!" in response to my constant attempts to have us spend every single moment of our lives like Siamese twins, joined at some strategic site.

One such incident happened not long after we were married when he remarked that he thought he would go downtown (Pikeville, a town of fewer than six thousand souls) to the record store. I thought that was a great idea and allowed as how I had some shopping to do at the drugstore, so I'd ride along. Once we were in the car, he said that he would drop me off at the drugstore, go to the record shop, and pick me up on the way home, to which I replied, "I can't go downtown by myself!" After all these years, I can still recall his astonished expression. I realize that anyone who has known me during the past twenty-five years would be hard put to believe this story, but I think it is a precise illustration of how very much *parts* of me have changed—just parts.

I returned to school with as much good grace as I could muster in the face of that miserable walk every day and took an overload in order to finish this tedious assignment as quickly as possible. Another noteworthy conversation ensued when I brought home six A's for my first set of grades after my marriage. Brett Dorse was astonished to find that I had received nineteen credits of A's, remarking, "Damn, Lee, I didn't know you were smart!" For two people who thought we had discussed everything, I suppose we must have omitted a thing or two.

Perhaps the issue that caused the most friction early on in our marriage centered around what I had thought was his intention to go on to graduate school at the earliest possible moment. Furthering his education, which he had apparently viewed as a far-distant goal, I had seen as an immediate plan. During my first two years of college, I had deciphered the unstated message that, money notwithstanding, a college professor was way up the class scale from a high-school teacher. I mean, that's what all that tea-serving crap was about. Thus, I was willing to return to school and obtain my degree, with the stipulation that Brett Dorse begin readying himself to go to graduate school as soon as I finished. Moreover, I wanted to get this plan into action—and I wanted it done now. As I saw it, I had not married a high-school teacher; I had married a college professor-in-training. Once we were married, however, my young husband seemed to have forgotten all about the promise of graduate school and appeared quite content to teach at John's Creek High School, work part-time at the A&P butcher shop, and spend every free moment on the golf course.

Arguably the best golf course in eastern Kentucky was located at the Paintsville Country Club, about eight miles from my homeplace. Consequently, every single Sunday of our married life found Brett Dorse carrying me sixty miles to my parents' house and dropping me off around 9:00 A.M. before driving back to the Paintsville Country Club, where he would play golf until dark. During the first year of our marriage, I spent far more time with my parents than I had in the year just before I married. Clearly, this marriage business was not going according to my plans. While golf was an obsession with my new husband, his graduate-school plans became an obsession for me. It took roughly an hour and a half of driving each way to make our little golf outing every Sunday, and I used that time to discuss our future plans—or, rather, *his* future plans for graduate school. He used that time to resolutely ignore me, which did not make for the most pleasant of trips Sunday after Sunday after Sunday for more than a year. When I was within three months of getting my bachelor's degree, Brett Dorse brought home the glad tidings that the principal at John's Creek High School had said he thought he could hire me—for twenty-seven hundred dollars a year—to teach English. As if that were not good news enough, my father-in-law offered to buy us a piece of ground directly across from the Church of Christ at Zebulon— a community near John's Creek very much like my home community of Two-Mile—and my daddy offered to help us build a house on that site. While at age fifteen such a prospect would have fulfilled all my dreams, by age twenty my future plans had undergone considerable revision. I had outgrown the Tim, Kim, Kay, and Buddy fantasies, but I still pictured a future with me as a happy homemaker in the Ozzie-and-Harriet mode. While I was quite willing to work outside the home early on, I could not conceive of my having a career in the future other than that of full-time wife and mother.

My immediate response to the rosy future painted by my husband and our families was to take the Federal Service Entrance Examination (FSEE) and sign a statement of mobility that said I would go to any city with a university where my husband could get his Ph.D. I still had no desire to go on to school myself and did not much care about what field of study Brett Dorse chose to pursue. I just wanted to get him to a place where he could *be somebody* and support our future family so that I would not have to work for money. Once again, I was saved by a standardized test. I got a job with Social Security, at fifty-six hundred dollars a year, that required me to report to Asheville, North Carolina, for training on the February Monday after I finished my last final examination on Friday.

I certainly did not look forward to being away from my husband, but I liked the notion of moving to the country and teaching at John's Creek High School far less. Although I may have been a little slow socially, it did not take a crystal ball for me to see that, once we took on the financial responsibility of a house, we were unlikely to pick up and move away in order for Brett Dorse to work on his doctorate. I could also anticipate that, if he continued to teach at the high-school level, my husband would never be able to support a family in the style I wanted very much to adopt, which would mean I would be stuck teaching at John's Creek High School for the rest of my life. In the face of that grim prospect, I resisted pressure from my parents, in-laws, friends, and husband, and for the first time in my life refused to go along. I recall thinking that I was not exactly sure what I wanted to do with my life, but I was dead certain that I did *not* want to spend it eight miles out of town with a couple of kids, a full-time job, and a husband on the golf course all the time.

I still had not learned to drive a car, and Asheville was three hundred miles away over mountain roads. Brett Dorse would have to remain in Pikeville and finish out the school year. Both his family and mine were appalled at the idea of my moving away, and he was not too thrilled with my leaving. Yet I never even considered not going. I had figured out by then that there was more of the world out there, and I desperately wanted to be part of it. It is hard to describe here just how scandalous my behavior was in the eyes of my friends, my professors, and indeed the mores of that time and place.

Not one friend or family member supported my decision; but Momma was the only one who said outright that, if I undertook this move, it was tantamount to leaving my husband. I believe this was the first time she issued the warning that she would offer me many times over the years I was married to Brett Dorse: "You married a good man and if you keep on with this, you're going to lose him." The prevailing notion was that a man just could not be left alone for very long, the implication being that if a wife were not right there to take care of his needs—especially his physical needs—he would be forced to look elsewhere. If the husband did find someone else in such a situation, the responsibility for the destruction of the marriage would clearly belong to the wife because it was she who was not holding up her side. Even if I had not been aware of my wifely duties before I decided to go to Asheville, lots of folks made sure I was informed. All of the warnings were clothed in euphemisms but Momma's.

If someone had told me when we married that I would ever consider taking a job that would keep me separated from my husband for three months, I would have been aghast. In the eighteen months we had been married, however, Brett Dorse had played a lot of golf, and I had learned to go downtown by myself.

*A*ll the wrangling over my leaving was forgotten, at least by me, when Brett Dorse drove through that last mountain pass and I got my first look at the Asheville skyline. It was only then that I realized I was moving to a city rather than a town, and I could hardly contain my excitement. We rented me a room at the YWCA, where I paid sixteen dollars a week for a room and three meals a day. The bathroom was down the hall, but the accommodations were surely as good as the Pikeville College dormitory room I had left when I married. In addition, the Y was only two blocks from my new office, so I deemed it perfect. The rules were very much like those of the old dorm—no men beyond the lobby, no food or appliances in the rooms—except that there were no "lights out" or curfews. Those rules suited me just fine because I did not watch television, and those were the days before hand-held hair-dryers and hot rollers. All I had to move in were the few clothes and cosmetics I owned. I had added one lavender wool skirt to my wardrobe in the first two years of our marriage, so I carried to Asheville almost the same clothes I had taken with me when I left home for college. It took all of an hour to get me moved into my little room, so I could not have had much in the way of worldly goods to cart along.

My days in Asheville might have appeared quite uneventful to an on-looker, but they were memorable for me. For the first time in my life, I had control of my clock, and I cannot overstate the significance of that. I worked only from eight to five, which left evenings and most week-ends unscheduled. Since I no longer had to cook or clean for a husband or study for classes, I was pretty much free to do whatever caught my fancy. Thus, I did what I had always done when left to my own devices: I read from the time I got home from work until I turned out my light at night. The Y was in the same general neighborhood as Thomas Wolfe's old house, so of course I had to read everything he had written. His admonishment that "you can't go home again" resonated for me, as did much of what I read. My free time in Asheville also gave me an oppor-tunity to get into a good many of the books that I had skimmed or missed entirely during my college years. Since the library was nearby, there were no assignments, and nobody was watching me or keeping score, I read whatever I wanted, mixing Agatha Christie with Euripides and Melville, with *Redbook Magazine* fiction thrown in for good measure. Just as I had no distinctive taste in reading material then, after all these years of life and formal education, I still don't.

My reading choices are as diverse as ever. I still read in my every free moment and find myself delighting in the interesting information con-tained in the least likely places. A recent trip to Barnes and Noble found me dragging home *A Whole New Life* by Reynolds Price and the latest attempt at autobiography by Pamela Des Barre—a sixties groupie who married a rock star (think "sugar-pie, honey-bunch"). It always makes me laugh to think of speeding through Japan on the bullet train a few years ago and taking note of my husband beside me reading some tome about the Ottoman Empire while I was losing myself in Ms. Des Barre's first work, *I'm with the Band*. I believe both Price and Des Barre will succeed in conveying to me a tidbit or two about what it means to them to make their way through life, and I certainly want to know about both. What's more, I'll be entertained by both.

Since I learned to read, I have never been bound by this body, not for a minute. I discovered in Asheville the meaning of freedom, which for me is time to read whatever I find interesting whenever I want and to slop around in my own aloneness. I say aloneness rather than loneliness because I think the Asheville experience set a precedent for me. If there is a book at hand, I am never alone. My leisure during the three months in Asheville was spent primarily in the lives of the characters I read about, and I reveled in it.

During the day, however, I was in training for my first real job, as a claims representative for Social Security. This was way pre-feminism, and, in a class of sixteen, there were two women—I should say one woman (Mary Claire Lentini) and one very green girl (Lee Scott). I was just twenty-one, fresh from the protective arms of my family, my husband, and Pikeville College. Although the Asheville YWCA provided some sanctuary, it was not close to the cloistering to which I was accustomed. The only preparation I had for being in the world on my own was what I had read. Once again, just as when I left home for college, I had to figure out how to pass for normal, how to fit into this new context, and how to keep folks from knowing I had no idea what I was doing while I figured out how to do it.

Unlike my trepidation upon entering college, this time I was convinced I could do the work. Whereas I had approached Pikeville College academically prepared but with years of social failure behind me, I began my career in Asheville a product of several years of academic *and* social success. That may not sound like much of a difference, but let me tell you that, from the inside looking out, it was a complete turnaround. Inasmuch as I had always felt confident in taking intellectual risks, I now felt confident in venturing into new social situations. I have always believed that Pikeville College is due credit for this change in my perception of my own abilities, because the college was small enough and protective enough to see me—and my schoolmates—as distinctive individuals who were not yet old enough or experienced enough to be able to make well-thought-out choices. Thus, their program was devised to allow us to make mistakes, both social and academic, in the context of a caring community that attempted to save us from our own disastrous choices before we made them. All the while they encouraged us to take on as much as we could handle, thereby bringing us along a bit at a time. For somebody like me, who needed precisely this kind of sheltering environment, Pikeville College—or some other place just like it—was essential to my development. Old PC readied me for the rest of my life, and I damn well appreciate it.

In Asheville, my workdays began at seven in the morning with breakfast in the basement cafeteria of the Y, where I would also prepare a bologna or tuna sandwich to take along for my forty-five-minute lunch break. I would then walk the two blocks to the Social Security Office for a day of classroom training in—and exams over—the rules and regulations of the Social Security Act. Later, interviewing claimants was added to the in-class training. Although the job wore me out, I found the classroom part of the work not too challenging, the interviewing interesting, and the acting like a grown-up with a real job the headiest experience of my life thus far. I mean, I loved it.

This was February 1962, and folks got all dressed up to go to work. Each morning found me in full regalia: long-line panty girdle, stockings, and three-inch high-heeled black pumps, appropriately accompanied by one or another of my high-necked, tight-skirted wool dresses, with necklace and earrings to match. Three of these dresses had served as my dress-up attire throughout college, and I found that I could alternate them, by using scarves and dickies, and they would get me through a five-day work week. It did not occur to me that I could have worn flat shoes for my walk to the office because that would have been frowned upon as unprofessional at that time. Every day I tottered the two blocks on those spikes repeating the words "hurt, hurt" to myself. Did the physical pain of that little walk make me miserable? No way! I would not have changed a thing. I recall thinking I looked simply wonderful and at age twenty-one, I could pass for twenty-five at least. Empowerment by dress code. Imagine!

Fortunately for me, several of my fellow residents at the Y were attending a local school of cosmetology. I worked out a deal to have my hair "done" once a week. My timing was perfect; teased hair was just beginning to be popular, and my beehive hairdo was right on the cutting edge. Sleeping alone also meant that my "do" would last a week if I carefully put toilet tissue around my head and covered it with a scarf at bedtime. I also learned many tricks of the trade—hairdo and beauty secrets—from my hall-mates, and I was a study in self-satisfaction. Why, you'd have thought I had planned the whole thing rather than fallen into it. Most of the residents of the Y were young women from rural areas surrounding Asheville who planned to work in beauty shops in or around Asheville until they met Mr. Right. I was the only woman there who had a college degree and the only married lady. Nobody was impressed by the degree, but they were openly envious of my having managed to get a man to marry me. Like all my family and friends, they also questioned my judgment for choosing to leave my husband for three months and expressed astonishment that he would allow it. I did not spend a lot of time with my fellow residents, however, because the job was so exhausting that I was not up for much other than solitary reading in the evening.

I have always felt lucky that my first job, straight out of the classroom, was with Social Security, because it was by far the hardest white-collar work I have ever done. The work began the moment the clock struck eight in the morning and did not end until precisely 4:45 P.M. That meant no visiting with colleagues and no hanging up of coats or retrieving of umbrellas on work time. If one of us arrived at 8:01, we were penalized one hour of annual leave time from the eighty hours allotted to us each year. We got one ten-minute break each morning, forty-five minutes for lunch, and one ten-minute break in the afternoon. If there were a newspaper to be read or a joke to tell a colleague, it had to be accomplished during those sixty-five minutes of freedom.

Over a five-year time span, I worked in five different Social Security offices. The rules were much the same in every one, which has often made me wonder about the widely held belief that government employees do not work very hard. It was also a perfect first job for me because it forced me to develop many of the work habits that stand me in good stead today. In addition, having had a job that required so much consistent effort has given me a marker against which I have been able to measure the requirements of all other jobs since that time.

The fourteen men in my training class made little or no impression on me, but the one other female was another of the educative forces in my life. Mary Claire was a twenty-nine-year-old Roman Catholic, with a master's degree in English from the University of Maryland. She had taught school for a time but was changing careers and had landed in

North Carolina following the breakup of a serious love relationship from which she needed space. She was born and brought up in Baltimore, had traveled all over the East Coast, and had even flown to California twice. She thought Asheville was the dinkiest little burg she'd ever happened upon. By contrast, at age twenty-one, the largest city I had visited was Lexington, Kentucky, three times—during the Kentucky State Basketball Tournament, on my senior trip, and on my honeymoon. I had certainly never been on an airplane, never even spoken to a Roman Catholic (as far as I knew), and I thought Asheville was just about the pinnacle of all that was urbane. Clearly, we had so much in common— proximity and gender—that we became fast friends.

I had never known anyone as sophisticated and polished as Mary Claire, and she had never known anyone even remotely like me. The two of us soon fell into the habit of going to dinner together after work on Thursday or Friday evenings, which provided us both with something very close to an anthropological study of an alien culture. Although television was on the scene, in 1962 it mostly showcased mid-American families—nothing too ethnic—and neither Mary Claire nor I fit into those neat little blank-faced boxes.

She later confessed to me that she was worried at first that I might "out" her to the Ku Klux Klan, who she feared would take out after her because of her religion. The Klan was an unknown quantity to me, too. I had never known anybody who had had contact with an actual Negro until I went to Pikeville College where, during my three years there, Garrett Mullins and Ron Terry comprised the entire population of color and, best I could tell, they were not all that much different from the rest of us.

Mary Claire and I also differed in a myriad of other ways, including diet, dress, and taste in just about everything from music to books. We did, however, agree upon one thing: We agreed that a woman had one role in life—to marry and have children. In that respect and that respect only—as a married woman—I was ahead of her. In everything else I was playing catch-up all the way.

In my Freewill Baptist Church, we knew about Jesus and His suffering in the days before the crucifixion, but I had never known anyone to "observe" Lent by giving up anything, and the fish-on-Friday thing was just beyond my comprehension. What any of that had to do with any kind of religious business made no connection with my idea of what religion was about. How, in the name of all that was holy, Mary Claire could call herself a good Christian and still drink alcohol was inconceivable to me. I had known people at Pikeville College who drank. In fact, my own young husband had a drink or two upon occasion; but he had not been saved, so that was to be expected. But here was someone who suggested that even preachers—priests, clergy, whatever-they-called-them—openly imbibed alcohol and did not consider it sinning! Well, let me say that I remained firmly unconvinced, enough so that I was twenty-two years old before I had my first drink. It took much longer before I stopped feeling guilty for enjoying an occasional glass of wine.

Mary Claire was also a seafood aficionado, and she certainly attempted—unfortunately, with little success—to broaden my horizons in that respect. I had eaten fish before I met Mary Claire Lentini (always river trout or catfish and always breaded and fried). The closest thing I had ever seen to shrimp, which she considered a delicacy, were the crawdads my friends and I had captured in Two-Mile Creek practically every summer's day of my young life. No way anybody I ever knew would taste anything like that—except for Herman Hunley, who once boiled and ate some of them, or at least that tale was told. And if I was scandalized by the thought of consuming shrimp, you can imagine my open-mouthed wonder upon seeing my first lobster! Mary Claire did get me to try broiled fish and crab cakes, but about the other seafood choices I remained adamant.

My lack of sophistication about such things as seafood and alcohol meant that often Mary Claire had to take apart and explain punch lines that would have been readily apparent to someone with a bit more experience. For example, I recall my confusion when she once told me a story of drinking too much beer with her boyfriend before going to his class reunion. Looking expectantly at me, she said, "You know what happened then? I was so embarrassed!" I had not a ghost of an idea. I guessed wildly, saying, "You ran into one of his old girlfriends?" Margaret Mead must have given her first Trobriander something akin to the expression this elicited on the face of my new friend, before she patiently explained to me that, when one drinks too much beer, sometimes the result is nausea—in this particular case, the lunch-in-the-lap syndrome. I learned a lot from Mary Claire, but I doubt she learned much of anything from me. It is hard to overstate my lack of understanding of the ways of the world.

When she proudly told me that one of the strengths of Catholicism is that, once a man marries a woman, the union is for life, since divorce is not an option in the Church, I surprised her by suggesting the same was true of most of the small sects of fundamentalist Baptists in my home community. They'd turn you out of the church—as in excommunicate—if you got a divorce.

Mary Claire was also the first person who ever suggested to me that it might be a good thing for a woman to wait until later in life to marry, inasmuch as a period of single life between college and marriage provided time for a woman to spread her own wings and find out what she really was about. Until that time, I had never heard anyone express such a view. When I became engaged at eighteen and married at nineteen, not one person—including my college professors—ever suggested any disadvantage in getting married so early. Indeed, by the standards of my community, mine was not an early marriage, and I certainly thought Mary Claire's view of women's appropriate age for wedlock was more than a little strange. Like lobsters, it was fine for her but had no place in my life at all.

And so my time in Asheville passed in a blur of new experiences, and in May 1962 I was sent to Louisville, while Mary Claire returned to Baltimore. She entered my life just once more, when, in December 1964, I was sent to Baltimore for my final two weeks of training. By that time, I had lived in Louisville for more than two years, given birth to a son, learned to drive, sampled my first mixed drink, and eaten at some moderately good restaurants. Although I still balked at shellfish, I no longer ordered my steak well done. I must say, I rather anticipated showing old Mary Claire how much I had learned, and she seemed to be looking forward to introducing me to the delights of Baltimore and Washington. All went well the initial week of my visit, and on Friday evening we headed to the District so that I could get a look at my nation's capital.

We went directly to Mary Claire's brother's place, where we were to stay for the weekend. He lived with a group of young bachelors in an old house out in the suburbs, where we enjoyed a great spaghetti dinner with red wine. After dinner, five or so of us were sitting around the living room with our wine when I was asked, "Since this is your first visit to Washington, where would you like to go tomorrow?" It was a great little softball question for me, since I had been reading up for weeks on Washington and environs. I confidently replied, "The zoo." At their incredulous stares, I felt called upon to provide rationale, so I added, "I've never seen a giraffe." Mary Claire's brother slowly shook his head, looked at her, and said, "Where do you *find* these people?" We all laughed.

The following day, I saw all the monuments, the Smithsonian, and Mount Vernon; I did not see a giraffe. After that visit, Mary Claire dropped out of my life or I dropped out of hers. A decade or so later, however, when I frequently flew into Dulles from London or Bangkok, I never failed to wish I had Mary Claire's number so that I could call her and report that I had indeed been to the zoo and seen the giraffe—on four continents.

It took no more time or energy to move me and my belongings to Louisville than it had taken three months earlier to move me to Asheville; I had not gathered unto myself anything more in the way of worldly goods. As a result of my experiences, however, I would suggest that I left North Carolina with so very much more than I possessed upon my arrival. When I moved into the YWCA in Louisville, I was not the least bit frightened by the fact that Brett Dorse would not be able to join me for my first month in the city and that it would be my responsibility to rent and move into an apartment; or that Louisville was a much bigger city than Asheville; or that in my new job I would have my own secretary (a benefit practically unheard of for women at that time); or that I would be earning, at age twenty-one, a larger salary than 75 percent of working women in the United States. This was pre–women's movement, so most women were not yet in professional careers. If I had learned one thing during my sojourn in Asheville, it was that I could take care of myself. Although I wanted Brett Dorse to join me in Louisville, I no longer needed his presence to prop me up every moment of my day. For me, this was one giant step.

After renting an apartment fairly close to the University of Louisville, I hit the next rough patch in my marriage when I obtained U of L's summer school schedule, took the bus—I still had no car or driver's license—to open registration, and enrolled Brett Dorse in two classes that began the Monday after he was to join me. He was not much appreciative of my saving him all the work of registration, because he had thought he might just take some time to get accustomed to the city and play a little golf that summer. Instead, since I had already paid the tuition and fees, he embarked, albeit grudgingly, on his master's degree. He adjusted by attending classes in the morning, playing golf all afternoon on weekdays, and staying on one golf course or another from dawn to dusk on weekends.

Meanwhile, my adjustment was not going so swimmingly. Since I had, by this time, never lived in a place that was air-conditioned, air-conditioning had not been high on the list of requirements in my search for an apartment. Louisville is located on the Ohio River; and, during that long, hot summer, I often felt I needed gills to breathe. I caught the bus to work by seven-twenty in the morning and returned home at five-forty-five, in time to figure out what to do about dinner before my golfer husband came home just after dark. Although Brett Dorse never pressured me to cook, the little voice in my head that told me what it meant to be a good wife would not allow me to get away with going out for burgers or settling for sandwiches in our hot apartment. Instead, having spent the day working in an air-conditioned office, I would hit the door of the apartment, peel off my workaday garb (which still included foundation garments more suitable to torture chambers of the middle ages than any modern-day activity), throw on as little clothing as I could decently get away with—windows wide open and all—and proceed to heat the place even hotter with my attempts to put a proper meal on the table. In this case, proper means a dinner worthy of either his mother's or my mother's table.

By the time Brett Dorse came home, I had usually succeeded in getting the food ready, exhausting myself, and making myself furious at him for all of the above. If divorce had been an option, our marriage would have gone down the tubes in one big hurry. I know how much fun I must have been as I rushed us through a meal neither of us wanted so that I could hurriedly wash and dry the dishes by hand and clean the kitchen before falling into bed near midnight, only to begin the same thing at six the next morning. It took more than a few years and a lot of misery before I realized that the person who was responsible for making me happy was the same one with the power to make me miserable—

namely, Linda Sue. Unfortunately this little bit of insight required serving my time during many such summers. I *said* I was a slow learner.

Over the course of that long, hot summer, Brett Dorse and I must have had more pleasant contact than either of us can recall, since autumn found me pregnant with our son. I was fortunate that the United States government had a work and sick-leave policy toward pregnant women that was the most liberal of that day. Most workplaces made pregnant women stop working as soon as they "began to show," would not allow them to return until the baby was six months old, and gave no sick-leave benefits for pregnancy. By contrast, the federal government allowed a woman to work up until six weeks before the birth, return to work six weeks after, and use all accrued sick leave. This was a blessing to the young Scotts because we literally did not have a dime. I worked up until my birthday, February 20. Brett Preston Scott was born on March 11, and I returned to work in mid-April, at the earliest possible moment.

Although physically my pregnancy was fairly uneventful, I was required to defy homefolks' traditions just a bit. When I was nearly four months pregnant, I was back home on Two-Mile for the weekend. Momma, Sister, and I decided to drive up to the head of Pigeon Roost and visit with some of Grandma Emmy's people. These cousins were close kin to us, but we seldom saw them because they lived past Grandma Emmy's homeplace thirty or so very rough miles off the main road. Since they had no telephone, we could not announce our visit, but they seemed thrilled to see us. We passed the mid-October afternoon laughing and catching up on all the family news. There were only two spots of difficulty over the course of the afternoon, and my pregnancy figured in both.

Aunt Susie Necessary was probably about eighty then but still sharper'n ary tack and delighted in giving us advice as well as a hard time. A midwife, she had delivered practically every baby on Pigeon Roost and on the head of Greasy as well. It had caused something of a fuss that Momma had not asked her to deliver either of her babies, choosing to have a physician in attendance with me and going to the hospital with Sister. Thus, for twenty-two years, Aunt Suze had had her nose a little out of joint because she believed Momma thought herself too good to have a mere midwife deliver her children. Of course, Aunt Suze would not address this slight directly, choosing instead to question me about my health and the delivery of my soon-to-be-born baby. When she heard that the child would be born in a hospital in Louisville, she was aghast and suggested that when a woman had a baby in one of those big-city hospitals she could never be sure that the child she took home was her own, given that they were thrown together in those nurseries and nobody much kept an eye on which was whose. We got past that without taking issue, and then she asked, "Are you going to have him scarified at that hospital or are you going to bring him back here to have it done?"

Up until that time, I had never even heard the word "scarify," much less planned to do such a thing with my baby. Aunt Suze explained that, shortly after a baby is born, the midwife takes a sharp knife and cuts a place in the small of the baby's back to "let th' pizen drain out." What's more, she said babies who were not scarified were more likely to take sick or to die because those "pizens" multiply. At this point, Momma spoke up, saying neither of her girls had been scarified and both of them were just fine. But Aunt Suze wouldn't let it go and suggested that if I didn't want a puny little old baby, I'd best be getting him scarified as soon after birth as possible. Thinking the subject needed changing quickly, I brought up the naming of the baby, saying if it was a girl, I planned to name her Amanda. I had not yet settled on a boy's name.

"Oooohh Honey," Aunt Suze exclaimed. "I've got a favorite boy's name but I didn't never know it till after my last'n was born." (Her "last'n" was her twelfth, and she named her Duzeena). She went on to say, "It sure would do my heart good if you'd let me name your boy. It's going to be a boy because you are carrying him low." When I tentatively inquired as to the name she had in mind for my first-born son, she replied, "Why don't you name him Arkie Joe?" I said I'd talk it over with Brett Dorse.

Shortly after Christmas 1962, one of Aunt Suze's granddaughters gave birth to a son whom she named Arkie Joe, so I was able to name my son for his father. Praise be.

Brett Preston Scott was due on April 1, 1963, but he chose to arrive three weeks early so as not to be born on April Fools' Day—at least that's the story I choose to believe. My pregnancy was one of the happiest and healthiest times in my life. I never had a day of morning sickness, and it was perhaps the only time in my life I have ever taken care of my health quite so well. I had been required to take a health and hygiene course in college, but I never thought twice about what I had memorized in that course until I got pregnant. Then, for the first and last time in my life, I made every effort to eat properly. I had always hated liver and had never even tried brains. But as soon as I found out I was pregnant, I bought both liver and brains, had it ground with hamburger, and made it into chili, which disguised the organ meats enough so that they would be palatable. I also made every effort to eat fish at least twice a week and increased the fresh fruits and vegetables in my diet.

The doctor had suggested I gain between fifteen and twenty pounds, and I was right on target when the baby decided to come early. This was well before I had ever heard of Lamaze, so the only choice I was given was between ether and a spinal (saddleblock). When my water broke and I went into labor, the doctor gave me a choice about what to do about the pain. He said that, while the ether or spinal would not hurt a full-term baby, it might be just enough to make a tiny infant pretty sick. Since I had only gained twelve pounds, he reasoned that the baby would in all likelihood be quite small. Then he left it up to me. Did I want to be medicated or not? It would have been difficult to have chosen a painkiller under such circumstances. Forty-some hours later, through no fault of my own, I delivered my son by "natural" childbirth. He lacked an ounce and a half weighing nine pounds. Given that was our introduction to each other, it's a wonder my son and I bonded at all.

I think both Brett Dorse and I were completely unprepared for the intensity of feeling we had for that baby. It is one of those factors that makes me happy that I did not have a child any earlier in my life. I believe it was important, both in my life and in the life of my son, that I had those first educational and career hurdles behind me and could focus on him. I may not have been the world's best-prepared mother, but I never resented Brett Preston or thought of him as having kept me from some great destiny.

Although I believed financial necessity required that I return to work, I was able to concentrate on nothing but my son in every leisure moment. For the first five years of Brett Preston's life, I had no interests outside him; he was first, and there was no second, third, or fourth. I think I learned my mothering from those pigs I had taken care of all those years before, and I was able to enjoy the time I had for the mothering business. It is hard for me to imagine how single parents manage to juggle the emotional commitment to their children and have the psychic resources left over to attempt new romantic undertakings. Since Brett Dorse was still working toward his degree and still playing golf, I think he was probably relieved to have the full force of my not-so-inconsiderable attention off him. In any case, there have been few experiences in my life where I believe I did precisely the right thing at the right time. Those early years of parenting are an exception to a life where often I just did the best I could and my best had to be good enough. I think that early total concentration on nothing but my son enabled him later to feel confident enough to push off on his own. My relationship with Brett Preston is without question my greatest success.

I was lucky in that Brett Preston Scott was a good baby. He slept through the night early, laughed far more than he cried, and was easily cared for. Some of my most satisfying memories are of sitting in our big green overstuffed rocking chair with him cuddled up under my left arm, reading Dr. Seuss books and singing. I come from a long tradition of rocking, reading, and singing, and I do not suppose it will end with me. Although my son is now in his thirties, I can still recite long segments from the good doctor's work. In my opinion, most folks' parenting would profit from a read-through or two of old Horton and his adventures. My little round son used to nod his head up and down in cadence each time I read, "I meant what I said and I said what I meant. / An elephant's faithful, one hundred per cent."

Brett Dorse, meanwhile, never lost his passion for golf, which meant that from March to November he was hardly ever home before dark on any day and was generally unavailable dawn to dusk on weekends. Other than late evenings, he might as well have been serving on a nuclear submarine for all we saw of him. Today, I would be highly critical of this behavior, but, given the context of the times, he didn't know any better, nor did I. So it seemed normal to us that we spent little time together during those early years of Brett Preston's life. As I describe this period, it may sound as if I were close to being a single parent. If judged purely in terms of time, I suppose I was but with one very significant exception: Brett Dorse was my greatest source of emotional support, particularly when it came to issues regarding Brett Preston. I never questioned that he loved our son at least as much as I did, and he never questioned any decision or action I took in regard to Brett Preston. I never felt that Brett Dorse's absence meant he was avoiding being with us; it just seemed a natural occurrence. Brett Preston never once heard me ask his father to stay home with us, and I never suggested to anyone that if his dad really loved us he would make more time for us. Much of the time in the summer, Brett Preston and I had dinner long before Brett Dorse was off the golf course, but, come winter or a big rain, we knew old Dad would be back with us. When he *was* with us, Brett Dorse was a lot of fun, so our son grew up believing that family members were pleasant to each other and took pleasure in being together. It has been my observation that, for all some families claim to love one another, they don't much enjoy being around each other; watching that sort of tension between parents cannot be good for children. It seems to me that perhaps the best thing a parent can do for a child is love that child's other parent— and if that is not feasible, at least be kind to and speak well of him or her.

The summer after our son's first birthday, the Louisville Social Security office was downsized, and I was transferred back to Pikeville. Although I was happy to move back near our families—we had been making the eleven-hour round-trip home from Louisville every other week since our son was born—I had learned to enjoy the amenities of a city the size of Louisville. After finally getting my driver's license in the summer of 1963, I had fallen into the habit of driving Brett Preston on short trips around the city—over to the airport to watch the planes, to the petting zoo at the local shopping center, or to get ice-cream cones at the first air-conditioned mall in the state of Kentucky. Moving back to Pikeville meant there would not be that much for my son and me to do in our leisure, but I would have more time with him because the commute to work would be much shorter. Once we decided to return to eastern Kentucky, Brett Dorse took a job in Pikeville as a probation and parole officer.

During the year and a half we worked in downtown Pikeville, with our offices less than one block from each other, Brett Dorse and I never ate lunch together—not one time. Although from time to time we ran into each other at lunch, it never occurred to either of us that spending our lunch hour together would be a desirable option. I still loved him, and he still loved me, but by this time we had apparently grown to love each other more in absentia.

As I reflect on those early days of my son's life, it appears that the time constituted a training program for me. If the purpose of such a program had been to create a self-sufficient, whole person, it could not have accomplished that job more efficiently. The Lee Scott who a mere four years earlier had not believed she should finish her bachelor's degree, thought herself unable to go alone to downtown Pikeville, and wanted—indeed, *needed*—her husband to be physically present with her whenever he was not at work had clearly been through some changes.

My job in Louisville had required me to go into the office every day and interview claimants and process and adjudicate applications for Social Security benefits. With the exception of learning to deal with the varying personalities of the claimants and fellow workers, the job itself was the same day after day. Not so the task in Pikeville. When I reported to the Pikeville office, I was assigned a "Contact Station," which meant that one day a week, accompanied by a secretary, I traveled to an area some distance from the Pikeville office and served as that site's Social Security office. There, I not only performed all the tasks I had handled in the Louisville office, but I was also responsible for going into the homes and interviewing folks who were unable to travel to the contact station; conducting background checks on questionable claims; checking courthouse records for birth, marriage, and other necessary proofs; and appearing on the radio to explain changes in the law or to answer other questions about Social Security.

My first contact station assignment was in Salyersville, Kentucky, fifty miles from Pikeville and some thirty miles west of my homeplace, working with folks just like my people, just like my family, and just like me. Although I had obtained my driver's license and had driven around Louisville on occasion, I was still quite nervous and uncomfortable driving a car. I had told myself that my nervousness was because I always had my son with me and was afraid we might get into an accident and hurt him. The truth is that I was almost as scared of driving as I had been in all those pre–driver's license years, when it seemed everybody was telling me that I needed to get my license, while they were questioning my ability ever actually to drive a car without hurting myself.

Although I trusted my competence academically and at the office, and I was ever gaining confidence in my ability to care for my son, I was still more than a little shaky when it came to the driving thing. Every time I took the car out in Louisville, all my confidence was on the line. I felt that members of my family and Brett Dorse's were just waiting for me to prove that I had taken on something that was too much for me. My poor old daddy always adored me, but over the course of my life he was against practically everything I ever attempted because he was so afraid I would fail and be hurt by the failure. My in-laws were also loving and supportive, but the truth is that nobody in my family or Brett Dorse's thought I should be working in the first place. They were appalled that I had returned to my job after Brett Preston's birth, and they said so repeatedly and with vigor. Believe me, the subject came up all too frequently.

Perhaps the reason all the rationale for my continuing to work outside the home comes to me so readily is because I spent virtually all of Brett Preston's growing-up years justifying it to both the Prestons and the Scotts. My parents and my in-laws, to a person, could hardly be with me without suggesting that I was neglecting my duties as a mother by continuing to be employed. Neighbors on Two-Mile also were quick to offer an opinion in this matter.

Bud Holbrook, Gwen's brother from across the road, and his wife, Augustine, "Teen," had a baby girl, Cindy, who was born two months before Brett Preston. One Saturday when we were visiting Momma and Daddy, all of us were gathered on the Holbrook front porch with Bud, Teen, and Cindy, who were in from Columbus, Ohio. (All except Brett Dorse, that is. He was playing golf.) Somebody, probably Momma, chose that time to criticize working mothers—specifically me—and they all piled on—Aunt Exer and Momma and Bud and Teen and four or five others who joined in for the sport of it. Since Brett Dorse was absent and Brett Preston was preverbal, I was left to take up for myself. As I recall I was doing okay until Bud said, "Well, I tell you right now workin' rurns [ruins] a woman. They get out there and they start makin' money and they just get way too big for their britches. I've got this to say for Teen, though, she didn't let it all go to her head. As soon as she got big with Cindy, she quit her job (as a telephone operator) and I've not heard a word about it since." It was on that very porch a little more than a decade earlier that Bud Holbrook's father and namesake, Keenis, had had the last word about the capital of Maryland, and it just seemed fitting that his son settle the issue of working mothers; I retreated. I did, however, keep my job.

Although I had no clear idea of why it was okay for me to work, I knew that Brett Preston had good care during the hours I was at work and that I enjoyed him all the rest of the time. I should point out that this was the only disagreement I ever had with my in-laws, who accepted me into the family without condition and were never less than supportive of me until they died. I knew that both my family and my in-laws loved my little nuclear group, but I thought they were wrong about my working. As I saw it, my son was happy, I was happy, my husband was happy; who else had any say in this anyway?

Brett Dorse was my staunch supporter in the ongoing conversation with our families about keeping my job, and he was good about the driving thing too. I sensed, however, that even he had trouble believing I was capable of handling the big red Pontiac Bonneville with white leather interior that was our prized possession. All the driving controversy was solved by the move to Pikeville and my every-Thursday assignment sixty miles from home. Throughout my life, I have consistently avoided growth at every opportunity, but when the boss said, "If it's Thursday, you must be in Salyersville," despite all my fear and obsessing, I drove to Salyersville. I think it took all of three weeks of making the Salyersville run before I was in that car, driving myself and my son everywhere.

The first time I drove Brett Preston home to visit my family—fifty miles away—was one of the happiest events of my life and of my parents' lives too, I think. I pulled in on the driveway, across that little wooden bridge, with my parents apprehensively watching me from their hot-pink metal lawn chairs and sixteen-month-old Brett Preston bouncing up and down on those white leather seats. Although Momma and Daddy did not say so, I am pretty sure Brett Dorse had called to tell them we were coming and that they had been waiting and worrying. No Olympic runner ever crossed the finish line feeling more accomplished than I felt as I hefted Brett Preston out of the big red Bonneville that day. Baby steps. It's all about baby steps.

Although I had never intended to work outside the home—and I still planned to quit as soon as we could afford it—my work was looming ever larger in my life. I didn't just do it; I was good at it. I was finding that I also got a real feeling of accomplishment from getting my work done quickly and well. All that time, when I thought I was working only for the money I made, I was also becoming competent at my work and confident in my ability to take care of myself financially. Ultimately, that competence and confidence were far more valuable to me than the money.

Freud said the most important things in life are love and work. During the five years between my twentieth and twenty-fifth birthdays, I was fortunate to have had just the right mix of the two. My responsibilities increased in precisely small enough increments both at home and at work. Had they been larger, I might have become frightened of failure and backed away.

Despite all my conflict with our families about my working, I really did not believe in my own heart that I *wanted* to work, and I worried constantly that perhaps our parents were right and my son would be in prison by his twelfth birthday as a result of his working mother. Brett Dorse, however, was grinding out his thesis—a master's degree still meant something in the early sixties—and my earnings more than doubled our income. By this time we were also saving a little money, buying up small pieces of property, and we even bought a second car—a four-hundred-dollar '53 Chevrolet.

I think one problem with the world I grew up in—not just my little community but the larger culture—is that, when it came to love and work, men were encouraged to put all their energies into work and women were encouraged to invest all their energy in love, which resulted in two half-people. That particular equation often works out only on paper. In reality, what begins as the two becoming one changes over the years of completely different roles and frequently becomes two separate halves in a union held together because of need rather than want, with both parties resenting the hell out of it. For all our research and theories and for all the apparent professional strides women have made over the last thirty years, I don't see the answers to this particular problem becoming any clearer either to our society or to the poor, overworked young parents who deal with it on a more personal level.

While in my case, through seemingly random experiences, I was fortunate enough to have grown into a satisfying relationship both with my child and with my work, the marriage did not make it over the long haul. I cannot deny that my growing sense of independence contributed to the ultimate breakup of my marriage, but a finished relationship is not a failed relationship. While that divorce was perhaps the most painful experience of my life, both Brett Dorse and I floundered our way through and came out stronger on the other side. Then again, Bud Holbrook may have been right. Maybe working just "rurns" a woman.

s I was growing more competent in my work, Brett Dorse was becoming more successful at his job. After a little over a year in Pikeville, he was offered a promotion to supervisor of probation and parole in the southeast region. Pikeville was not included in that region, so we had to move to a town somewhere in the southeastern part of Kentucky. Because he would be setting up the office from scratch, Brett Dorse was able to situate his office in whatever town he chose, so I immediately put in for a transfer to any town within that region. It turned out that Social Security was preparing to open a new office in Middlesboro in December, and I would be allowed to begin work in Corbin, fifty miles from Middlesboro, during the two months before the new office opened.

Brett Dorse also liked Corbin. It was in the middle of his region, and Middlesboro was on the edge. We decided that we would move to Corbin for the first few months and look for a permanent base later somewhere between the two towns. We rented a house in Corbin, Brett Dorse established the office there, I found a baby-sitter, and, in October 1965, we moved.

For the first couple of months, all went well. Both of us were within five minutes of our offices; the Corbin Country Club, which we joined immediately, was inexpensive and convenient; and the area puts on a show of autumnal color to rival Vermont. Then the big day came for me to transfer to my permanent assignment in Middlesboro. Fifty miles is not a long way by interstate highway or even when the road is straight. Let me tell you, the fifty miles from Corbin to Middlesboro was forever. Each morning, I left home at six-thirty and returned at six-thirty that evening if the weather and traffic were good.

The only reason I was able to continue working at all was that I had found two saints to care for Brett Preston. Gladys Johnson and her husband, George, were in their forties and had just sent their only child to northern Kentucky to study cosmetology. They made a living by cleaning offices in the evenings, and I hired them to work days taking care of my son and my house. Brett Preston soon took the place of the daughter they missed terribly, and they lavished love on him to such an extent that both he and I will be owin' those two wonderful folks for as long as we live.

Although my days were long, they were made bearable by the fact that when I returned home at six-thirty, Brett Preston was happy, the house was clean, and supper was on the table. Brett Dorse traveled a lot in his job, and he still played golf, which meant he was seldom there in time to eat with us. My son and I had most evenings to ourselves to read or watch television or play games. Home movies of that era show Brett Preston singing his ABC's and in his element at Christmas, Halloween, and birthday celebrations.

The two years we lived in Corbin passed in a blur. I worked in Middlesboro three days a week and manned a contact station in Harlan—seventy-five miles away—the other two days. During that time, I was also involved in three automobile accidents—none judged to be my fault. The last one almost killed me, which finally convinced me that I could no longer continue to drive more than six hundred miles a week no matter how badly we needed the money. I rounded a blind curve while heading home at sixty miles an hour and happened upon a woman who was test-driving a car she was thinking of buying. At the stop sign, she hit the gas instead of the brake, and we collided almost head-on. I was wearing a seat belt, else I would probably not be here to report the incident. But this was before shoulder belts; my head hit the dashboard, and I suffered a concussion. The other driver was not wearing her seat belt, and she left five of her front teeth just above the windshield in the roof of her car. Neither car survived. Careening around curves in the wailing ambulance on the way to the hospital, I felt my head puffed up like a misshapen muskmelon. I recall thinking that I needed to live in order to take care of Brett Preston. Directly on the heels of that thought came the insight that Gladys and George could and would care for him as well as I could anyway.

Although I began looking for work when I left the hospital, I continued with Social Security for seven months, until I landed a job teaching at Sue Bennett, a Methodist junior college six miles from where we were living. The job was contingent on my completing a master's degree over the next two years, so I left Social Security on a Friday in June and registered the next Monday for six credits of English courses at Union College in Barbourville. Somehow it has not always been my good fortune to be able to take time to think about what I am doing; often I have to jump right in. Thus, it was not with happy anticipation that I charged into school that summer of 1967.

Although I still believed that money was the reason for my not quitting work and being forced back to school, I think a good part of my decision had to do with my assessment of the difference between my life and the lives of other women my age. I had a fairly clear window into the lives of some of my cohorts in Corbin because, for the first time in our five-year marriage, Brett Dorse and I had made friends as a couple. In Louisville and in Pikeville, each of us had had individual same-sex friends, but we never spent our leisure either with each other or with any other young couples. Brett Dorse had spent his free time on the golf course; I had spent mine alone reading or with our son.

In Corbin, however, there were interesting young women my age whose husbands spent virtually all their time either working or playing golf. Most of them had children Brett Preston's age, so we would often get together on Saturday and Sunday around the pool at the country club while our husbands were on the golf course. In the late afternoon two or three of us would go to one or the other's house and prepare dinner as we waited for our husbands. Elements other than age and proximity brought me together with these young women, not the least of which was the almost complete absence of our husbands from our everyday lives. All of us were married to men who were well on their way to becoming professionally successful leaders in the community, we each had at least one preschool child, and all our husbands were avid golfers, which meant they paid not the slightest attention to us or to their children.

I don't want to sound angry about the absent father business, because I was probably as much at fault here as was Brett Dorse in that I did not make that much fuss about it. I think at some level he most likely knew I would have preferred that we do more things together as a family. But if given a choice, I could not have defined what "things" I would have liked to do, so we just drifted along. Between work and golf there did not seem to be a place where any family activity could be sandwiched in; golf *was* our family activity because it involved all three of us.

Beginning with the second weekend in May through the last weekend in October, there was a golf tournament somewhere within a two-hundred-mile radius of Corbin every single weekend. Brett Dorse and our other male friends usually competed in two or three tournaments per month. The script was almost the same week after week. The men, in groups of two to four, would leave work early Friday and drive to the tournament site that afternoon to play their practice and qualifying rounds. If the tournament was within a two- or three-hour drive, they returned to Corbin that night. Otherwise, they took a room and stayed over. On Saturday morning the wives and children got together and shared rides to the town in which the tournament was being held, where we would then sit by the pool all afternoon while our husbands golfed and our children swam. Around five o'clock we gathered up the children, took them somewhere for supper, picked up a previously arranged baby-sitter, showered, got ourselves up in our best party dresses, and drove, with our husbands' dress clothes hanging in the back seat, back to the club. The dinner usually began around 6:00 P.M., and we were almost always there by seven.

Since our husbands were good golfers, they teed off late and were hardly ever off the course until well past eight. This meant we sat for an hour or more watching everybody putt out on number eighteen, while the not-so-serious golfers and their wives drank, ate, and partied. Although I always took a book to read by the pool, it was considered bad form to read while waiting on number eighteen because the golf action was presumed to be riveting and a book might indicate boredom. The ritual was not over when our husbands finished playing, however. Before they were ready to shower, dress, and eat, they had to go get a drink and re-play for us and each other every single shot each one of them had hit on all eighteen holes.

I do not know about the other wives, but for me those endless hours when I sat starving and sober waiting for each flamboyantly dressed golfer, with the ubiquitous gin and tonic, to relive his day in the sun serve as a high-water mark for misery in my personal history. I never once said, "Could we just, for Godsake, eat, already?" I spent just about every weekend for eight summers of my life engaged in this waiting game, until my son began playing organized baseball and gave me an excuse to get off number eighteen, at least occasionally. I realize that I was the one who chose to spend those weekends in this manner, but at the time an alternative did not occur to me. The door was there all along, but I just did not see it.

Though I had not looked forward to attending summer school, one positive aspect was that I had assignments to complete, books to read, and papers to write. I was able to take that stuff along and work on it while sitting in the sun beside some country club pool or another, which made that summer of 1967 one of the better ones. I was not looking forward to teaching either, but, by this time, I could see that, for all my thinking that I did not want to be working, my life just seemed more interesting than the lives of those nonworking golf-groupie wives. For one thing, Brett Dorse always invited Brett Preston and me to go along with him to the tournaments, while some wives had to manipulate, scheme, or politic to go. Although unstated, it was pretty well known that some of the husbands—those less serious about their golf game—did not want their wives along because that enabled them to pick up on the local talent common at every club—damn common at that.

One evening a woman I'll refer to as Carla Johnson, wife of a notorious womanizer, and I had just returned to the country club, all dolled-up for the party, and were checking our make-up in the rest-room mirror when two local women walked in, still in their Bermuda shorts. They had been working the concession stand on number eight tee. They were standing directly behind Carla and me, recapping their day on the course, when the short one with the frosted hair said, "God, did you ever see anything like that bearded guy? Thinks he's God's gift to women!" The tall, tanned one replied, "He sure was all over you. I thought we'd have to throw a bucket of water on him!" Gales of laughter followed.

Carla's husband was growing a beard for an upcoming centennial celebration, and, from the time Ms. Frosted-hair said "that bearded guy," Carla had paled and stopped dead-still, with her lipstick halfway to her mouth. It took our two rest-room companions a few beats to notice that the make-up-freshening activity had ceased on the part of one of the parties. I was still going through the motions of diddling with my hair, trying hard to ignore the whole scene. Ms. Tall-and-Tan said, "Uh, maybe we're saying something we shouldn't." To which an expressionless Carla, in a cold, even voice replied, "I think you're talking about my husband." The two women fell all over themselves, making comments about just kidding around, several men with beards, and so on, and quickly fled into the shower stalls. Carla and I walked out of the rest room.

Once outside, I remarked on the menu for the dinner that evening. Carla said, "I cannot believe you are not going to say anything about what just went on in there!" Whereupon I pooh-poohed the whole thing, as in it probably wasn't him; and, moreover—guys, whatcha gonna do about 'em; and everybody kids around; and. . . . That was just one incident in a long list of things of that sort that happened at golf tournament parties. I honestly do not think there is as much fooling around at golf tournament events as there is at other alcohol-saturated social occasions. I know of few serious golfers who would choose sex over their golf game—which is one of the reasons I never believed the newspaper story of Vice President Dan Quayle's purported Florida tryst. Hey, old Dan was there to play golf, and even Cindy Crawford couldn't get any action from a man with golf on his mind.

Of course, there were always some men who went to the tournaments to get laid by somebody other than their wives, and there were a few women who were looking for love from somebody other than their husbands. To me, we all seemed pretty much interchangeable. As I saw it then, marriage was marriage, men were men, and women were women; I saw no reason to do a round robin divorce-remarriage-divorce-remarriage when it appeared to me that it would all be just more of the same with a different surname waiting on number eighteen.

Still another aspect of these marriages was the control thing. From many around-the-pool conversations, I had gleaned that money was a source of ongoing conflict for most of the couples. The women often told of sneaking some new item into the house and fibbing to their husbands about where it had come from. There were also many stories about the man of the house complaining about the cost of one thing or another and insisting that the item be taken back. Such a mandate was usually followed by the wife buying something even more expensive and simply not reporting it. There was also more than one woman who had to make frequent trips to the rest room to smoke, for their husbands forbade their smoking.

It was hard for me to get a bead on such activities. Brett Dorse never once in our marriage *forbade* me to do anything, and he never, ever suggested that something I bought was too expensive. He had always treated me as an adult even when I wasn't one. Thus I had come to see myself as a separate, independent person, as capable of making financial decisions as he was. In addition, he had never once hinted that he might not have wanted his son and me to accompany him to a golf tournament, which I would have taken as an indication that he was on the make for some woman.

I would like to think that if he *had* made such a suggestion, I would have thrown both a fit and my clothes in a suitcase and, with Brett Preston hanging on my hip, left Brett Dorse's bed and board. In truth, I was far too practical for that. I doubt that I would have bestirred myself enough to get furious if Ms. Frosted-hair's comment had related to my husband instead of Carla's. I lost my romantic visions of happily-ever-after somewhere on number eighteen. If remnants of such dreams still lingered when we moved there, my time in Corbin saw them die for good.

I never got the chance to fulfill the contract I had signed with Sue Bennett College. In July 1967, Brett Dorse was contacted by Eastern Kentucky University and asked to come there and help set up the new Department of Law Enforcement. Eastern could not hire me because I had only a bachelor's degree, but, in order to entice my husband there, they gave me a graduate assistantship and an opportunity to get my master's degree. I suppose they just assumed that someone who was already doing graduate work, with a husband in higher education, would want to get a graduate degree. In any event, August 1967 found us living in a small duplex apartment one block from campus, with Brett Preston in nursery school, Brett Dorse writing and teaching, and me teaching twelve hours a week and taking classes Monday, Tuesday, Wednesday, and Thursday nights and from eight to one-fifteen on Saturday. The little Scott family was busy.

Though it sounds like an awful time, for me it was the happiest period in our marriage. In the morning, I took Brett Preston to nursery school at eight and taught from eight-fifteen till eleven-fifteen, when I picked up my son and went home for lunch. Then Brett Preston and I had the afternoon to ourselves, when we could explore the seemingly endless delights of Eastern's campus. We'd look at the snakes and lizards in the biology building, play on the playground equipment at the University School, or sit in on storytelling over at the early childhood department. Whenever either of us had some critical assignment due, I exchanged play dates with the student-mother of the little boy who lived in the other side of the duplex. Then, around 5:00 P.M., Brett Dorse came home, we ate dinner, and I went to class, leaving father and son to fend for themselves.

We had not yet joined the Richmond Country Club, so Brett Dorse played golf only on Saturday afternoons and Sundays, when he drove twenty miles or so to a club in Winchester or Lexington. Furthermore, for the first time in our married life, Brett Dorse did not play golf every Saturday afternoon. Instead, the three of us regularly attended Eastern's home football games. During this nine-month period, my husband spent more time with his son than he did in all the rest of Brett Preston's life put together, and they bonded in a way that has been lasting throughout all our lives. Although now the three of us count that year as significant for their relationship, it was unplanned and went unnoticed at the time.

A home movie made during the Christmas holidays 1967 shows the three Scotts romping in the snow, throwing snowballs at each other, and sleigh-riding down the hill of the amphitheater on Eastern's campus. I think if I had been offered a job at Eastern when I received my master's, the marriage might have held together, because that was the only time I recall our functioning as an Ozzie-and-Harriet perfect family. Such an offer did not transpire. Instead, the University of Kentucky had a last-minute resignation, and the fall semester of 1968 found me and my brand-new master's degree teaching twenty-five miles away at the Big U.—and that made all the difference.

The June day I received my master's degree, with me donning my hood and Brett Dorse resplendent in his academic regalia, was one of the happiest days of my life. I thought we had really made it. I wondered which thing I was happier about—that the two of us had advanced degrees or that we were finally getting a home of our own. Before coming to Richmond we had saved quite a bit of money, so, in the spring of 1968, we bought five acres in a new development on a lake about four miles from Eastern's campus and broke ground for our first home.

I should, perhaps, make it clear here that I was very happy about having obtained the master's because of the job opportunities it opened up for me, not because of what I had learned. I *still* had not tied the book-learning stuff to my real life and had pretty much memorized my way through my graduate work just as I had done in undergraduate school some years earlier. My thesis was a statistical comparison of one group of students with another group, and the fact that I can recall no more specifics about it suggests the depth of my involvement with the learning. (I think it had something to do with freshman grades.) Indeed, on graduation day I repeated to myself the pledge I had made to myself after I finished my last exam at Pikeville College: "I will never sit in another classroom as long as I live." At that time, a number of university faculty did not possess doctorates, so I saw no reason for doing further graduate work. I saw a graduate degree purely as a ticket to get into a job I was sure I could do, nothing more. I had the good sense not to tell anybody that I felt this way, but, at age twenty-seven, with two degrees, I had learned some things in school and some things in life. Clearly my thinking in one was somewhat funded by the other, but I was still blind to it.

The summer of '68 was just full of happenings for the Scott family: We moved into our new house, we paid cash for our first Mercedes, I began the job at the University of Kentucky, and Brett Preston won his first blue ribbon in swimming. We also joined the Richmond Country Club, and that was the beginning of the end of the marriage. I recall that the day we brought the Mercedes home, I was so in love with it that I did not put it in the garage. Instead, I parked it in the driveway, where from time to time over the course of the afternoon I could steal to one of the front windows and get a glimpse of it. With my big, new four-bedroom, three-bath house—paid for except for a small bank note—complete with the requisite white columns (which I still called *col-yumes*) and the new silver-gray 280SE Mercedes in the drive, I was sure there was nothing else I could ever want. There have been just enough times in my life when I felt this way, only to discover later that I have changed my mind, that I have come to enjoy the all-too-fleeting pleasure of such times without worrying that they too may pass. That's part of the *being there* thing that I think is so important. My years at UK taught me to be there.

I began work at the University of Kentucky in August 1968 and was assigned to share an office with another instructor, Janice Carter, who was the nearest thing to a hippie that I had ever seen. The sixties had been banned at Eastern Kentucky University by President Robert R. Martin, who had announced at the opening faculty orientation meeting the year before, "If anyone feels uncomfortable with the rules here, let me say to you: This is Eastern. Love it or leave it!" He was powerful enough to make that sort of thing stick. The University of Kentucky, however, was another world. While there were a number of faculty still around who believed in traditional forms of teaching, dress, and decorum in the classroom, there were just as many who had already bought the whole sixties package of free love, revolution, and let's get high on everything—especially ideas. At that time, however, most of the changes had to do with form, not substance. We were more invested in "the canon" than ever.

My office mate and her husband were in cross-disciplinary doctoral programs that were pretty radical even for the sixties. They took courses from several departments and integrated the disciplines in their thinking and writing. The thing that impressed me, however, was not that they took classes, read books, and wrote papers but that they never shut up about what they were doing. They talked incessantly about philosophy, and they applied it to whatever topic came into the conversation. Soon our office became a gathering place for folks of all stripes from several schools and departments to toss around, argue over, and laugh about issues and ideas. My first response to this gathering was irritation. I could not escape them. Nor could I get into the ongoing conversation, because I had no inkling of what they were talking about. Now and again I would catch an allusion to some fact or another that was part of my repertoire, but the stuff they were doing with said fact was always way out of my cognitive comfort zone. For the first time in my twenty-seven years, I was in constant contact with folks talking over my head, and I was not amused. Here I was having a veritable salon in my office, and I could not even participate. I mean, to hell with that business! In December 1968, after an entire semester of attempting to get a seat—or at least a handhold—on this intellectual train, I went to the UK Library and checked out forty books, which I carried on holiday with me.

I put those books in a bright-blue shopping bag with a psychedelic flower on the side. I took that shopping bag full of ideas home to Two-Mile for Christmas, to Florida to see in the new year, and back home to my favorite chair in Richmond. I read and read and read. On Two-Mile, as my family watched TV and read *U.S. News and World Report* and *Southern Living*, I muddled through intentionality. On the beach in Florida, while Brett Dorse played golf, Brett Preston played with his buddies, and the golfers' wives polished their toenails and read *Vogue* or *In Cold Blood*, I attempted to sort out Nietzsche's will to power. By the time I returned from Florida and settled into my favorite reading chair in my den in Richmond, I still did not know enough to hold my own in conversation with my office mate and her verbose friends, but I knew enough to phrase a question. And with that, my former life, my marriage, and everything I had ever thought I knew and believed changed forever. One more time: *Education, if it takes, changes the inside of our heads so that we do not see the same world we previously saw.*

Thus it was that my own education was able to give me exactly what I had been looking for all along: love, and through that love, salvation. I read those books and truly fell in love for the first time in my life. I fell in love with ideas and with a world where such thoughts appeared to be in infinite supply—the university. If ever there were a time to lust after ideas, it was the late sixties when universities became nerve centers for much of the activism that was going on. I also think I had my little epiphany at just the right time in my life—age twenty-seven. Most of the folks with whom I bandied about ideas were graduate students who were around my age and had some of their growing up behind them. We were only peripherally involved in the social movements — Vietnam, civil rights, and personal freedoms. Much more time and energy were spent in thoughtful exploration, argument, and justification of various positions on those issues than was spent attempting to *do* anything about them.

This may sound as if we accomplished nothing of substance, and I suppose you could look at it in that way. But I believe most of us sincerely thought the central role of the university was to study issues, look at all sides, and pick them apart in discussion. Once that had been done, the rest of the world would go along with what we had determined was clearly the "right" thing. Day by day, we pursued the truth, and, for most of us, it was not just enlightening, it was fun. (Only the Marxists were dour, and they were to be avoided at all costs.) The whole endeavor — changing the world — was accompanied by an infectious enthusiasm and optimism for the future that today seems naive and inconceivable in the light of what we now know of cultural shifts and the tendency of the human condition toward selfishness and greed and insularity. But that is now; *then* we genuinely believed all we had to do for the world to make itself better was to point the way — at least I believed that. What's more, if we were wrong about the probabilities for making the world better, so be it.

I am still glad I was there in that place in that time because it led me first to learning and then to teaching as well as to a belief that, however small my contribution, I can indeed make a difference in the future. Did I say we were high on ideas? Well, I suppose I still am. Each semester for more than three decades now, I have been issuing the altar call to those folks who sit in my classroom for them to come on down and I'll turn them on to ideas too. Just like church, not everybody heeds the call, but enough do to make me believe they are ready to let ideas make a difference in their lives. If this is couched in the language of my religious fundamentalist past, it is because I think that education offers the same sort of transformation. All that reading and memorization I had done up through my master's degree served as data I had gathered, and I finally had a place to put it.

So — one more time — I went back to school. Unlike the other times, I did not have to be forced into the classroom. In the summer of 1969, I began a doctoral program at the University of Kentucky, and, although it has waxed and waned, I have not since lost my passion for the world of ideas. In the intervening decades, I have had the good fortune to come into contact with a number of other folks who believe as I do that there is still hope for this planet and its creatures and that the basis of that hope lies in the promotion of better understanding on the part of every human being of his or her own capacity for love and hate. Until we come to terms with our own emotional range, we are dangerous to each other; and we'd damn well better pass the word along about that. We cannot always love folks, but we can be unfailingly kind to them and, in so doing, try to understand and thereby control our resentment of them.

If all this sounds just way too Mary Poppins, let me say that controlling my own selfish impulses and evil tongue is just about the hardest thing I have to do, but I do believe that knowing that about myself helps me keep a lid on it sometimes. Furthermore, I believe that the more I know about what it means to be trapped in the human condition, the more likely I am to be able to help my students connect what they think they are looking for to what they seem to be finding. Having wandered for so long in the wilderness myself, I still only catch a glimpse of the Promised Land from time to time, but those glimpses sustain me and grant me fortitude.

While I have said that a lot of folks found my exuberance hard to take during my growing-up years on Two-Mile, I had calmed it down considerably—some would say I had matured—by the time I entered the doctoral program at the University of Kentucky in the summer of 1969. The closest I have ever come to acting like a lady was my year at Eastern, when I was so ladylike that I was asked and agreed to sponsor a sorority. You might figure that just when I was close to gettin' it all, the good Lord raised the bar or something came up. For me, that something was that I finally got the call to teach. Now, it wasn't like the preachers back home described their call from God Almighty. I didn't hear a voice tellin' me to go out and teach the heathen—nothing like that. It was more like figuring out at long last where I fit into the scheme of things, as well as finally seeing where all my experiences up to that point came together.

Remember that I had been teaching for two years before I went back for my doctorate, and I honestly thought I had been a fairly good teacher—

nobody had run screaming from my classroom. Nobody had even complained—probably because they were so zoned out by the time the class was over that they had not the energy to complain. During those first couple of years, I patterned my classroom behavior after what I thought were mature and serious lecturers. I even bored the daylights out of myself, so you can imagine how exciting it was for my students. Indeed, as I think back on some of those classes, it occurs to me that if old Elvis Presley had just had me to lecture to him for about ten minutes every evening he would never have developed a need for those sleeping pills and just might still be around today.

I ought to point out here that I mean no disrespect to those teachers whose classes I took prior to entering my doctoral program; many of them were excellent. For the most part, they were plugged into their disciplines, and they did a pretty good job of making certain I memorized the material that was critical background for me to begin educating myself. I appreciate their efforts, and I am thankful for the educational structure that existed in that day, else I would never have been able to self-educate once I got the chance. The chemistry, art, and English professors at Pikeville College were particularly outstanding in their dedication to their work, and they succeeded in not turning me *off* to their subject matter. If you consider where I was in my development at that time, not turning me off to learning was no mean accomplishment.

One of the problems of finding something that is life-changing in a positive way is that it often makes something of a preacher of the one whose life is changed, which can—and often does—irritate the devil out of those folks who must hear the gospel according to whomever over and over. Well, like a full moon on a werewolf, my graduate work at the University of Kentucky brought out all those personality traits I had spent ten years systematically phasing out of my being. For me, the program was transforming. Every day I was in it I became more certain that my mission was to preach the gospel of education throughout the land. If that sounds over the top, it probably is—and over the past decades, I have perhaps calmed down a bit. Remember, though, that I come from fundamentalist country where the saved are called to witness to all who have not been saved so as to keep the latter from roasting in Hell forever. Well, I think that salvation business is what teaching is all about. If you don't feel that passionately about it, that tells you that the world would probably be better off if you just did not teach. I mean, do research or writing or get a job you believe in.

I know I have called time-out on the story of my life and fallen to preachin' for a bit, but I do not see how I can explain my travels in and my infatuation with the world of ideas, as well as my desire to get the word out about what I had learned, without explaining about the philosophy of teaching that evolved as a result of my graduate-school experiences and my years of testing what I learned there. Professors profess; at least this one does. What can I say?

*B*rett Dorse and I agree that, although our marriage lived on legally for many more years, the life went out of the relationship quite early in my time at the University of Kentucky. We disagree, however, on the question of why the marriage didn't make it. It could be glossed over by saying that we developed in different directions or that we just grew apart; both statements are correct as well as factual. Nevertheless, I believe our marriage fell apart as the result of several big changes that happened in our lives right at the end of the sixties.

Brett Preston Scott turned six years old in March 1969, shortly after my washed-in-the-blood-of-ideas Christmas reading frenzy. He was in kindergarten and beginning to prefer spending his free time exploring the boundaries of his little five-acre world with Keith Kidd and Crisper Nelson rather than hanging out with his mother. While my son still needed me, he was on the way to needing me less and less. Our efforts to have another child had not worked out, which cleared some big-time space in my schedule. In addition, a pretty good seam of coal had been found on some property we owned, which meant that, for the first time in our marriage, Brett Dorse and I had enough money coming in so that I did not have to worry quite so much about our personal finances. We had built, decorated, and moved into a brand-new house that needed less of my time and attention, and Brett Dorse had returned to his lapsed golf game with a vengeance. What with his work and graduate studies, once again he had no time for me at all.

As I reflect on the Lee Scott of that time, I had everything I ever could have thought or dreamed to want. Nonetheless, the person who should have been so happy living in her big new colyumed house, sneaking peeks at the Mercedes in the driveway, just was not enjoying that life nearly as much as she had thought she would. Given that context, is it any wonder that existentialism washed over me like the waters of Lourdes? Brett Dorse says it never occurred to him that I was not happy with my position on number eighteen until I dragged him to what he terms one of my "hippie parties" over at the university. He says he was amazed by how bored and out of place he felt and equally surprised at how perfectly I seemed to fit in. I agree with him on that one, too, but once again we disagree as to the reasons. Brett Dorse thought I fit in because of the people, but, in my opinion, I fit in because of the ideas. I was drawn to the people, yes; but I was interested in them for what they were reading and interpreting and thinking about and talking about. I found the discussions interesting and lively and a logical extension of the classroom. For all the day-to-day misery of doctoral work, I loved it far more than I hated it, and I felt a real sense of belonging there. Graduate school also seemingly rooted out the last vestiges of my Appalachian essence, though I did not know it at the time.

Passing for normal—not hillbilly—was a journey I had embarked upon when I entered Pikeville College, and each year thereafter I had moved a bit closer to my goal. At the time I really thought I was doing quite the opposite. After all, I had maintained my ties by continuing to visit my parents every other weekend, I had remained faithful to the dialect of my youth, and I always had admitted where I came from. In Kentucky, when rural folks from the Appalachian counties move downstate, they often respond to questions of their origins by claiming to be from the town closest to their homeplace. My way of being assured that I had not got above my raisin' was to keep reminding myself that I never, *ever* professed to be from Paintsville. It didn't matter to anybody else anyway, because even my closest friends had no idea about the class and cultural differences implied by the town-country background distinction. I never thought to educate them because somewhere along life's way I had conveniently forgotten the differences myself. I had been away from the country for more than a decade and had grown so accustomed to the life I was living that I honestly believed my background was not that different from Brett Dorse's. Although the little Scott family had lived one year in Pikeville and two years in Corbin—both Appalachian towns— we had lived *in town,* and we had lived as if we were both *from* town. The University of Kentucky graduate-school experience then put the final gloss on a transition that had all but taken place before I got there.

I received my doctorate in May 1972, and my first tenure-track university teaching appointment began the following fall semester at Kentucky State University in Frankfort, where I was hired to teach general psychology, human development, and personality theories. The job was a typical university appointment. In addition to teaching three classes, I was expected to do research and "publish or perish." My graduate training had taught me that the most important part of the job was to find time to eke out the requisite publications in order to get tenure. Although universities give lip service to the importance of teaching, the truth is that most administrators and professors attach little value to time spent advising students or in the classroom. That was the case in 1972, and it is still the case; research, grant-writing, and publication are the most valued endeavors at so-called research universities. However effective teachers may be in the classroom, they will not be tenured if they fail to excel in the research mode.

I had learned that lesson well when one of my best professors at the University of Kentucky was denied tenure for lack of publications and was only able to get a job teaching philosophy at a community college. In academe, to go from the major research university in the state to teaching at a community college is a precipitous drop in academic standing, and those of us who had unsuccessfully protested that tenure decision did not need further warning about the results of wasting our time teaching and advising. You might say we got the message.

As a graduate student, however, the whole teaching-researching-publishing thing had looked pretty easy to me. After all, I had been teaching two courses while working on my dissertation, so technically the new job meant only one added course. Thus, I reasoned that I could simply plug the research and writing into the slot left open by the dissertation. This plan worked out about as well for me as I had expected, and I was able to teach my classes at KSU and do my research around Brett Preston's school schedule. I also took on a few counseling jobs with some of the small rural churches in the county, keeping my hand in the therapy side of the profession.

There was, however, one difference between Kentucky State University and the universities where I had taught before: KSU was a traditionally African American university, and I was the only white female Ph.D. on campus. Although they had hired white female faculty before me, the women either had been adjuncts or did not have the terminal degree. This may sound like a small point, but at that time it was not. I found that one of the most difficult things about teaching at Kentucky State was being thrust into the position of representing *all* white women, while facing my own set of preconceptions about *all* black folks.

One way they tested me early on was that students, particularly male students, would come into my office and stand close behind me at my desk, sometimes reaching over my shoulder to shuffle through papers lying in front of me. This behavior also occurred in the classroom immediately before and after my class lecture. While I found such conduct strange and slightly annoying, I decided to ignore it and wait to see where it was going before I called attention to it. By the end of my first few months at KSU, it ceased. A couple of years into my tenure, a student told me that it was common knowledge that white folks were made uncomfortable by the nearness of black folks—especially by being touched by black males—and the students had just wanted to see how a white woman would handle such behavior.

Some of the white-woman myths widely accepted by my students were that white women seldom engaged in any physical work, had sex only when they had to, hardly ever reached orgasm, and were "after" black men to give them sexual satisfaction. Once they came to trust me, a number of my students, and even some of my teaching colleagues, asked me about these convictions. Although I believe I was able to dispel some of the myths with some of the people, a few declared that while I might not fit into the stereotype, I was an exception. Teaching at Kentucky State taught me about making connections with students whose culture was different from my own while letting me see just how similar my background was to theirs.

Early in my tenure several incidents happened to remind me that I had indeed immersed myself in another culture. The first month I was there, Michael, one of my male students, came by my office to discuss an assignment; our meeting lasted until time for class. We left my office and were walking downstairs to the classroom when we encountered four other male students who began to give Michael a hard time, commenting, "Hey, man, what you doing with that white stuff?" "That sweet white stuff, man?" and the like. Michael was clearly appalled by the remarks. After sputtering for a few seconds, he demanded, "Shut up, man, you shut up! This ain't no woman; this here's a *doctor*!" Although I tried to maintain my composure, the incident broke me up, because it had never occurred to me that earning a Ph.D. had de-sexed me.

I had only had minimal contact with black folks before my tenure at Kentucky State, and one of my most surprising discoveries was how very much I had in common with some of my students. If you did not see the difference in our skin color, we were remarkably similar. Many of them were, as I had been, first-generation college students; they too had never planned to go to college; they believed income was the only marker of success; they didn't much trust anybody outside their own families; and, where higher education was concerned, they also wanted to "get in, get over, and get out." Had I been able to make a list of such characteristics when I had gone away to college some fourteen years earlier, it would have been virtually identical to the qualities I noted in these students. It took me a year or so as a faculty member there to see any of this well enough to try to take advantage of it in my classroom. All that remained then was to make these similarities known to the students without being obvious about it.

All of this took me by surprise. By 1972, prior to going to KSU, I had become so thoroughly assimilated into the culture of academe that with the exception of my still-distinctive speech patterns, I was well-nigh close to passing for normal—as in non-hillbilly. As a result of my six years at Kentucky State University, I rediscovered the hillbilly girl sequestered since my early days in Pikeville and found that I could use cultural insight, long repressed, as a bridge to understanding more about ways my students came to know. I like to think that I would have unearthed and retrieved that same strength in my heritage if I had found my first real teaching job at a different sort of school, but I doubt that would have been the case.

Kentucky State University also provided lessons of another kind. My colleagues appeared to have at least as much distance between and among each other as there was between them and me. Since I had never spent much time around black folks, I had accepted the academic liberal view that, since they had experienced such discrimination, they were all inherently better than those of us whose forebears were more fortunate. Not surprisingly, I found some good folks and some bad folks at KSU, and I made some long-lasting friends and bitter enemies — both with good reason. I also got close enough to some folks that we were able to get beyond stereotypes and to investigate long-held biases that none of us even knew we carried around.

I must say, too, that some of the very best teaching I have seen in all my years in academe went on at Kentucky State, as well as some of the worst of what passes for teaching. There were such professors as Dr. Henry Cheaney, who had taught at KSU when the school had no offices or storerooms for teachers and had had to walk from his home in the colored section of Frankfort, carrying the historical maps he used in his classes. I used to stand just outside his classroom and listen to his inspiring lectures, and I saw how much time he gave to any student who dropped by his office for support or guidance. Dr. Cheaney was not alone in his concern for students and his commitment to passing along the word; he was just the best example of that group. Conversely, KSU was also afflicted with its share of faculty who used their color as an excuse for any failing and as reason for unearned special privilege. In this respect, Kentucky State was the same as any other institution of higher education — only the excuses were different.

After my first year at KSU, I was appointed director of Research in Education and Psychology, charged with setting up a research unit, and given my own suite of offices, with a secretary, an administrative assistant, and an assistant director. Over the next five years, our little unit wrote grant proposals, brought in funding, and did research on the effects of culture and cognition in a number of different places—including my home county in eastern Kentucky. Not surprisingly, such research strongly indicated that the culture we grow up in affects our expectations and aspirations and provides boundaries for the things we are able to allow ourselves to know.

One of the best things about being the director of a research unit was that it provided an opportunity for me to test out personal theories as the research went forward. One of my strongly held beliefs was and still is that people can be taught almost any concept or skill if they can be convinced they are capable of understanding it. I have long believed that blocks to learning are often more emotional than cognitive; folks are afraid to risk trying to learn, thus, their fear of failure gets in the way of their learning.

The research center received several grants to do research on the effects of culture on cognition, which required us to hire thirty-two folks to administer several IQ and achievement tests in the school setting to groups of first-, fifth-, and ninth-graders. Then our field workers visited a sample of the students' homes, took background statements, and interviewed the parents of those students. There was no particular educational requirement for those field workers, but in areas where there was a college, we hired folks with bachelor's or master's degrees. In my home county and neighboring counties, however, we did not even attempt to find folks with degrees. Instead, I spoke with the county agricultural agent and some of the teachers at the consolidated county high school and obtained names of women who had been good students in high school but had not worked since their high-school graduation. From an initial list of around eighty names, I tracked down about twenty women and interviewed them. I hired six to work in our project. We then trained those six to administer the tests, conduct the interviews, and put together the data.

We found that the six non-degreed field workers carried out their research responsibilities as well as or better than those field workers who had bachelor's or master's degrees. When the project ended, four of those six field workers went back to school and earned bachelor's degrees; three of them are teaching now. I know I cannot say with any degree of certainty that their competence in testing, interviewing, and generally doing their jobs *caused* those four women to enter college after many years out of school, but I certainly believe it played a part. After that experience, I have tried to look for folks who can be trained to do a job and not to use lack of letters—A.B., M.S., Ph.D.—to screen them out. This is yet another example of the almost accidental influence that can be brought to bear on individuals when the stated goal—in this case, researching the effects of culture on cognition—is something else entirely.

During my five years heading the research center, I was able to present papers on this research and a number of other topics, and I received tenure and promotion at the university. In addition, because of the income from the grants I helped bring to KSU, coupled with the visibility of my professional presentations and publications, I was often invited to apply for other positions. I was not interested in moving because Brett Preston was in a good private school in Frankfort, and it did not seem wise to chance a move. I could see the boundary of this period rapidly approaching, however. Brett Preston's private school ended with the eighth grade, and Brett Dorse and I were not impressed with the quality of the local public schools. During my son's seventh-grade year, I visited and sat in on classes at high schools within a sixty-mile radius of Frankfort trying to find one that was acceptable. I recognize that very bright, highly motivated kids graduate from every one of those schools I visited. But it's a crap shoot, and his father and I agreed that we wanted to take no chances with Brett Preston's education. Thus, we took two weeks in December of our son's eighth-grade year, and the three of us visited seven boarding schools in New England. Brett Preston applied to three and was accepted by all. In September 1977, he enrolled in St. Mark's School in Southborough, Massachusetts.

Driving away from St. Mark's that Sunday afternoon was one of the most painful experiences of my life. Although I firmly believed that Brett Preston's education was the most important single gift I could ever pass along to him, leaving my baby son with that bunch of snobby, cold-blooded Yankees—no bias here, of course—was excruciating for me. The next three months were also very difficult, for I had little or no life outside my work. As a result, I accepted the very next job offer that came along. During the summer of 1978, I took a job as director of the new Institute for Appalachian Studies at East Tennessee State University.

Much of what has happened in my life has come about as a result of a fortuitous set of circumstances, and the job at ETSU was just such an occurrence. In the spring of 1977, I was asked to speak about culture and cognition at a conference on regionalism at the University of Wisconsin-Milwaukee. The conference was scheduled in July when Brett Preston was in camp, and I had done some consulting at UW-M and had friends there, so I thought it might be a fun thing to do. When I arrived at the conference, I was asked by the director if I would mind serving on a panel in addition to my scheduled presentation. No problem there; the panel was in response to a paper about regional spending habits, and I looked forward to hearing what the presenter had to say.

I found myself along with two other professors sitting in the front of an auditorium listening to a paper on "The Cultural Implications of Doorbusters at K-Mart Stores," where the author had done a study of the differences between regional responses to K-Mart advertisements. It was reasonably interesting stuff until the presenter reached the part about Appalachia—specifically Kentucky and West Virginia. She said that *western* Kentucky pretty much conformed with the Midwest in their response to advertisements for doorbusters (advertisements for paper products—kitchen napkins, paper towels, and toilet tissue—brought the public flocking to K-Mart). The presenter further declared that *eastern* Kentucky was more in keeping with the Appalachian region, which responded more vigorously to sales of candy. This particular statement got my attention right away because I was sitting there with three Snickers bars in my purse. To this day, I am hardly ever without my chocolate fix, and it has long been the case that candy sales will indeed suck me right into the store.

When it was my turn to respond to the presentation, I began by saying "My name is Linda, and I am an Appalachian." I took the Snickers from my purse, one by one. After I gave my own presentation later in the day, I was approached by some people from Mars Hill College in North Carolina and asked if I would come there in November and speak on Appalachian culture. Although I had studied and spoken about the effects of culture on cognition, this was my first clue to the uniqueness of my own culture. Baby steps; it's all just baby steps.

With that in mind, I began applying what I knew about studying culture to my own very distinctive background, and, of course, I was hooked. Consequently, by the time I spoke at Mars Hill College, I was in full hillbilly mode. I had rediscovered my roots completely, and by that time

I was taking another look at the twists and turns my life had taken in the light of this new knowledge. The folks at Mars Hill had been steeped in Appalachian lore for a long time, so my visit there was a rousing success. In January 1978, I received a telephone call from someone who had heard my speech at Mars Hill asking if I could come to East Tennessee State University in Johnson City the first Saturday in May to give the keynote speech for the founding of ETSU's new Appalachian Institute. This particular gathering was to be held in conjunction with the week-long festivities leading up to the inauguration of ETSU's new president, Arthur H. DeRosier Jr. That date fit well with my schedule. I had already scheduled a presentation in Hot Springs, Arkansas, on Friday morning of that week, and I figured I could fly from Arkansas to Johnson City on Friday afternoon—connecting, of course, in Atlanta.

In May I went over to Arkansas on a Wednesday and was having such a good time that I really was a little disgruntled at having to cut short my visit there. As a result of a long brunch and much good humor, my hosts almost caused me to miss my plane. I arrived in Johnson City, though my luggage remained in Atlanta, and was met by an ETSU professor who must have been all of twenty-four years old. After she had collected me—sans luggage—and put me in the car, her first words were "So, what are you going to talk about?" When I replied that I would probably say some things about the region, its distinctive cultural heritage, and the like, she halted for a stop sign, turned her disbelieving face to me, and said "Haven't you written your speech?" When I replied, "Not exactly," she exclaimed, "You are giving the keynote address at eight o'clock tomorrow morning and you haven't written your speech?!?!??"

This interchange was repeated several times in some variation or another during the twenty or so minutes it took for her to carry me to the Camara Inn, where she left me, full of ill will but not much else. (In my rush to make the plane, I had not eaten since my lengthy brunch at ten o'clock that morning.) I distinctly recall stripping off all my clothes—in case I had to wear the same things the next day—pulling out my yellow legal pad, and thinking, "For this, I left a great group over in Hot Springs. No food, no clothes, they're paying me all of one hundred dollars, and they send a child to make me feel guilty for not having my speech engraved in stone! At least I won't be sticking around here for long." My little welcoming committee had left me with all the specifics about ETSU's new president and his dream for the founding of an Appalachian center to serve the region. Although it sounded interesting, I had no time to explore it. I had scheduled a flight that left a short time after my speech. So I set to write.

The next morning, President DeRosier welcomed the two or three hundred folks gathered in his name in the auditorium, apologized for leaving early—press of business and all that—and, though he listened as I was introduced, when I got up to speak he walked out. It was a successful speech and a responsive audience. As I was being carried to the airport, I was asked if I would be interested in applying to be the new director of the Appalachian center. "Yeah, right!" I thought. My welcome the evening before had been so enthusiastic. I didn't even think twice about the invitation to apply for that position as I flew back to Kentucky and another busy summer. By the time I got home, Diane Nelson, a biology professor at ETSU, had called and left several messages for me to get back with her. While I may well have felt myself ready to get on with my life, the prospect of which included moving away from Kentucky, I was not at all sure that I wanted to move to Johnson City, Tennessee. One of the reasons had to do with ETSU's remote location in the northeastern corner of Tennessee, coupled with the small size of Tri-City Airport. By that time I had created a life for myself that included quite a lot of travel, both for business and for fun. For all the pride I had developed in my Appalachian roots, I now saw myself as a citizen of the world, and Johnson City sure looked to me to be more backwater than crossroads. I returned Dr. Nelson's call, certain that I had no desire to work at ETSU. Between the welcoming-committee-of-one's questioning my ability to put a decent speech together and the new president's not caring enough to stick around to hear what I had to say, I was less than interested in even re-visiting ETSU, much less working there.

I had met Diane Nelson only once and spent perhaps a half hour in discussion with her as she carried me to the airport after my speech, so I had no idea how determined she could be. This woman, who was to become one of my closest friends, was convinced that I should come to Johnson City. She pushed, pulled, and cajoled me, as well as the search committee, until July 1 found me driving myself and all my worldly goods to an "efficiency" apartment on Maple Street, about three blocks from ETSU.

I had hedged my bets, however; I had asked for—and Kentucky State had granted me—a one-year leave of absence from my tenured position as associate professor and director of research in education and psychology. Essentially, the move was lateral because I was appointed associate professor, with tenure, and director of the Institute for Appalachian Affairs. The salary and benefits were roughly the same as KSU's, and the leave of absence provided a safety net for me to see whether this new adventure would work out to my satisfaction.

One other thing had happened as a result of my growth and development over the decades since I had entered Pikeville College: You might say I had consolidated my identity. If that sounds unclear, let me explain by saying that I finally felt strong enough to deal with my early self, Linda Sue Preston, the one who couldn't get along in the world without an annotated field guide. Although I had never used the name Lee on any formal papers or in classes, I had *become* Lee Scott. After two decades of having leaned on my creation for strength, I finally felt ready to let her go; I went to my new job as *Linda* Preston Scott.

At ETSU, once again, as when I had been appointed director of the new research unit at Kentucky State University, I was given the opportunity to start up a whole new program. To say that I approached this new position with missionary zeal would be an understatement, because this time the program would have a direct impact upon Appalachia and its citizens—my folks. If you will recall the description of my evangelistic approach to teaching and just apply that times ten to my approach to the new opportunity before me, it may come close to describing the attitude I took with me to East Tennessee. Let's just say that I was tickled to death to become a part of that scene.

ETSU was a very exciting place to be at that time because President DeRosier seemed intent upon shaking the place out of its small-town provincialism and dragging it, kicking and screaming, into mainstream academe. Although he seemed to want the university to become a major player in the world of teaching and research, his founding of the Appalachian Institute indicated to me that he wanted the improvements to have a regional flavor. When I had interviewed for the job, the president had outlined an irresistible vision of the force the university could become in helping the citizens of Appalachia develop independence educationally and economically. In addition, there was already a structure in place at ETSU that included some of the finest teachers, writers, and researchers, who had been working for many years on Appalachian issues. I could hardly contain my excitement at the thought of working with these people, and they seemed just as turned on as I was to the possibilities for the new institute. As I saw it, East Tennessee State University had all the elements to bring about a number of necessary changes in the region. It was located in the extreme northeast corner of Tennessee, within a one-hundred-mile radius of the Appalachian areas of Tennessee, Virginia, North Carolina, and Kentucky. In addition to a fine undergraduate liberal arts program, a business school, and a dental hygiene school, the new medical school was just enrolling its first class.

As a result of President Johnson's Great Society programs more than a decade earlier, Washington had been throwing money at Appalachia. Hence, Appalachian centers of this or that had been set up in several locations, primarily to take advantage of the federal soft money, or so I thought. Moreover, it appeared to me that, although it was seemly to attempt to highlight and maintain the culture of the region, that was a minor function in light of some very real regional problems that first needed to be addressed. In other words, I was willing to have festivals and fairs where folks could play their fiddles and eat soup beans if I could also work on the physical health and educational limitations of the area. It has been my experience that a number of the folks who come from the East to reach down to Appalachia's economically and culturally impoverished population sometimes do more harm than good. They treat the natives as if money were the answer whatever the question. Thus, those who may truly want to help never get beyond a surface interpretation of what is needed. If economic independence were the answer, then those folks from Appalachia who got rich with the coal boom would still be rich and their kids would be having a better life than their parents did. Unfortunately, that has not always—or even often—been the case. One of the saddest scenarios is that of the hill folk who got rich on the coal boom. Five years before coal got hot, they were running around with the knees of their britches out. Then coal hit big, and with the coal money they bought new Cadillacs and built huge houses, furnishing them with giant-screen TV sets, gold leaf, and silk flowers and waterfalls in entryways. They did not get their kids' teeth fixed, and they didn't send them on to school. Then coal went bust, and five years later many of the instant rich folk were again running around with the knees of their britches out.

I think one of the hardest lessons all of us need to learn is that it ain't what you make; it's what you do with what you keep. What you do with what you keep is all about making informed choices, and my plans for the Appalachian center at East Tennessee State University had to do with making it possible for native Appalachians to think about choices and the consequences of same and enabling them to reach a place where they could inform their own choices. Specifically, the first step was to set up an Appalachian Studies minor so that students could take a class or two or a minor in the literature, sociology, psychology, economics, and/or history of their homeland. I did not want to offer a major, since I believed most students would be ill-served by not spending enough time concentrating in depth on one of the traditional disciplines. In agreement with the institute board, I worked to make certain that the Appalachian-oriented classes we would offer would have real meat to them so that they would be taken seriously by both faculty and students. Another of the programs I initiated was in conjunction with the dental hygiene department, which entailed taking our dental hygienists-in-training out to rural communities in the region and doing teeth-cleaning, x-raying, and referrals—kind of a bookmobile for teeth. The fact that this never got off the ground was probably my biggest disappointment at ETSU. Like practically every other issue concerning the institute, this was personal for me.

I was twenty-two years old before I had my first tooth filled, and then it was at the behest of Brett Dorse. By that time I had lost eight teeth. As I was growing up, when I would have a toothache, I would carry an aspirin in the tooth until I could get an appointment to go to town and have the tooth pulled—a practice engaged in by virtually everyone from my community. No wonder then that, by age fifty, practically all my neighbors had lost every tooth in their heads and sported a complete set of false teeth. Perhaps this can be justified when a family has no income at all, but this practice is still commonplace in the creeks and hollers of Appalachia. This has to do with values and is a quality-of-life issue that will not change unless it begins with the children. I will belabor this point no longer, but suffice it to say that I had great plans for a similar roadshow/clinic involving the medical school and centering on prenatal care and anti-smoking education, two issues of real need in Appalachian rural areas. It infuriated me to see funding go for damned soup-bean festivals when half the teenage women in attendance were holding a baby with one hand and a cigarette in the other.

In order to get the institute and its programs off the ground, I spent my first year at ETSU writing grant proposals, meeting with community leaders, and generally beating the public-relations drum for the programs we planned. Although I did not have much opportunity to meet formally with President DeRosier, we were both part of a group of about ten folks who met at the student center grill for coffee around seven every morning. Also, in promoting the university and the Institute for Appalachian Affairs, we both did a good deal of public speaking and often found ourselves on the same program. About three weeks after I began work at ETSU, I spoke at a luncheon meeting over in Virginia, where I was seated next to the president at the head table. We made conversation during lunch; he got up and made his speech, sat down, and then left as I got up to speak. For someone who had founded the Institute for Appalachian Affairs and purported to be such a great supporter of my program, his behavior struck me as odd.

On days when I was not working out of town, I went into the office around six in the morning and seldom went home before six or seven in the evening. I never became accustomed to fitting a social life around my workday, so most of the socializing I did was work-related and out of town. It was difficult for a woman to be taken seriously if she was seen as somebody's wife or girlfriend, so I preferred to engage in any purely social interaction out of town and on weekends, which left long hours to work during the week. Late one evening in November, ETSU's Dean of Student Affairs burst into my office in a panic. His office had a two-day regional on-campus meeting of three hundred student leaders, who were at that very moment converging upstairs in the ballroom for dinner fifteen minutes hence. The problem was that the keynote speaker was stuck in the Atlanta airport and would be unable to make the dinner. "Oh, please," the dean begged, would I come upstairs and give the speech? Never one to miss an opportunity to get somebody indebted to me, I put together some notes and headed upstairs. Once again, President DeRosier sat beside me at the head table; once again, he welcomed the group; and once again, he left as I began speaking. Now, that made three times the man had walked out on me. I recall telling Diane Nelson that the prez seemed to find my work acceptable, but he certainly did not appear to be very interested in what I had to say about it.

Although he did not seem to want to hear me speak in public, sometime during that first year of my tenure at ETSU, the president had begun calling me at the office, talking about the progress of the institute, and often asking my opinion on some of the little fires he was constantly having to put out on campus. I frequently suggested caution in going ahead so quickly with this plan or that because I could see that some of the folks he thought were on the team were not quite ready to do the needed work half as quickly as he was pushing them to do it. I honestly did not quite know what to make of this president. Clearly, he was a man of great vision, but it seemed to me that he just did not protect himself, giving his adversaries an easy target. Not long into my tenure at ETSU, I cautioned him, "When you make change you make enemies, and it looks to me as if you're making a lot of change pretty quickly."

Despite his having what I thought was a terminal case of naïveté, Arthur DeRosier was a real believer, and his passion and optimism for ETSU and its mission carried many of us right along with him. Like a number of others on that campus, I would have followed him anywhere. But then he asked me out. Scared hell out of me. It was after six o'clock on a Wednesday evening. We were on the phone, discussing I've forgotten what, when he said, "Why don't we go get some barbecue at KJ's on the highway near Bristol?" After a full ten seconds of suckin' air, I flat lied to the man. I claimed I had another engagement, hung up the telephone, took two Dramamine, locked my office, and scurried back to my little apartment, where I did not answer the telephone for the rest of the evening for fear he might call and find out I was home. I had heard the rumors of his messy divorce, his drinking, the women he was supporting, his fancy lady friend from Washington, D.C., and worse. While I had seen no signs of any of this behavior, I did not want to get close enough to be forced to ignore such signs. I just hoped this would not happen again. I liked and admired this man, but I also loved my job and knew that nothing good could come of involving myself with him in any romantic way.

Less than a week later, he asked me to go with him to a campus play. Again I said I was busy. Over the course of a month, he asked me out three more times, until I began to dread his telephone calls. I then decided the best thing to do was to confront the problem head-on, so I called his secretary and made an appointment for nine o'clock on a Monday, my rationale being that Monday morning was the least romantic time I could think of. The moment I was seated in the big chintz-covered wingback chair across the desk from him, I looked at him and asked, "Are you courtin' me, Chief?" He looked a bit startled but replied, "Why, yes, Linda, I guess I am." I suggested that this pursuit did not seem like such a good idea to me, considering that we worked so well together, and perhaps we shouldn't tinker with a professional relationship that seemed to please everybody. He said, "In other words, you don't want to go out with me." And I said, "It's not that. I just think . . ." And he interrupted, "Okay." And I got up and made a hasty exit. Another three-Dramamine day.

We then entered the period when he did not call me and I did not call him. When we met in the course of our work, we were pleasant and polite to each other. Then I got an invitation to a lunch for Rosalynn Carter, and a friend from campus offered me a ride to and from. When the friend picked me up, his wife was sitting beside him in the front seat, and President DeRosier was sitting in the back seat, at least as surprised to see me as I was to see him. He and I were not at the same table for Mrs. Carter's speech; but on the ride back to campus, we got into a conversation about what she had to say. We are of different political persuasions, and we continued our discussion after our friend had parked the car and he and his wife bade us good-bye. Then Arthur said, "What are you planning to do this afternoon?" I replied that I had to take some papers over to Marion, Virginia—about sixty miles away—and planned to return for a six o'clock bank party.

Arthur: "I have to go to the bank party too, so why don't I just drive you to Marion and back?"

Linda: "That doesn't seem like such a good idea."

Arthur: "C'mon Linda, do I smell bad or something? I don't understand your excuses."

Linda: "I'll tell you what. Why don't you pick me up in half an hour in front of my apartment. My address is. . . ."

Arthur: "I'll be there." He smiled, "How will I recognize you?"

Linda: "You figure it out, Chief."

I didn't call the man by his given name until well after we were married. I walked away from him that late afternoon with Grandma Emmy's words to Grandpa Lige running through my head, "You don't shit where you eat."

We took the papers to Marion, we missed the bank party, we stayed in Virginia for dinner, and we have been together ever since. Although our period of courting was not overlong, Arthur cannot say he entered the marriage without any warning. A few days after our trip to Marion, he invited me to dinner at Shelbridge, the ETSU president's home. There were three other couples there, and the cook had prepared a wonderful meal. When time came to open the wine, not a corkscrew was to be found; I offered my Swiss Army knife and all was well. The next morning when Arthur dropped by my office with a sheepish smile and my big red knife in his hand, I told him: "Other women might leave a delicate handkerchief, or perhaps some frilly lingerie. I left a knife and it might be a good idea for you to think about that before this goes any further."

Clearly, he took my cautionary suggestion to heart because four days after that evening, Arthur again appeared in my office at 6:30 A.M. and announced, "If our situation were not what it is, we'd get married right now, wouldn't we?" and I allowed as how we probably would. We were, however, adults, and we knew our union would be less than popular with more than a few of those who purported to love us. What's more, there was no hurry. We decided that we would continue to see each other and perhaps get married the following summer. Shortly after we agreed upon the idea of a summer wedding, I was going to my parents' house for Christmas break, and we decided that Arthur could follow me home to ask Daddy for my hand in marriage. Given my age, that may sound ridiculous to some folks, but it was important to me. I may have been thirty-something, once-married, divorced, and gone from the hills for awhile, but I was still not "broke from home."

Since I planned to stay with my parents through the first of the year and Arthur would be driving back to Johnson City on the twenty-third to spend Christmas with his children, we had to drive to my parents' house in separate cars. He showed up at my apartment early on the morning of December 21 with a big smile and a shiny-clean car. When I asked why he had washed his car, he said he wanted to make a good impression on my folks. Obviously the man had never followed a coal truck over thirty-two miles of twisted highway after a spittin' rain. I said, "Honey, by the time we get to my house, you won't be able to tell what *color* that car is, much less when it was last washed." That was the first lesson I taught Arthur about the Appalachia I grew up in. We stopped in a diner near the Head-of-the-River (Levisa Fork of the Big Sandy), and I introduced him to soup beans, onions, and cornbread along with fried potatoes and pork chops (yes, all together). If the man thought he was going to marry me, he had to develop a strong affinity for bacon grease, and I let him know it right there.

I was thirty-eight years old when I fell in love with Arthur DeRosier and he was slightly older than I was, and it didn't make a damn bit of difference. We might as well have been seventeen. We were both blindsided by what we felt for each other. Neither of us saw it coming, and we paid for it with two careers that up to that moment had been on a trajectory that seemed unlikely to peak anytime soon. I think we might have salvaged some of what both of us had worked so hard for, but my husband is not known for his patience—wasn't then, hasn't changed. We went to Momma's on December 21. Arthur talked to Daddy on the twenty-second and returned to Johnson City on the twenty-third. The visit went as expected, and we planned to get married sometime the next June. Arthur called me on Christmas Eve, and we saw our first Christmas in together, albeit from different places. Late on Christmas Day, I changed my plans and drove back to Johnson City. The next morning, we got the clerk to come into the courthouse, persuaded a doctor to complete our blood tests, and married each other that very evening.

A lot of folks I had known over the years asked, "Why him?" Why did I marry Arthur rather than somebody else who might have appeared more suitable? Well, between marriages I did have an admirer or two and once fancied myself in love with a wonderful man who appeared to return the favor. I did not put my emotional life in the safekeeping of that man because he lacked something I didn't even know I was looking for at the time—a certain urgency, if you will. I married Arthur DeRosier without thinking twice because he had that so-absolutely-Arthur urgency to be with—to be with immediately, to be with completely, and to be with forever. I guess I got hooked on that be-with urgency because I had never had that before—not with anybody.

I believe Brett Dorse loved me; he didn't drink too much, beat me, or run around on me. In all the ways I knew to judge, he was a good husband, and he continued to be a good husband for as long as we were together. But however much he may have cared about me, Brett Dorse never did want to spend a whole lot of time with me—not ever! It wasn't about sex, either; the sex in my first marriage was just fine. Instead, it was about doing things together and calling each other at the office maybe once in awhile to say, "How's your day going?" Except for sex and Christmas, Brett Dorse and I just flat didn't do anything together for fun.

One summer in the late sixties, during the unraveling time of our marriage, I decided that I would get him to take a Saturday afternoon off the golf course and join Brett Preston and me by the pool at the country club. Brett Preston was not old enough to go to the swimming pool unsupervised, so, along with practically every other mother my age, I spent three or four hours a day, seven days a week, by the pool. Monday through Friday the pool was peopled almost entirely by mothers and children, but on weekends many of the fathers came along with their families—except for the golfers, of course. Now and then, between rounds, Brett Dorse would stop by and watch his son's latest diving accomplishment, but for the most part, he was on the golf course long before Brett Preston and I got to the pool and stayed well after we had gone home. Anyway, for some reason I got it in my head that it would be nice for our little family to spend an afternoon poolside, along with the other families. Brett Dorse resisted, his reason being that he would get sunburned. Bear in mind that this is a man who kept a "golfer's tan" year-round, never wore sunblock, and routinely burned his face, arms, and legs two or three times a summer. I was adamant. I assured him that, with all the sunblocking agents available, there was no way that two or three hours by the pool could hurt him. Finally, he acquiesced.

On the appointed Saturday, the three of us trooped to the pool, where I spent three hours coating my husband with Presun for babies (the strongest sunblock then on the market). Brett Dorse was a good sport about it, swimming and diving with Brett Preston, laughing and talking with the other families by the pool. When he was not in the water, after I had coated him with sunblock, Brett Dorse wore a hat and kept his shirt on. But he burned; oh, he burned bad—not badly, *bad*; he burned his ears and his shoulders and the tops of his feet. He got burned, and so did I. And, you know, I should have known better in the first place. There was plenty of love in my first marriage, but if ever there was be-with urgency, it was gone way before Richmond, before Corbin, and even before Pikeville when we spent a year working in offices one block from each other and never thought to have lunch together one time.

I often remind Arthur that the Arthur DeRosier who couldn't seem to force himself to stick around for the first three opportunities he had to hear Linda Scott speak in public has paid for it by being sentenced to hear her talk for the rest of his life. I know that be-with urgency is still alive, because after almost two decades we still work mightily to fashion our schedules so that we can spend as much time together as possible, and neither of us has ever quite finished a conversation with the other. Our jobs consume a great deal of our time, so you will not always find us right up next to each other. But after nearly twenty years together, I am still what Arthur tries to get away *to*, rather than what he tries to get away *from*. And for me that makes all the difference.

I did not want to have a negative effect on Arthur's career, so I approached first ladyhood as I approached every other job in my life: I went to the library and tried to research it. There I found a few books on college or university presidents but virtually nothing on their wives. In several of the books on the academic president, I found short pieces on matters of family, each of these warning about high visibility and lack of privacy for spouses and children. Part of the problem Arthur and I faced was that we had to work out a complex configuration of former spouses and children, and we had to do it with the press as well as colleagues, alumni, and the general public training a microscope on us.

When Arthur and I married, our family picture in no way resembled a Rockwell painting. My new spouse brought to the union three daughters and a son. Deborah, age twenty-seven, and her husband, David, lived with their two little boys (one toddler and one baby) several hours away in Middle Tennessee; Marsha, age twenty-four, and her husband lived just across the border from us in southwest Virginia; Charles, age twenty-two, and his wife lived about a mile from the president's home in Johnson

Our 1980 Christmas card picture taken in Idaho. (Left to right) Arthur, Linda, Melissa, and Brett Preston.

(Left to right) Uncle Mitchell, Daddy, and Uncle Glen at Auntie Irene's funeral.

Brett Preston, Momma, and Daddy, Christmas 1989.

Back (left to right) Ryen, Linda, Sister, Brett Preston; Front (left to right) Daddy, McKinley, and Momma, Christmas 1990.

(Left to right) Arthur, Brett Preston, and Brett Dorse, Christmas 1990.

At the wellbox, 1992.

Across the creek from Meade Memorial School, 1992.

With Momma, McKinley, Sister, and Daddy on Decoration Day in May, 1992.

With Sister, McKinley, Momma, Brett Preston, and Daddy, 1993.

Momma and Daddy, Christmas 1993.

(Left to right) Melissa, Brett Dorse, Marsha, Arthur, and Deborah, Christmas 1995.

With Brett Preston and Arthur, Christmas 1995.

With Gwen Holbrook (center) and Sister, 1996.

(Left to right) Granddaughter Rebecca, son-in-law David, Deborah, Brett Preston, Linda, and Arthur at Chatham Hall in 1998.

Sister with her son, Ryen, and husband, Michael, at Chatham Hall on her daughter McKinley's graduation day.

City; and Melissa, age fifteen, moved in with us two days after we m
ried. I brought to the marriage Brett Preston, age sixteen, who was aw
at boarding school in Massachusetts but would be joining us for sur
mers and holidays.

This all took place in the days before they even coined the phras
"blended families," and it certainly preceded most folks' approving o
such an arrangement—especially for those of us who were supposed to
be providing a model for more than eleven thousand college students.
The situation was complicated by the existence of two former spouses,
one of whom lived in the same town. While Brett Dorse and I had remained close, supportive friends, Arthur and his former wife did not
exchange valentines. An angry ex-spouse is not an ideal situation for
anybody; for someone in a high-profile position, it is especially volatile.

On the positive side, our children, parents, and siblings saw how much
we cared about each other and forgave us our haste. On the negative
side, hardly anyone else did. Most of our friends were appalled at our
headstrong behavior, and our colleagues thought we'd lost our collective mind. It was rumored that he had married me for money and I had
married him for position, which is ironic since both of us divested ourselves of any money we might have brought to the marriage and then
gave up the best professional positions we were ever likely to have. The
truth is that we married because we had no choice. If either of us had
thought we could have gotten over the other, we damn sure would not
have risked this union. We do not have a loving sentiment engraved inside the gold rings we have worn for nearly two decades; our rings say
no matter what, and that pretty much says it all.

I married twice out of curiosity: the first about sex, the second about
everything else. Arthur is of infinite variety; his strengths are his weaknesses and in that respect he has not changed one whit since I urged
caution on him twenty years ago. He never thinks about what he *should*
say; he says what he really thinks. That drives me crazy, but I admire
the hell out of him because of it. Over the years I have watched him
make decisions that were detrimental to him—and sometimes to me—
because he believed those decisions were for the good of whatever college or university he happened to be running at the time. I would have
called it differently and justified it, as I believe practically everybody else
would, but my husband is not made that way.

When we decided to marry, we knew we could not stay in East Tennessee where we had both been high-profile people, because we could not do our jobs the way we believed they should be done and be married to each other. Arthur was very disappointed with the pace of the progress at ETSU and the amount of resistance he had encountered with every minor change. As we discussed what we wanted to do with our future, we decided to look for a smaller school, where there were not so many layers of ingrained faculty and administrative investment in the status quo. Because of what Pikeville College had done for me, I wanted to go to a liberal arts school much like Pikeville, and I also wanted to get far enough away from East Tennessee that I would not try to second-guess the person who took my place as director of the institute. I did not want to know about the path the next institute director would be following, and I reasoned that if I were far enough away I would get over my proprietary concerns. While it broke my heart to lose the institute, I must admit that I also felt the need to put space between myself and just a whole bunch of folks who had called themselves friends of mine but who just could not seem to get any kind of clear vision of me with Arthur, blocked as they were by what Arthur did for a living.

The College of Idaho met these few criteria, so, in the summer of 1980, we moved to Caldwell, Idaho. When the East Tennessee newspapers announced our leaving, I received a telephone call from a female community leader in Johnson City who said, "If you follow Arthur DeRosier to Idaho, you will set our women's movement back twenty years." At the time I suggested to her that I thought she might have overstated it a bit. In truth, what really happened was that I set my own movement back twenty years—no, *more* than twenty years. Moving to Idaho was a definite Linda Sue.

New Ground

And so, almost two decades ago my body left Appalachia for new ground beyond the Mississippi. Admittedly, it was not by wagon train, but it was nonetheless traumatic. Momma and Daddy never quite got over the fact that both Sister and I moved out of the county, much less across the state line. Before I moved in the summer of 1980, Sister and I talked at length and agreed that our parents were mistaken about the impact of my move. As we saw it, Momma and Daddy were just of a different time and could not understand that, with modern transportation and telecommunication, they would hardly know I was gone. And we were right—for awhile. My family passed along certain physical predilections, and in so doing they also passed along the expectations that accompany those conditions.

Both my maternal grandmother and my mother had breast cancer. Grandma Emmy had died of it when I was in high school, and Momma had had a breast removed in 1967. Momma was forever sick in some way or another. But after the cancer surgery, she was down more than she was up, and, as country folks will, she attributed every ache and pain to the cancer. So, before I left for Idaho, I made an appointment with her oncologist in Lexington to discuss my impending move. At that time her doctor told me that there was really little I could do for my mother. He said he would estimate that she would probably live no longer than three years, but that she could well die in three months or three weeks. He suggested that, since my sister was living in Frankfort, she could monitor the situation and keep me informed. It was clear to me that the doctor did not see the state of my mother's health as having anything to do with my moving nearly two thousand miles away. But, then, he was not a creeker and could not be expected to know the agenda.

My first years in Idaho were very full, what with teaching full-time at the college and providing support services expected of the president's wife. I was not so busy, however, that I was unable to keep up with what I saw as my responsibilities to my parents. While Sister carried on with going to the hills at least once a month, I made the trek back to the homeplace every two months or so; both of us phoned Momma and Daddy at least once a week. The first two years we lived in Idaho, Arthur and I drove back and forth across the middle of the United States eleven times—and that is in addition to the times I flew back just to check in with my parents. The reason I recall those travel and telephone statistics so clearly is because they are emblazoned on the area of my brain that will always carry guilt for having moved so far away from home. I was brought up to believe that taking care of aging parents was one of the most important things I would ever do in my life. I still believe that, as does my sister. Our mistake was that we thought we could do that caretaking function from a distance.

When they discovered Grandma Emmy's breast cancer, the doctor said it was too late for surgery, so he sent her home to waste away. From that time until my grandma had to go to the hospital just before her death, my mother spent nearly every afternoon cooking, cleaning, and visiting with her. After cooking supper for Grandma Emmy, Momma came home and cooked supper for Daddy, Sister, and me. When we had eaten and cleaned up our dishes, all four of us went back around to Grandma Emmy's to wash her dishes and sit with her until bedtime. Then, if my grandma felt particularly bad on any evening, I simply spent the night with her instead of going home. Much the same schedule was followed when Pop Pop was down sick a few years after Grandma Emmy's death. This was—and, to some extent, still is—the standard pattern in my community. Though it is a routine that does not require a great deal of planning or extra effort if all parties live within a few miles of each other, such is not the case if long distances separate family members.

In December 1986, I received the first call: "Sister, we got problems." My sister went on to say that Momma had experienced what the doctors thought was a mild heart attack and was in the hospital. I flew home, stayed four days, then returned to Idaho for a week before Arthur and I headed back to Momma's for the Christmas holidays. While Sister and I were home for Christmas, we hired a person to come in twice a week to help Momma with the *housekeeping*. In truth, we were more interested in having somebody keep an eye on our parents. Our cousin Tucker, his wife, and their two boys lived next door, and, along with the housekeeper, they were able to give just enough attention so that Momma and Daddy could keep some semblance of their independence.

Then, in early December 1991, another call: "Sister, we got problems." This time there was no way we could go on pretending our parents were ever again going to be able to take care of themselves. Momma was in the hospital, completely irrational, and Daddy was so confused that he didn't even recognize Sister. From that time until three years later when my parents died a scant three weeks apart, my sister and I lived in a state of apprehension, dreading the next telephone call. Although we patched things together—hiring three caregivers to work in shifts, 'round-the-clock—we were never able to satisfy either ourselves or our mother that we were doing all we could or should. I flew back from Montana once a month, and Sister drove up at least once a week, but Momma insisted upon believing that we were not doing our part. Then I made everything worse by going back to school.

I was a long time making the decision to go back to school, and there is no doubt in my mind but that it was the most selfish choice I ever made. It was not that I chose to do it without considering anybody else; it was the arrangement or ordering of those folks whose welfare I considered that made my decision self-centered. It was clearly a me-first choice. The only person who saw it as such, called it what it was, and reminded me of my excessive self-indulgence repeatedly was Momma—and she died mad at me over it.

Here is the way I remember the situation. Sometime in October 1993, I realized that I had a sabbatical coming up in the '94–'95 school year. At the same time, it occurred to me that this would be my last sabbatical before I turned sixty years old. I suppose the idea of going away to school—not just going back, going away—had been germinating for years. As I saw it, I was fifty-two years old, and ever since I had married Brett Dorse Scott thirty-three years earlier, virtually every decision I had made about what to do with myself and where to go to do it had been centered around somebody else—husband(s) and child(ren). I am not whining here—I hope—nor am I suggesting that I regret those choices—mostly good ones—that have marked my road from was to is. I'm just telling what the Lord loves, and that's the truth. That's what I said over and over to Momma, and she bought not one word of it, repeatedly reminding me that I was going to lose another good man if I didn't cease my foolishness.

My reasons for moving two thousand miles away from my husband were well nigh inexplicable to my mother and are indicative of the gap that lay between the two of us. Call it the difference between the person I had become and the person my mother was. Maybe I should say here that I am damn near a clone of my mother. I look like her, I sound like her, I even run my house—and some might say my family—very much as she did. One major difference between us, however, was the way we regarded time. Because Momma was everlastingly sick, she was certain every day of her life that death was imminent. Therefore, she did not do much planning for the future or even thinking about it, trusting in the Lord to bring it all on however he might.

I, on the other hand, have always seen time stretching out infinitely in front of me, and I have just planned my head off, living each day as if I would always have plenty of time to do all the things I was sure I wanted to do before the old physical plant shut down. Then, when I turned fifty, I began receiving catalogs featuring comfort items: corn pads, button extenders, canes, pads for overnight incontinence, and shoe inserts. My first reaction was to complain to Arthur about being on the mailing list for such catalogs.

Now, maybe it was because that "last sabbatical before age sixty" phrase had such a finite message, or because both my parents were near death, or because I caught a glimpse of my reflection in a mirror in Macy's and momentarily wondered what my mother was doing in New York City, or because Arthur reminded me that I had in fact bought a couple of button extenders and shoe inserts from the very catalog I was complaining about. It could have been any of those things or all of them added together. I strongly suspect that it was time—or my beginning to see the lack of it—that sent me running back to school. At the time, I explained the decision—to others and myself—as an academic or intellectual journey, but, upon reflection, I think it was more accurately my attempt to run away from the now-you-see-me, now-you-don't truth of the human condition. After all, being a student implies a future that does not include the contemplation of a corn pad purchase for a very long time. Although I would prefer to deny it, I may well have been attempting to shirk those routine responsibilities of womanhood—caring for everybody older and younger than myself. Perhaps I just wanted to be in the world for myself, for a change, to manipulate the minutes so that they fit around me rather than the other way around. In any event, I had a sabbatical coming, and I proposed to take a year to study and think about teaching and learning alongside some of the very best teachers and learners. 'Y doggies, I was going back to school.

After reviewing the requested catalogs, I realized that not much had changed since I had applied to graduate school in the mid-sixties; the first thing I was required to do was re-take the MAT or GRE. That in itself was quite a hurdle for someone fifty-three years old, who had last taken such an exam nearly thirty years earlier. But rules are rules, so I retook the exam and secured letters of reference from my present and former academic deans. One thing that was unusual was that I had to obtain recommendations from former students rather than from former professors, because many of the people who had taught me in undergraduate school were either retired, dead, or had not enough memory left to recommend anybody for anything. In due course, I jumped through all the hoops and was accepted to Harvard. In September 1994 I matriculated, driving my little Subaru, filled with books, denim, and computer equipment, from Montana to Massachusetts.

The story of my experience with the computer is perhaps the first of my graduate-school tales, for I think it says much about my own approach to learning. During all my years as a student and professor, I had managed never to take a typing class, never even to attempt to type, and never to turn on a computer until I bought my own little Gateway 486 on June 1, 1994. I then bought a book, *Idiot's Guide to Windows;* fooled around—untutored—with my new machine all summer; and carried it to the East, confident that I could handle anything I was assigned. I *know.* That sounds preposterous to me, too, but it's the truth. Since I was on my own and had nobody to help me, I spent a great many hours just testing out what the computer would do and learning through trial and error how to use it. The fact that I was able to do that was one of the more important things I learned, the essential element being, I think, the importance of having enough confidence in myself to take risks and try to master something new.

Academically and intellectually, the year could not have been better; emotionally it could hardly have been worse. Because Momma and Daddy were down sick, I had worked out a plan to visit them in Kentucky two weekends a month and fly home to Montana on alternate weekends. I had reasoned that, since Massachusetts is much closer than Montana is to Kentucky, my move would enable me to see my parents even more often. I had planned those biweekly visits to Montana in order to see my husband and to take care of some of the social responsibilities that are an integral component of the role of a college administrator's wife. Although I was taking on the responsibilities of graduate school, I had no plans to allow any of my family responsibilities to slide. In retrospect, I cannot believe my naïveté.

From August through January, I spent only three weekends in Cambridge. The rest of the time, my Thursday evenings through Sunday evenings were spent in airports or hospital waiting rooms. Throughout those weekends, I was doing homework. With my backpack full of books and my laptop, I was able to do my work and complete the assignments without asking for or receiving a single extension. Momma and Daddy were dying. Homework was therapeutic. I honestly believe that the press of work helped to distract me from some of the emotional drain of my parents' illnesses and subsequent deaths. While I did all I could for them, I did not spend time in helpless frustration over things I could not change.

Okay, I *did* spend some time in that way but not as much as I might have.

I moved to Massachusetts the last week in August, and Momma died November 11; but she never gave up her crusade to coerce me to see the error of my ways and leave New England immediately.

Six weeks before her death, I was back in Montana for the weekend when my mother telephoned. Arthur answered just as I picked up the phone in time to hear the following interchange.

Arthur: "Hello."

Momma: "How're you holding up?"

During the last three months of my mother's life, that's the way she saw it. In her view, she, Daddy, and Arthur were forced to try to "hold up" under the weight I had willfully placed on them by running off to go back to school. My first duty was to be at home taking care of my parents, and I should feel great regret for having moved so far away as to make that almost impossible. I might have been excused from some of that guilt by virtue of the fact that it was necessary for me to be in Montana to care for my husband, which after all is a wife's first duty. Taking off to live alone and go to school full-time, however, meant that I was shirking my responsibilities to everybody who was supposed to mean something to me. As far as Momma could see, it just didn't get much worse than that, and she never forgave me for it.

She would call two or three times a week, asking, "When are you coming home?" She did the same with Sister. Once we were actually at her side, it became clear that Momma did not really want to talk with either of us; she just wanted us to be there and *stay there* to take the place of the caregivers. I was in school full-time, Sister owned her own business, and both of us had stretched our schedules to the breaking point to try to care for our parents. Momma refused to understand that neither of us could just drop what we were doing and move back home for an unlimited stay. Daddy was less rational each time we saw him, often asking Momma or the company at large to take him home. Meanwhile, Momma refused to admit that Daddy was confused, insisting that he was completely fine when we were not around. Daddy was still chain-smoking and had to be watched every minute to make sure he did not drop a cigarette and burn the house down on top of them. Sister and I agonized over each new cigarette burn we discovered and put off accepting these signs that Daddy needed more attention than the caregivers could give him while they were busy with Momma. The situation deteriorated until one night in early October 1994 when our mother somehow got hold of a gun we didn't even know they owned, slipped out of the house, and headed down the road, saying she was not about to be taken alive. The caregiver could not leave Daddy by himself, so she called the police, who picked up my eighty-seven-pound, nearly eighty-year-old Momma, packing heat, and took her to the hospital. Thank God, she didn't shoot anybody! In a late October letter to a close friend, I outlined the situation:

I don't know how much I have told you about the situation in Kentucky, but I'll be meeting Arthur there over Halloween, when we go down to close up the homeplace. The situation has been absolutely terrible for the last several weeks. A couple of weeks ago, my mother's mind finally snapped (In my view, it was caused by the strain of the past three years of denial that anything was wrong with my daddy) and she was taken to the hospital in a very confused state. So, last Thursday, my parents were taken to a nursing home about half an hour from their house.

I flew back there that evening, and Sister, Brett Preston, and I appeared before a judge on Friday morning and had both Momma and Daddy declared incompetent. From there, we went to the nursing home to take them some pictures and clothes, in order to make the place seem a little more like home. When we walked into their room, they were both sitting on the side of my mother's bed staring forlornly at the floor. Looking at those two little wizened people, with absolutely no control left over their own lives, was the worst experience I have ever had.

We stayed for about four hours and all three of us did everything but a soft-shoe to entertain and engage them but nothing worked. My mother's confusion was somewhat better than when she was taken to the hospital but Daddy was completely disoriented. On Sunday morning, as my sister took me to the airport at five A.M., I remarked: "Well, Sister, there is comfort in knowing it can't get any worse." When I got to my apartment that afternoon, there was a message from my sister on the answering machine, saying: "Sister, it's worse." It seems that Sunday morning, they found Daddy lying in the floor, with a broken hip and a gash on his head that required fourteen stitches. He had surgery on Monday to put a pin in his hip and, as of today, they expect to release him back to the nursing home next Monday.

Daddy never returned to the nursing home. Within three days of his hospitalization for the broken hip, Momma was also taken to the hospital with breathing problems. The first of November, we checked them both out of the hospital and brought them back home to finish out their lives together. Since my parents were both in terrible shape, we hired seven caregivers, who worked in overlapping shifts to care for them. It is a testament to my sister's organizational skills and tenacity that we were able to get and keep the help necessary for my parents to die at home. At one point, Sister remarked that each time she picked up the *Paintsville Herald*, the local weekly newspaper, she expected to see a picture of herself designated as the largest employer in Johnson County. That is precisely the kind of remark my daddy would have made in such a situation. Although the new arrangement made my parents more comfortable than either the nursing home or the hospital, their condition did not improve. Momma died November 11; Daddy, December 5.

While Sister and I had been dealing with our parents' dying for three years, we were not at all prepared for their deaths. After Daddy's funeral we went back to their house, changed into our traveling clothes, vowed to come back *sometime* during the approaching holidays, and headed out of the hills. Though we did come back to visit the graves Christmas Day, we stopped by the house only briefly on our way back downstate. We hired a local person to keep up the yard and the outside of the house, but we made no other changes; the house sat empty for almost two years. We did not disconnect the telephone or the electricity, nor did we empty the refrigerator. I don't know about Sister, but I kept thinking I would one day wake up and realize what Momma and Daddy would want us to do with *their* house. My parents died in their *new* house, and neither Sister nor I felt any emotional pull toward it. It was much too close to the Paintsville city limits for our liking.

When my daddy was laid off by Princess Elkhorn Coal Company in 1962, he built a spec house up on the property he had bought from Grandma Emmy's children. When he sold that house, he built another one. By the time he was called back to work several months later, Daddy was doing so well building houses that he never went back to the mines. Then, in 1965, he bought a hollow over near the river narrows and had it dozed out. The following year, he built the first house in what was to become Preston Estates.

Sister and I have no special affinity for that house, but Momma and Daddy loved it. It was big, it was fancy, and it was the culmination of their dreams. For that reason, we wanted to handle it very carefully until we could get some idea of what would be the right way to proceed. We felt the same way about our parents' furniture and cars. Although their furniture did not fit in with our own, Sister and I took the pieces we felt had special meaning for our parents, and I bought Daddy's last Cadillac from the estate. That car was important to my Daddy, and I expect to keep it in the family for as long as it lasts. I'll bet I'm the only college faculty member in America who drives a white-on-white Cadillac, with red leather interior—and a big old wheel on the back! I don't need vanity plates to identify me; I have a vanity car!

During the short period that Momma and Daddy were in the nursing home, I was visiting with them and had to drive back through Two-Mile on my way downstate to catch a plane to Montana. Uncle Keenis and Aunt Exer Holbrook's house had been torn down years before, and their daughter Gwen and her husband, Wallace, had built a modern brick ranch house on the property. As I drove past the homeplace, I saw Gwen sitting on her porch across the road. I was in a hurry—as always—but I stopped to say hello to my oldest friend. I walked over and sat down on the porch with my old partner in crime. She got me a Pepsi, and we visited a bit about my parents and the state of their health. As we talked, I looked across the road at the scene of so many of my memories. Pop Pop's house was long gone, and the house Daddy had built after the fire and sold ten years later had also burned. The shell still stood, but little else gave testimony of our ever having been there.

After about fifteen minutes, I stood up to leave. Gwen asked me to sit a while longer. I said I would really like to but I was in a rush—and I added, "just like everybody else, these days."

She responded, "I'm not."

And I said, "Oh, sure you are. You're probably doing different things, but I'll bet you rush around a lot."

She said, "No, I just come out here and sit on the porch and watch the world go by."

I have thought about this interchange ever since, and I believe she was telling the truth. There was that sense of no-hurry that existed in my youth and still exists, to some extent, in my home community. Although it seemed we were eternally busy, there was no rush about getting things done; and there seemed to be all the time in the world to reflect and to talk to folks—while skinning beets, stringing beans, bugging potatoes, or carrying water. Each chore had to be done in a timely fashion, but most things could be done in concert with friends or family; if done alone, there was time for thought or daydreaming. Perhaps the very mindlessness of the tasks enabled us to be more mindful of relationships. Currently, all of my real work must be done in solitude, or, if others are a part of a project, we must stay on task during the time we spend together. It may well be those very detours from task that give life its meaning, by providing the glue that bonds folks together. At this point in my life, the only time I have in which I feel free to do something other than what I *must* do comes in fifteen-minute increments—usually in the early morning or late at night—making it increasingly difficult for me to remain connected to those folks I care about. Even when I am talking to family or friends on e-mail or the telephone, there is some sense that I am taking away time I should be spending planning for class, writing checks to pay bills, or working on my taxes—all the activities that have a lock on my time during the day. Although Brett Preston visits me and I visit him, we get far more relating done by telephone or e-mail than when one of us is physically present in the same town as the other, because those things we *must* do always take precedence over those things we may *want* to do. Thus, if one of us takes time out to have lunch with the other, both feel guilty about the time taken away from what we "should" be doing.

Daughter Marsha has a close friend of twenty-some years who recently told her and some of her other friends that she was calling time-out from seeing them because she was just overwhelmed by her work and family responsibilities. Marsha was hurt by this, and, as she related the story to me, my first response was that I wish I had the courage to do that. Instead, I try to cover all those friendship bases and end up not giving anybody time enough by half, resenting the time I do give, and losing sleep worrying about all of it.

My son's theory is that this time crunch is felt by all folks who are passionate about their work. In Brett Preston's view, most careers differ from jobs in that a career is really a twenty-four-hour-a-day commitment, and it preempts every other thing in a person's life. Even our most personal relationships get pushed to the margins. That means we can only relate, he says, to those folks whose careers are as all-encompassing as our own, because nobody else can understand being put on hold so often or for so long.

My sister suggests that perhaps the fond memories she and I have of ample time, an extended family, and a close-knit childhood may have as much to do with class as anything else. From working with folks trying to rent subsidized housing, Sister has noticed that the less money folks have, the more likely they are to depend on pooling their resources—time, money, and talent—just to get by. This runs the gamut from child care to ride sharing to shared housing. These people and their children spend hours and hours daily working together as they try to negotiate their way through the system of living. Upward mobility to them means being able to get their own apartment, buy and drive their own car, and send their kids to day care instead of leaving them home with a relative who works another shift. As their dependence upon each other lessens, so does their bonding. Sister suggests that maybe what has happened to us is that we just "moved on up to the East Side."

Over the years, each move I have made has found me adopting new policies and procedures for taking control of my time. While moving requires going through, picking up, and packing up all material possessions, it can also provide an opportunity for re-thinking all other aspects of individual lifestyle. At least I have always used a physical move in that way. Each time I have moved from one place to another, I have tried to bear in mind what I wanted to take and what I wanted to leave behind, and I'm not just talking about stuff here.

I grew up believing that life pretty much happened *to* me; I was born into this ready-made world, and—like a birdie in a badminton game—I had little or no control over the order and organization of my time or of the folks with whom I spent that time. I was led to expect that my adult life as a woman would be organized around a pre-set structure; three meals a day would be cooked—not at a time of my choosing but when they were due, and I would be expected to plant or pick or preserve fruits and vegetables based on nature's whimsy, not my own. Had I been a man who worked out in the world, I would have had still another layer of organization imposed upon me by the power structure that made decisions about acceptable clock-in and clock-out times. By the same token, I was led to believe that my emotional network would also be ready-made by my extended family and community. During my growing-up years, I do not recall anyone's ever moving into our local area who was not kin to someone else who lived there. What that means is that whenever someone *new* moved in we already knew his lineage, sometimes even better than he did, so there were few if any surprises in that realm. We went about our days relating to those kith and kin who worked alongside us or who decided to drop by. With the exception of an occasional insurance man or vacuum-cleaner salesman, we saw the same folks day after day. There were no locked doors, and the only folks who even knocked on doors were traveling salesmen. The proper way to visit on Two-Mile was to walk through either front or back door, call out "Anybody home?" and march on in. To have made a more formal entry would have been considered pretentious because it would have been seen as calling unnecessary attention to one's self as somehow special.

One of the first things I learned in college was that I needed to knock on the door of my hallmates rather than burst in unannounced. At the time, this practice seemed a little ridiculous to me since we were, after all, living under one roof, but I figured out the system soon enough. When Brett Dorse and I moved into our first apartment, the front door was locked, but all our family and friends felt welcome to drop by at any time and spend the night—or even longer—if they chose. This system of almost-constant open house remained our personal policy for virtually all our married life, and it is still in effect in Brett Dorse's house. I do not recall anyone's ever telephoning to announce a visit, and I've never called ahead either.

Moving so far away from home has made it necessary for me to impose an organization on my time that has little or nothing to do with the natural order of things. Whereas my Grandma Emmy's days were delegated by when the sun rose and set, I am required to adjust my sleeping and waking in accordance with the requirements of my job rather than the laws of nature. As a college professor I have more control over my clock than many folks; but I cannot spontaneously decide to spend a day with a friend, and I am unable to leave my job for weeks at a time even in an emergency situation.

One Friday evening last summer, I was packing my bags for a business trip to Breckenridge, Colorado, when the telephone rang. I don't answer the phone anymore because I have no desire to hear the latest offer from Visa, MCI, or the folks who want to pave my driveway or put siding on my house, so I listened through my message. At the tone, I caught a voice that I had never before heard on my answering machine. "You don't know who this is, but . . ." I snatched up the phone and said "Gwen Holbrook!"

"Why, you. . . ! Were you standing right there listening to me?" she demanded.

It is not unusual for me to talk with Gwen by telephone because I check in with her every few months, but this was the first time she had ever called me long distance. You see, I am the one who moved away, and it is always the responsibility of the leaver to call the left—at least that's what feels most comfortable to me. That put some degree of importance on this particular telephone call, and indeed it was significant. My old grade-school buddy announced, "I called because I want you to worry with me."

She went on to say that she had been diagnosed with advanced bladder cancer and was scheduled for surgery the next Tuesday. We spoke for perhaps half an hour that evening until I hung up the phone and continued with my packing. Gwen got it right, though; she now had me "to worry with her." I spoke with her from Colorado on Saturday and again on Monday afternoon. I checked in with her daughter in the hospital waiting room shortly after the surgery and talked with her husband or her sister or sometimes with Gwen herself almost every day of the four weeks she was hospitalized. While I continued to telephone regularly, it took more than four months for me to find a way to reconfigure my schedule to include a visit to Two-Mile to sit for even a short spell with someone who means a lot to me. Contrast my scheduling problem with the "goin' to stay all day" custom followed by my momma, aunts, and grandma when I was growing up.

However much a woman had to do around her homeplace, it was not unusual for her to declare, say, on a Wednesday evening, that on the morrow she thought she would take the kids and go over to some friend or family member's house to "stay all day." The friend would not have been notified of the plan, for there were no telephones; indeed there *was* no plan until it entered the potential visitor's head the evening before. The next day after morning chores had been done, the woman would clean up herself and the children and set off for her friend's house. In Grandma Emmy's day she would set out walking; in Momma's, she would catch the bus or drive her car. When she and her brood arrived at the friend's house, everybody was thrilled to see the visitors.

I can recall squatting in the middle of the potato patch, bugging potatoes, and spying Auntie Lizzie, Lois Ann, and Tucker comin' 'round the curve on their way to Grandma Emmy's. I was jumping up and down with excitement as I shouted the news of their arrival to my grandma. Such an unexpected visit did not call a halt to the daily routine of the hostess or her kids. Indeed, it brought both companionship and help. If the host family was putting up beans or bedding out sweet potatoes or pickling kraut, the chore was made lighter by having someone to share it. A good hostess did not go out of her way to do anything special just because she had a visitor, though she might just stir up a little sweetbread to go with dinner (the noonday meal) so as to be thought *clever*.

When homefolks speak of a hostess being clever, they do not mean witty or bright; they mean she knows how to entertain. Since practically all visits—even overnight ones—are of the drop-in variety, a clever woman always has a little something in the fridge or the pantry that she can serve up to let the visitors know she's glad for the company. In Grandma Emmy's time, "goin' to stay all day" usually meant through suppertime. By Momma's day, folks generally left in late afternoon so that they could be home in time to get supper for the family.

Old habits are the hardest to break, and even today I have to remind myself to sit down at my own table and pick up my fork so that folks can get on with eating while I rush back to the kitchen to attend to some last-minute oven emergency. Some table manners make little sense if the point of visiting is for me to enjoy my guests while I show them I'm glad for the opportunity to have them at my table. It took more than a few years for me to figure out the protocol surrounding something as simple as a drop-in visit, especially as it concerns who eats what and when. Momma, Grandma Emmy, and everybody else I knew always kept something in the pie safe or the oven or the fridge, left there just for somebody who might come by right after dinner or supper but had not yet eaten. It was also not unusual for a visitor to drop by bringing his own food and just wanting to sit and visit while he ate. Such a caller would offer to share what he had, and, if we had still not eaten, we would share; otherwise we'd get him a glass of water or milk or lemonade and sit with him while he ate his food at our table.

An incident that happened during my stay in Asheville suggests that, though Pikeville College might have taught me about knocking before entering, serving tea, and writing thank-you notes, I still had a ways to go in the manners department. One Friday evening, after a hallmate at the Y had set my hair, I took her out for pizza. Actually, she took me out—it was her car—but I bought the pizza. After we had picked up the largest pepperoni and double-cheese pizza Papa Gino's could produce, I suggested that, instead of taking our pizza back to the Y, we stop by and share it with my friend from work. Since I knew Mary Claire particularly loved pepperoni pizza, this seemed a splendid idea. When we knocked at her apartment door bearing pizza, Mary Claire invited us in, said she had just finished dinner, and reminded me that she could not eat meat on Friday anyway, so pepperoni was verboten. Did the two of us country girls slink on back to the car and return to the Y with our prohibited booty? Nope; sorry. Instead, we accepted Mary Claire's invitation and her soft drinks, and we sat ourselves down and ate that big ol' pizza right in front of her. The only explanation I can offer in my defense is that on the Creek it was common practice for folks to drop by unexpectedly right around suppertime, and, if we had already eaten, we would just dish up some leftovers for them and sit with them while they ate. I also think that somehow the fish-on-Friday thing seemed to me to be such an insignificant rule that I really thought Mary Claire would join us if she actually wanted some pizza. In the light of what I know now, it just looks like a case of extremely bad manners and blatant insensitivity on my part. It also suggests to me that my companion, who was from a rural area in western North Carolina, was as unaware as I was of the proper behavior in such a situation.

The custom of dropping by for the afternoon, the night, or the next week is so completely at odds with the way my world operates today that my notions of what to expect of myself and my own family seem caught somewhere in between. While the whole family knows what the expectations are when it comes to Christmas, weddings, and graduations, if I want to see my sister or my children other than for big events, I must engage in an elaborate rearrangement of my own schedule; and I must notify them early enough to get on their agenda, too. What's more,

I don't even remember the last time it would have been *convenient* for me to visit or be visited unexpectedly.

Moving out into the big world required learning a whole new set of rules for what was expected both before and after an actual visit, and it took me awhile to crack that code, too. The widespread custom of writing notes of appreciation to those who have entertained me is another of those requirements that, for me, has turned something pleasurable into just another duty. While Ann Landers and her sister continue to insist that those visitors who do not send a thank-you note the moment their host's door closes behind them are just ungrateful jerks, I do not think that is necessarily the case. If somebody has been to my house, had a good time, and said so, she does not have to send me a handwritten assurance; she also doesn't have to be in any rush to reciprocate my hospitality. I hate everything about this scorecard approach to getting together, and I think one reason for my resistance to it can be traced directly to Two-Mile Creek and the kind of casual interaction that implied that we were all family and would be delighted to see each other whenever, whyever, and for however long.

EPILOGUE: COMIN'-HOME SPIRIT

*O*ver the course of my life, I have been lucky in that I have seldom managed to get exactly what I wanted; instead, I have most often been able to grow to appreciate what I got. Many times what I perceived as failure at that moment turned out to be success clothed in camouflage. What comes clear to me in these pages is that I have always been a slow learner everywhere but in the classroom—taking baby steps, often in a doubtful direction. In those clue-gathering years when I was failing everywhere but in school, I tried very hard to sort through and learn from every failure. Along the way, I plotted and planned my life and went back and revised and refined those plans time after time after time. Before I talked about it to myself—sometimes for *years*—all the while thinking out what I would do if A happened, what I could do if B happened, what I should do if . . . and so on. For all my plotting and planning, I ultimately was unable to live out my life that way. Almost as soon as I was sure of the precise thing that would make me completely happy forevermore, I got that thing and was disappointed in it. Even more frequently, I did *not* get what I wanted, yet found myself remarkably satisfied. Such experiences certainly made me doubt my judgment until I realized that I was attempting to be consistent, and consistency simply meant that I had learned nothing. I wanted to tie things down in my life, fix it so that I would not have to worry about the future. It was never enough that my needs were taken care of in the now; I worried about whether they would be met in the next two hours, too, and next week, and next year, and. . . . Well, there's that forever again. My early attempts at figuring out how to act, through reading books for clues and directions, did not work because there was no book about somebody like me, no manual that I could use as an absolute guide. But while I may not have been able to see clearly where I was headed, the origin of my journey was never in doubt.

I once heard a speech about organic systems illustrated by a slide depicting a stand of aspen trees in Colorado that was claimed to be the largest living system yet discovered. While most of us would see this stand of aspen as a grouping of separate trees, they actually are interconnected by a complex root system that gave birth, while remaining connected, to every tree. This is certainly true for me. Although I may appear to be separate and on my own in the world, I am still strongly connected to my root system. I was long in coming to understand much about myself or about the world at large, and this look back at the early part of my life has been a way of seeing for myself what I have kept and what I have left behind. One thing I know: The hills of eastern Kentucky and the values and customs of that place and those people remain a central part of me today. It is left to me, then, to recognize that fact and draw strength from it or attempt to deny the connection, thereby cutting myself off from it. In either case, it exists.

As I have become reacquainted with Linda Sue Preston, one thing is clear: The scene in my rear-view mirror is considerably different from the vista I beheld through the windshield. If you have stayed with me thus far in this rambling narrative, you have been privy to a number of changes in my world, in the world at large, and in the identity of Linda Sue "Lee" Preston Scott DeRosier—changes in the way I saw myself, defined myself, and presented myself to everybody else. It seems that the older I got the less certain I became of who I was and the more I questioned my early goals. The world kept changing on me, and I kept changing with it as each fresh set of experiences brought new insights into the past and visions for the future. I would climb for a while, then reach a plateau and peer out, only to see that the terrain had changed markedly since last I looked. However painful or pleasant those insights and visions may have been, I never . . . ever . . . lost my feel for home.

You might say that, for all the sacks of iris rhizomes from Grandma Emmy's, the yellowed pages of lye-soap-making specifications, and the family recipe for hogshead souse that I have carried with me all these years, the most valuable commodity I brought from home is my Appalachian consciousness—my spirit, if you will. My internal landscape was drawn way back by the old ones, artisans who only knew to draw in the old ways. And while the outside of me may look considerably changed, all the parts of me that make sense of the world I live in were formed early on. Thus it is impossible for me to separate my life from the context of my people.

In the beginning there was my family: Momma, Daddy, Grandma Emmy, and Pop Pop. When Auntie Amanda died recently, she left only Uncle Mitchell as representative of that generation; at age ninety-two he may not make it all that long. That leaves it up to Sister and me to create and pass along family and our ideas of what family means in the twenty-first century. My world today is somewhat larger than the one Grandma Emmy passed on to me, and blood is no longer the password for entry, although such a tie remains important. In answer to the question "Who are your people?" I would have to begin with Pop Pop and Grandma Emmy—but, Lord, how that definition has grown on my watch.

Recently on my way to work, I saw the Hale-Bopp comet radiant in the heavens over the butte, and I wondered what would be left of me and my people to see that sucker the next time it comes around in the night sky. Hot on the heels of that thought came the wondering where I should be and what I should be doing that I'm not. Right now, for all the things that drive me crazy, overall my life is pretty close to the way I want it. For so many years, the life drained out of me drop by wearisome drop on number eighteen—and that was supposed to be the *fun* part of my existence. What took me so everlasting long getting off number eighteen was that given my baseline I just could not envision anything *better* being out there. But there was better. And it had nothing to do with the man I was with and everything to do with the woman I was. That woman was waiting around for somebody else to provide the action in her life, refusing to take over that function for herself.

One of the ways I have enriched my life over the past thirty years has been through expanding my extended family to include connections with a number of folks who are not blood kin. Since I gave up wifing and went to teaching, I have sent enough of my psychology majors to graduate school that I could have a nervous breakdown in almost any state of the union and have my mental health restored by a former student. That image is perhaps more comic than comforting, but a whole lot of those former students have become friends of mine. Hardly a morning goes by that I don't pull up my e-mail to hear of some wild-eyed adventure from one of those students or from Sister or Brett Preston or somebody else who feels close enough to tell me things that cannot be shared with just anybody. Often they report on their successes, and I tell them they're lucky that I'm so good at "vicarious," else I'd have to kill them. But I think the reason I have grown so adept at vicarious is because my own life is so full of energy now that I am no longer depending on somebody else to energize me.

Each morning as my clock goes off at four-thirty, the lupus I have wrestled with for the past forty years reminds me that I am far from free of it. I turn off the clock and think, "I can't go to work today." Then I turn over to see Arthur getting out of his side of the bed, and I insist, "As bad as I'm hurting, they can't expect me to come in today." Then I turn back over and drag my sorry self out of bed and go to work. My job is different every day, and just doing it engages every part of my being. Every year they're eighteen. Every year I'm a year older, and I am passing along all I know of the world and what it means to be in it to another generation of young folks who are just beginning to make sense of their inheritance. I teach psychology, but it is psychology filtered through Appalachian sensibilities and shaped by my Appalachian heritage.

While it may be true that I live far from where I grew up, the things I learned there still fund my every move. Two-Mile is such an integral part of my consciousness that no behavior is without its Appalachian foundation. My notions of kin and connectedness are grounded in my experiences of family and community, in the dinners-on-the-ground, in the stories told in graveyards, in the songs of summertime with everybody home.

Perhaps the place Two-Mile shows up most in my life today is in my notion of kin and how that concept is defined. I have never sought liberation from my people, however far I may have strayed from the homeplace. I have left no one behind. Instead, my sense of family has simply expanded to include a lot of folks I have met along life's way, some of whom were just not lucky enough to have been born in eastern Kentucky. Indeed, if you are ever in my life, you are always in my life. My configuration of family may not be shaped exactly as was Grandma Emmy's, but we are family nonetheless. Once, as I was trying to explain to a friend who all I was going to be visiting over Christmas break, she termed my kinship network "a combination of the homespun and the implausible." Well, maybe it is.

Brett Dorse, for example, remains an important part of this family and a part of my life, as illustrated by events that took place about two months after Arthur and I moved to Idaho. At that time, Melissa, Arthur's youngest daughter, was a sophomore at Chatham Hall in Chatham, Virginia. Chatham fathers' weekend was a tradition at the boarding school and fell on the same weekend in October as the President's Trust Fundraiser at The College of Idaho—a mandatory attendance event for Arthur. What's more, Melissa's *parents'* weekend was a scant two weeks after the *fathers'* weekend, and Arthur and I were planning to fly to Virginia to attend the latter event. Although we would be seeing her two weeks later, Melissa was sad not to have her father present for the special fathers' weekend. When Brett Dorse heard of our predicament, he volunteered to stand in for Arthur at Melissa's fathers' weekend celebration. On Thursday, he drove from his home in Frankfort, Kentucky, to Bristol, Virginia, to watch Marsha, Arthur's middle daughter, in a play. Then, on Friday morning, he and Marsha drove on to Chatham to spend the weekend with Melissa and participate in her celebration. Yes, I know it is hard to sort out my former husband's kinship to my stepdaughters, but there is a bond there. True, it ain't Walton's Mountain, but we do have our own kind of extended family, however implausibly defined.

This sense of connectedness is never clearer than during the Christmas holidays when we try mightily to get together, as illustrated by the Christmas after our youngest grandbaby, Benjamin, was born in November 1995. Through masterful manipulation of everyone's calendar, Sister and Deborah, Arthur's oldest daughter, had managed to get every member of our *blended* family to Sister's house for the holidays—everybody, that is, except Melissa, Jim, and their two babies. There was every good reason for their absence that year. After all, their older son, Jefferson, was barely two years old, Benjamin was practically newborn, and the round-trip from North Carolina to Kentucky was twenty-six hours long. Unbeknownst to us, however, Jim, Melissa, and their little brood made the trip and surprised us by showing up. It was the very best Christmas present they could have given us!

And so we gathered at Sister's: Deborah from Middle Tennessee, Marsha from South Carolina, Brett Preston from Washington, D.C., Melissa from North Carolina, and Arthur and me from Montana—along with sons-in-law and grandchildren—to wait for Santa Claus. It was just like those Christmases of so long ago with Grandma Emmy and Pop Pop. Sister's family was there, of course, and Brett Dorse, and ninety-year-old Auntie Amanda to oversee it all. The saying in the hills is that "Hillbillies don't marry *off*; we marry *on*," and the connections grow ever more complex. There is a comin'-home spirit that is an essential part of growing up in Appalachia; if you grow up there, you never doubt where home is. I carry that spirit of place, and I perpetually call upon that spirit to address every new experience in my life. I live in Montana now, and I deeply appreciate the beauty of my adopted home. But much of what I love about this place I never would have noticed had it not been for my growing up on Two-Mile.

The house I live in now is nestled under four hundred feet of rock cliff. I suspect that, once you look beyond the tiny green handkerchief that is my backyard, not much about the two-hundred-foot field of boulders that leads up to the rock face—or the cliff itself—has changed since man moved in. I probably spend more time than I ought to looking at those rocks, watching the morning sun gradually overtake the butte that lies to the west, and later watching the purple shadows of evening shift as the boulders play hide-and-seek with the setting sun. At night those rocks turn white and seem to glow in the moonlight as I sit on my back porch and think about all the folks who have come and gone while those old rocks have stood guard. In a now-you-see-it-now-you-don't world, those rimrocks are now-you-see-'em, now-you-see-'em . . . now-you're-gone. The ridges of home tell different tales from my rocks, but I would never have noticed one without the other. I learned to look for and to think about such things on Two-Mile, with Pop Pop telling Sister and me about old-growth timber long before either of us could make any real sense of such a lesson. You cannot grow up as close to the land as I did and not notice your natural surroundings, and you cannot grow up Primitive Baptist without seeing time stretched out before you and behind you and pondering the world's meaning and your own. I know, for example, that I have been extremely lucky in this life: lucky to have been born into a time and a place where folks may not have had much in the way of material things to pass along, but they handed down a sense of belonging that cannot be taken away even by disapproval or hostility.

Sister and I have often talked about our growing-up years, when it seems that the two of us fought about twenty-three of the twenty-four hours in any given day. Out of my earliest feelings of resentment toward that three- to ten-year-old child Momma made me drag along everywhere, coupled with my blatant jealousy of the precocious and curvaceous adolescent she became, Baby Sister and I have forged one of the strongest bonds in my life and in hers. That closeness, however, was long in coming. It was not until we both passed twenty that Sister and I became best friends. I have no doubt that part of the reason the relationship survived, turned positive, and flourished was because of the hillbilly family thing. In the hills, we were taught to keep close, however much we might dislike and/or disapprove. Since both of us were taught that loyalty to family is primary, we loved each other even when we did not like each other very much.

Some years ago when I was living in Idaho, I took a weeklong summer workshop in Greensboro, North Carolina. Since Sister had business in that area, I flew into Kentucky, and we drove to North Carolina and spent the week there together. All went well until we were on our way back to Kentucky and got into an intense discussion about I-don't-recall-what. We were on the interstate in deep Carolina woods, and it was raining—hard. We were between towns, and the foliage was thick and tall on both sides of the road when Sister pulled that big old BMW over on the right shoulder of the road and said, "Get out."

"What?" I replied.

"Get *out*!" she repeated—loudly.

When I just stared at her, she said it again. "GET OUT!!!!"

"Sister, I am not getting out of your car. If I did, we'd just lose an hour or so, because it'd take a lot of time for you to double back and get me."

Hands on the wheel, she stared at me with that Ward lower lip stuck way out.

"I am your sister and I am always going to be your sister, so you may as well just pull this big 'chine back on the road 'cause no way you're ever gonna get rid of me."

She pulled back into traffic, and we went on to the house.

Though our feelings of affection may wax and wane, the attachment remains strong. Indeed, it is my faith in that very connectedness that has enabled me to tell some of the stories I have told here, full in the knowledge that some of my people are going to intensely disapprove of what I have committed to paper. There will be folks I love who will be furious at me for telling so much, but I have faith that they will still love me though they may not be liking me for awhile.

Once when I called Momma from Idaho she told me they were filming a "woman coal miner story" on Two-Mile, and everybody was fire mad over it. When I asked why folks were so aggravated, she said, "Well, they're showing some people eating dinner and they've got all the men eating at the table before the women eat." I said, "But Momma, that's the way it always was, after church." Then she said, "I know that, Linda Sue, but you know how that looks." There was nothing left for me to say.

The life and living I have set down here is put to paper the way I saw it, as I lived it, and there are some who will recall it differently or will make sense of it in an altogether different way. But that's their story, and this is mine. I give thanks both for my past and my present, which brings me to still another area where I have been lucky: Arthur.

My marriage to Arthur may be the "implausible" part of that "homespun and implausible" designation. On the face of it the marriage doesn't make a lick of sense, but it works. He continues to be politically as far to the left as I am to the right and resolutely optimistic in the face of my cynicism. Over the course of our marriage, we have had our share of sorrowful times, including the death of his son, Charles, and the loss of all four of our parents. Although nothing can compare with the tragedy of losing those we loved deeply, we have also had some interesting career ups and downs centering around Arthur's job, including being not-so-gently ushered out of one post and damn near canonized in another. Moreover, both of those things can happen in the same place—and nearly have, I might add.

For me, one of the most challenging aspects of being along for this particular ride is that the highs and lows of his job come so quickly on the heels of each other. Sometimes, if you hang in there, they're glorifying your name before you can get the tar and feathers washed off—and you'd best not get too accustomed to that glorifying business either, because you're perpetually about one good rumor away from disaster. To be more specific about such matters would be to tell Arthur's story for him, and though I'd often like to, I will restrain myself here.

After nearly twenty years together, we share a passion for living, for our work, and for each other that, frankly, continues to surprise us; after all, we're old folks. We have had some powerful screaming matches—he once accused me of throwing knives at him; in point of fact it was a *fork*, and it slipped out of my hand as I was gesticulating in order to make an important point—but we do far more laughing than shouting. A couple of times a month Arthur will slip away from work in late afternoon, pick me up at my office, and take me to the Cracker Barrel for pinto beans, onions, and cornbread. And he won't even subtly suggest that the blackberry cobbler and ice cream that follow those beans will go straight to my hips. After our soup-beanfest, if there's time, we'll stop by Barnes and Noble or the used-book store on our way home. I should note that the time and money we spend in bookstores is no more worthwhile than the time and money some folks spend on golf courses, but when we go to Barnes and Noble neither of us is waiting for the other. Perhaps that is what convinces me that we are well suited—well, that and the fact that when he is out of town, I often call up Arthur's voicemail and listen to him telling the world, "You can call the switchboard to seek another who might be of service to you," as only Arthur could say in just that way. In truth, I sometimes think that this marriage works because Arthur is very large of spirit, and just being married to him has made me live up to goals I never would have thought to set.

As I look hard at the specter of sixty looming just ahead, I remain in negotiation with my own set of issues every moment of my life. As a child growing up on Two-Mile, I often felt that I had been born into the wrong world because everybody else seemed to fit in so much better than I did. Over the years, I have managed to make a place for myself in a number of different locations, and each place has had its own advantages and disadvantages. While at the moment I am pretty well satisfied with where I am and who I am, I still wrestle with my fitting-in-and-belonging demons. Predictably, I think about Two-Mile and wonder if I could make a better fit back on the creek now that I have played out most of my choices.

Sister and I flirt with returning home for our retirement. Our most recent venture has been to make an offer to buy all of Pop Pop's property, including our old homeplace, on the south side of Two-Mile Creek. Appalachia haunts the both of us, albeit in somewhat different ways, and we speak to each other of regaining possession of what we lost upon leaving and of building us a cabin up the holler where the pigs used to be. We agree that owning the property would at least give us daydreaming rights about going flower-picking or looking for 'simmons with our grandbabies, telling them not to wade the creek or go back in the coal bank, and for Godsake to watch for copperheads, showing them Brett Preston's footprints in the concrete bridge their grandpa poured when my son was not quite two years old, and telling them about their Pop Pop and what it was like to prick blacktop bubbles with your toes while barefootin' it down to Leonie Wallen's to get a big Pepsi and wait for the mail.

One of Sister's e-mail messages to me about the purchase of the homeplace says much, I think, about the two of us—what is important to us, what we can never get rid of, and what we want to pass on: "Seems like Two Mile just might provide me with a place and time to do some daydreaming of climbing to the rock cliff with our grandkids. Truth might be, it would just be another place to let the weeds grow up and pay taxes on, but I've dropped a lot more money on a lot less to dream about. So it will be mine, or ours, or our kids' or grandkids' or all of the above; you choose."

And so I will choose, using my best judgment at the time. If there is one thing I have learned as a result of living my life, it is how very right I can feel one day, only to be proven wrong by information discovered the next day or the next year or the next decade. That leads me to perhaps the best thing I have learned, which is to accept the new information without feeling that I wasted all the time I spent living with and fighting for the old information. In my mind, that is all a part of engaging with folks with all the truth that I believe in at that specific moment.

Although I am late in my sixth decade, I do not see myself foreclosing on my future at all. Instead, I see myself as undergoing still another transition, one that I believe this exercise has helped me put in perspective. In a class I took a couple of years ago, we were asked to imagine ourselves back in adolescence and "describe yourself, to yourself." In response, I wrote, "I am a sixteen-year-old daydreamer who is smart, skinny, funny, active, lazy, taller than I'd like to be, and not very popular. I love to read and to eat, especially chocolate." I wrote in my notes later in that class that the professor spoke of a female writer's reflection on her adolescence as "an adult woman looking back over life and feeling a sense of loss. She has lost her sense of having been a free spirit as she has developed a sense of self-watchfulness."

My own story is perhaps just the opposite. The more I attempted to lose my sense of myself as a free spirit, the more tenaciously that characteristic has clung to me. The harder I tried to suppress my sense of humor, the more it bubbled up and overcame me. I have dissolved in laughter in the most inappropriate of places. Today, considerable years past adolescence, many of the same descriptive terms apply to me. I am still a smart, skinny, active, lazy daydreamer who loves to read and eat chocolate. I am not, however, "taller than I'd like to be" anymore, because somewhere along the way I got comfortable looking everybody squarely in the eye.